Michael Twaddle

PROLETARIANS AND AFRICAN CAPITALISM

Perspectives on Development is organized by and
edited from the Centre for Developing-Area Studies, McGill
University, Montreal, Canada. The primary focus of the series
is on economic, social and political development in third world
countries. The series includes works of a broad, comparative
and interpretive character as well as specific institutional and
empirical studies which stem from research activities of the
Centre. However, the series also includes other works judged by
the Editors to be valuable contributions to our understanding
of the development process.

Series Editors

R. Cranford Pratt, Professor of Political Science, University of Toronto, Chairman
John A. Barnes, Professor of Sociology, University of Cambridge
Irving Brecher, Professor of Economics, McGill University
Peter C. W. Gutkind, Professor of Anthropology, McGill University
Ben Higgins, Professor of Economics, University of Montreal
Kari Levitt, Associate Professor of Economics, McGill University
Richard F. Salisbury, Professor of Anthropology, McGill University

1   I. Brecher and S. A. Abbas, *Foreign Aid and Industrial Development in Pakistan*
2   T. C. Bruneau, *The Political Transformation of the Brazilian Catholic Church*
3   A. Jeyaratnam Wilson, *Electoral Politics in an Emergent State: The Ceylon General Election of May 1970*
4   R. Sandbrook, *Proletarians and African Capitalism: The Kenyan Case, 1960–1972*

PROLETARIANS AND AFRICAN CAPITALISM

THE KENYAN CASE, 1960–1972

Richard Sandbrook

University of Toronto

Cambridge University Press

Published by the Syndics of the Cambridge University Press
Bentley House, 200 Euston Road, London NW1 2DB
American Branch: 32 East 57th Street, New York, N.Y. 10022

© Cambridge University Press 1975

Library of Congress Catalogue Card Number: 73-91818

ISBN: 0 521 20428 3

First published 1975

Printed in Great Britain
at the University Printing House, Cambridge
(Euan Phillips, University Printer)

Contents

Tables

Acknowledgements

I have incurred many debts of gratitude in the five years devoted to this study. One of these is to the Canada Council and the Sir Arthur Sims Fellowship Fund, administered by the Royal Society of Canada, both of which supported my research in Kenya either in 1968–70 or in the summer of 1972. Thanks are also due to the University of Toronto's research administration, who responded promptly and favourably to my requests for small sums to cover the many costs incurred in preparing a manuscript.

Of the many Kenyans who assisted me, I will mention only four by name. Two of these are Clement K. Lubembe and J. D. Akumu, M.P., each of whom served successively as Secretary General of the Central Organization of Trade Unions (Kenya) during my research. Without the assistance and co-operation of these two men and many other union leaders, this study would have obviously been impossible. I also wish to thank Dr F. R. S. DeSouza, the former Deputy Speaker of Kenya's National Assembly, who was invariably helpful in his encouragement and introductions to politicians. As well, I frequently benefited from discussions with Dr John J. Okumu, until recently Dean of Arts at the University of Nairobi. Not the least of the personal rewards of field research is the opportunity to make the acquaintance of people such as these.

Professor Colin Leys, now Chairman of the Department of Politics at the University of Sheffield, provided invaluable advice and criticism at every stage in the preparation of an earlier version of this study as a doctoral dissertation. Helpful comments on various drafts of the manuscript were also received from Professor Cranford Pratt, Professor Henry Bienen, Dr E. A. Brett, Professor Ralph Campbell and Professor M. Crawford Young. The contribution of my wife, Judy, to this enterprise has been immense. None the less, as I am well aware of the alacrity with which she excises all clichés from my manuscripts, I had best keep my thanks to her off the printed page.

1974   R.S.

Abbreviations

AATUF	All-African Trade Union Federation
ACIE	Association of Commercial and Industrial Employers
AFL-CIO	American Federation of Labour-Congress of Industrial Organizations
AWF	African Workers' Federation
CAPU	Coast African Peoples' Union
COTU(K)	Central Organization of Trade Unions (Kenya)
CPP	Convention Peoples' Party
CPWU	Coffee Plantation Workers' Union
CSACSU(K)	Common Services African Civil Servants' Union (Kenya)
DATA	Distributive and Allied Trades Association
DWU	Dockworkers' Union
EAFBCWU	East African Federation of Building and Construction Workers' Union
EARH	East African Railways and Harbours Corporation
EATUC	East African Trades Union Congress
FKE	Federation of Kenya Employers
GAWU	General Agricultural Workers' Union
ICFTU	International Confederation of Free Trade Unions
KADU	Kenya African Democratic Union
KANU	Kenya African National Union
KAU	Kenya African Union
KAWC	Kenya African Workers' Congress
KAWU	Kenya African Workers' Union
KCGA	Kenya Coffee Growers' Association
KCWU	Kenya Chemical Workers' Union
KDCWU	Kenya Distributive and Commercial Workers' Union
KFL	Kenya Federation of Labour
KFPTU	Kenya Federation of Progressive Trade Unions
KFRTU	Kenya Federation of Registered Trade Unions
KLGWU	Kenya Local Government Workers' Union
KPOWU	Kenya Petroleum Oil Workers' Union
KPAWU	Kenya Plantation and Agricultural Workers' Union
KPU	Kenya Peoples' Union
KQMWU	Kenya Quarry and Mineworkers' Union
KTGA	Kenya Tea Growers' Association
KUCFAW	Kenya Union of Commercial, Food and Allied Workers
KUSPW	Kenya Union of Sugar Plantation Workers

LAB	Labour Advisory Board
L. & S. Co.	Landing and Shipping Company of East Africa
M. of L.	Ministry of Labour
NCMU	Nigerian Coal Miners' Union
NUTA	National Union of Tanganyikan Workers
PEA	Port Employers' Association
RAU(K)	Railway African Union (Kenya)
SCPWU	Sisal and Coffee Plantation Workers' Union
SEA(K)	Sisal Employers' Association (Kenya)
SPWU	Sisal Plantation Workers' Union
TPWU	Tea Plantation Workers' Union
TUC(K)	Trade Unions Congress (Kenya)

Note: Where Kenyan pounds are used the K£ is equivalent to KSh20.

PART I

The economic, social and political context

1. Workers, unions and dependent capitalism

For Frantz Fanon the unionized urban workers in Africa are not the exploited, deprived class depicted in studies of the primitive stage of Western capitalism, but 'the most comfortably off fraction of the people'. The significance of their putative privileged position, Fanon believed, is that urban workers and their unions thereby gain a vested interest in the colonial and neo-colonial *status quo.* While workers strove for independence, their struggle was limited to the constitutional path of peaceful transition to neo-colonialism. And in the era of abortive independence – when the national liberation struggle fails to transform itself into a socialist revolution – 'the workers...do not know where to go from there'. They simply want 'more', but they fear that their demands would 'scandalize the rest of the nation'. Hence the trade unions, which are subjected to increasing state regulation, either 'merely mark time' or turn to (often subversive) political activity in order to wrest more of the fruits of neo-colonialism from the national bourgeoisie. The peasantry at this stage is merely a spectator.[1]

This study seeks to assess the validity of Fanon's schema, particularly as it relates to the period of political independence. What is the relationship between organized labour and the national bourgeoisie (what I will call the 'political class') in poor African countries following a capitalist strategy of development (or underdevelopment, as some would have it)? I seek an answer to this question within the context of Kenya, a country which has often been considered the archetype of dependent capitalism in Africa. In this chapter, I first demonstrate the appropriateness of applying the term 'capitalist' to Kenya by exploring the main features of its political economy and development strategy. I then turn to a closer examination of the role of unionized labour within this political economy.

The political economy of dependent capitalism

The economic base

'Socialism', like 'democracy', is a term with a very positive connotation, especially in former colonies which have experienced the hegemony of one of the leading capitalist powers. It is hardly surprising, therefore, that even African governments who show scant sympathy for such socialist principles as public ownership of the means of production, social equality and democracy should none the less refer to themselves as 'African socialist'. Kenya possesses such a government which, though publicly committed to socialism, pursues a manifestly capitalist development strategy. The generic

[3]

economic elements of such a strategy are the following: a conception of development as, at least in the short run, maximizing production rather than ensuring social equality; a decision that development in this sense can best be stimulated by the prod of the profit motive and the associated institution of private property; a considerable reliance upon foreign capital and expertise to modernize the economy; and the official encouragement of indigenous entrepreneurship in both the urban and rural areas. This strategy has unquestionably led to substantial increases in output in Kenya; the growth rate since independence in 1963 has averaged about 6.5 per cent per year in real terms. Yet what has developed in this country is a dependent capitalism whose potential for continued growth may be limited. Kenya's economic dependence derives in part, as we shall see, from its reliance upon the inflow of foreign resources – both capital and skilled personnel – from a few advanced capitalist countries. This dependence is accentuated by the concentration of Kenya's trade with a few industrialized states, a trade in which Kenya supplies mainly primary products (coffee and tea usually constituting about half of its exports) in exchange for manufactures. Since this dependent economy is interconnected with a distinctive social structural and political context within which organized labour functions, we must briefly examine its main features. The logical place to begin is with the colonial economy.

During the colonial period the economy was built around the immigrant settlers and the so-called 'White Highlands'. In general terms, the settlers contributed capital and some managerial skills while the colonial government provided the land and the cheap labour. The land was acquired partly by the physical movement of whole tribes and partly by the restriction of the 'natives' to reserves. Although Kenya covers an area of about 225,000 square miles (roughly the size of France), almost three-quarters of this territory is unfit for agriculture. Most of the Europeans settled in the 7.5 million acres of fertile, well-watered land in the highlands of central Kenya. One of their chief demands was for a supply of cheap labour, a demand that the colonial government tried to satisfy through such indirectly coercive measures as the imposition of hut and poll taxes.[2] Wage labour for Europeans was often the easiest way for an African to discharge his tax obligations, even though wages were pitifully low. By 1960 there were about 3,400 white farming units (coffee, tea and sisal estates, mixed farms and cattle ranches) with an average size of 2,400 acres and a total African work force of about 250,000.[3] Most of the marketed agricultural output at this time was derived from non-African farms and estates: K£36 million out of a total of K£46 million.[4]

Industrial growth was limited, since Britain conceived of Kenya, as of its other colonies, as a market for metropolitan industries. The little industry that existed before 1945 was concentrated in the processing of local primary products. A few small factories in Nairobi and Mombasa produced such items as clothing, footwear, furniture and aluminium hollow-ware, but their contribution to the national income was negligible.[5] Kenya enjoyed a period of considerable economic expansion after 1945, prompted partly by the large investments of international corporations. By 1963, 13.8 per cent of the Gross Domestic Product was produced by industry.[6] While this is a small proportion in world terms, Kenya at independence possessed an industrial sector considerably larger than that in either Uganda or Tanganyika, a consequence of its larger and more affluent immigrant population who provided a local market for consumer goods, its more developed infrastructure, and its access to a protected East African market for manufactured goods. Its industrial sector, however, was still composed mainly of processing and last-stage assembly plants, and was still concentrated largely in the vicinity of Nairobi and Mombasa.[7] The union movement would not be able to rely upon a large industrial base for its strength.

What then were the main elements of the colonial economic heritage which influenced the nationalist government's decision about an appropriate development strategy?[8] One obvious legacy was the dominance of oligopolistic overseas corporations, mainly from the United Kingdom, in the import trade, banking and manufacturing. These firms enjoyed many advantages in establishing themselves; some of these were simply in the form of easy communications with governmental officials and local Asian and European businessmen, while others were the result of governmental concessions. A second and equally obvious legacy was a remarkable inequality in the distribution of wealth. In 1961, for example, the wage bill for the 22,000 Europeans (who represented under 4 per cent of total employment) accounted for about one-third of total wages and salaries. A final legacy – that relating to the creation of new values and aspirations – was perhaps more subtle, though crucial in understanding the current pattern of development. As the I.L.O.'s recent report on 'Employment, Incomes and Equality' observed (p. 87):

Kenyan attitudes and aspirations had perhaps been moulded more than was realized by the style and ethos of the divided economy, by the colonial experience of having to accommodate oneself and to work within the existing structure of the economy rather than to change it. Thus, when national independence was achieved the political aim of taking over the economy became merged almost imperceptibly with individual aspirations to take over the jobs, positions and life styles which the economy made possible.

This then is the historical context within which the government of Jomo Kenyatta had to choose an appropriate development strategy. That this government decided not to transform the colonial economy is evident from its key policy statement on development strategy, 'African Socialism and Its Application to Planning in Kenya' (Sessional Paper No. 10, 1965). Although this white paper refers to socialism, it actually outlines a capitalist mode of development. It shows that the ruling elite hopes to rely upon private ownership (but with considerable governmental regulation and participation), the profit motive, substantial inputs of foreign resources, and indigenous entrepreneurship to increase output rapidly, with the expressed hope that, in the long-run, the increased output will permit more social welfare and enhanced social justice.

In the short-run, however, priority is to be given to production over equality in the belief that social justice can only be achieved by sharing wealth, not poverty. Although the white paper specifically affirms the centrality of the goals of equality and justice at several points (see pages 1, 2, 5), the whole thrust of the paper is to give precedence to the maximization of growth regardless of the consequences for social equality. For example, the policy statement specifically commits the state to uphold the right of individuals to accumulate property and wealth – in the name of 'human dignity and freedom' (p. 12). The document also declares that 'growth...is the first concern of planning', and that 'the bulk of Government development expenditure will be channelled into directly productive activities in order to establish a foundation for increased and extended welfare services in the future' (p. 52). But these are just hints; the emphasis throughout the paper is on economic growth. As one perceptive commentator aptly observed:

In interpreting the principles of African Socialism...the paper consistently chooses whatever investment of resources will earn the greatest increment of national wealth. If well-paid foreign experts, incentives to overseas firms, loans to the most progressive farmers, investment in the most fertile provinces, and a tax structure which enables the enterprising to enjoy the reward of their efforts will best promote the development of the country, then the paper is singleminded in endorsing them. But would this not mean that social justice and human dignity are, after all, to be compromised for material ends, in the faint hope of reinstating them more fully in some distant future?[9]

To augment economic growth, the government places great importance on the inflow of foreign resources in the form of private investment, aid and skilled personnel. The official expectations (or, more accurately, hopes) about the contribution of foreign capital can be gauged from Kenya's *Development Plan, 1970–1974.* In this document (p. 161) the projection of the inflow of private foreign investment over the five-year period is K£140. Since the inflow of private capital in 1969 was only K£13, the magnitude of the projection is quite remarkable. As well, the development plan (p. 163) projects the foreign aid contribution to the central government's development expenditure in 1970–4 as amounting to K£95 – over half of the projected official development expenditure in that period.

To attract the requisite foreign private investment, the government has provided a number of guarantees and incentives. The Foreign Investment Protection Act of 1964 constitutes in effect a bill of rights for foreign investors, guaranteeing freedom of repatriation of profits (in proportion to the foreign share of equity), interest and repayments on foreign loan capital, and abjuring expropriation without good cause. On the subject of nationalization, Sessional Paper No. 10 of 1965 (pp. 26–7) musters a range of arguments to demonstrate that expropriation of foreign concerns is a fool-hardy strategy; this leads to a promise to nationalize assets only under certain unusual circumstances, and then only with full compensation. Foreign companies also benefit from incentives, including a tax allowance of 20 per cent based on depreciation, market protection in the form of tariffs and quotas on imports, and special permission (often granted) to import duty-free capital goods and materials unavailable in Kenya.[10]

These policies are doubtless partly responsible for the impressive scale of foreign investment in Kenya. In the agricultural sector foreign control of the large coffee, tea, fruit and sisal estates was still extensive even after a decade of resettling landless Africans on former European land.[11] In the import–export trade the bulk of transactions are still handled by a few oligopolistic trading companies. Most of these also have direct links with banks, insurance firms, steamship companies and manufacturers in ad-vanced capitalist countries, especially Britain.[12] Foreign control is parti-cularly pronounced in the 'modern' – capitalist-intensive, technologically sophisticated – industrial sector. As I mentioned previously, this sector, though limited in scale, is still large and sophisticated in East African terms. However, a large part of manufacturing activity is still devoted to processing local raw materials: foreign companies predominate in the processing of the export crops, in the canning and preservation of fruit and vegetables, and in the production of such commodities as cement, soda ash and salt. But the greatest part of foreign investment in recent years has been in the import-substituting manufactures, especially textiles, footwear, clothing, paper products, assembly industries, petroleum refining and pharmaceuticals. Most of this manufacturing depends upon the import of parts and raw materials.[13]

The extent of foreign control is considerable regardless of the measure one employs. The top decision-makers in the manufacturing sector, for example, are mainly non-Kenyans: of the fifty most influential directors of Kenyan operations in 1967, only seven were Kenyan citizens and only four were Africans.[14] Another measure of the influence of foreign enterprise is the ratio of manufacturing investment involving foreign capital (even though it may also include local capital) to total manufacturing investment. One report estimated that, in 1967 and 1968, projects involving foreign invest-ment accounted for about 60 per cent of total manufacturing investment. In addition, enterprise with foreign equity participation accounted in 1967 for 57 per cent of the gross product of manufacturing firms employing over fifty workers, and for about 73 per cent of the total profits. Moreover, this same report asserted that the proportionate importance of foreign enterprise was increasing.[15]

The Kenyan economy is also dependent upon the inflow of foreign aid, in the form of grants, loans and technical assistance. The major donor has always been the United Kingdom, though its share of the total disburse-ment had declined to just over half in 1970. Aid as a percentage of the government's total development expenditure has remained fairly constant over the past few years: while aid accounted for 95 per cent of development expenditure in 1964–5, this proportion had decreased to 39 per cent in 1969–70 and 37 per cent in 1971–2.[16] If the government is to reach its target in the current planning period, foreign aid will undoubtedly have to remain at about 40 per cent of development expenditure. Kenya is still far from self-reliant.

Another aspect of Kenya's economic strategy relates to the retention of foreign expertise. While Sessional Paper No. 10 advocates Africanization throughout the economy and administration, it also frankly contends that the maintenance of rapid economic growth requires reliance upon skilled expatriates for some considerable time. One can certainly appreciate the government's quandary, arising as it does out of the injustice of the colonial period. The power structure in colonial Kenya created and perpetuated a racial stratification of employment with Africans at the bottom. Most of the posts requiring special skills were officially or unofficially reserved for Europeans and Asians. Even the artisans and white collar employees were mainly Asian prior to independence; Asians in fact enjoyed a virtual monopoly in some skilled trades, a monopoly maintained by the recruitment of apprentices from amongst their own people.[17] Africans, having minimal educational opportunities and few chances to learn skills, generally played a subordinate role in economic activities. Kenya thus arrived at independence with very little skilled African manpower.

The response of Kenyatta's government to this situation was to institute various training programmes and negotiate technical assistance agreements with foreign governments, firms and individuals.[18] As a consequence the total number of expatriates serving under technical assistance schemes has increased: from about 2,700 advisory, operational and voluntary personnel in mid-1968 to over 3,700 in mid-1971 (about 60 per cent of which came from Britain).[19] This level of dependence is unusual even in the African context; in 1970, Kenya apparently maintained a larger number of technical assistance personnel than any of eight other African countries (including Nigeria) for which data is available.[20] How influential these advisers are in the decision-making process is, of course, difficult to judge. One study estimated that just over 20 per cent of the high-level posts in Kenya's civil service were held by expatriates in 1969 and about 13 per cent in 1972. It concluded that the technical assistance personnel are 'functional' to the maintenance of the present regime and socio-economic system, but that their presence tended to undermine Kenyan self-confidence, thus perpetuating the dependency syndrome.[21]

A final element of the capitalist development strategy is the official encouragement of indigenous capitalism in both the urban and rural areas. In its white paper on 'African Socialism and Its Application to Planning in Kenya' (p. 29) the government committed itself to 'establishing Africans in a firm position in the monetary sector by ensuring that a large share of the planned new expansion is African owned and managed'. The paper then suggested a number of specific policies to ensure African participation, most of which have been implemented since 1965. The government has provided aspirant African businessmen with various training schemes and with technical advice and assistance once commercial or industrial activities have been undertaken. It has made capital available to Africans at low interest rates through the Industrial and Commercial Development Corporation, established in 1965. It has also provided such other special assistance to African businessmen as the following: the reservation of certain categories of government contracts to Africans; the restriction of trading licences for certain types of trade to citizens with a deliberate bias in favour of African applicants; and the extension of a quasi-monopolistic position to African businessmen dealing in certain items of trade or involved in road transport or construction.[22] I will return at a later point to the implications of the ruling elite's attempts to foster a commercial and industrial bourgeoisie.[23]

The rural areas were also to be 'developed' by means of individual enterprise and predominantly private ownership of resources – in this case land. Whereas before independence the bulk of the export crops (especially coffee, tea and sisal) had derived from foreign-controlled, large estates, Africans were now to gain a much greater share of their production. Since Sessional Paper No. 10, 1965 had affirmed the government's intention to build upon tradition in constructing African socialism, one might have expected a communal or co-operative approach to African participation in commercial agriculture. Traditionally, after all, land had not been owned individually; individuals had possessed rights only to the use of land which belonged ultimately to the clan or lineage. Yet the white paper on 'African Socialism' specifically rejected the efficacy of African tradition in this respect, opting instead for individual ownership and enterprise and reserving the co-operative element mainly for the marketing of produce. Traditional communitarianism, the paper revealingly argues (pp. 10–11), 'cannot be carried over indiscriminately to a modern, monetary economy. The need to develop and invest requires credit and a credit economy rests heavily on a system of land titles and their registration. The ownership of land must, therefore, be made more definite and explicit...'.

To this end the nationalist government continued and expanded the colonial government's programme to consolidate and provide a title deed for the scattered landholdings of African farmers. The Swynnerton Plan, instituted at the height of the Mau Mau Emergency in the mid-1950s, had originally aimed at creating a conservative landed middle class among the Kikuyu of central Kenya.[24] After land consolidation and registration, the colonial government had intended to assist progressive Kikuyu farmers with credit and extension service facilities. This scheme was extended to the rest of the country just before independence under the auspices of the African government.

At the same time, the Kenyatta government created parastatal bodies to foster indigenous rural capitalism. For instance, it established the Kenya Tea Development Authority to encourage tea cultivation by Africans, the Agricultural Development Corporation to provide credit at low interest rates, and an expanded extension service to advise African farmers on husbandry. Predictably, these services have benefited 'progressive' farmers the most, ensuring that those who succeed become even more successful.

In sum, there are firm grounds for holding that the government of Kenya has pursued a capitalist mode of development in its first decade of national independence. It has emphasized the Africanization of the pre-existing economy rather than its transformation. This strategy has undeniably succeeded in expanding production at an impressive rate relative to other African countries. Yet the benefits of economic growth have been very inequitably distributed: while about 63 per cent of Kenyan households in the 12 million population earn annual incomes of under K£60, just over 1 per cent of the households earn over – mostly well over – K£1,000 per year.[25] As one authoritative report on the Kenyan economy has rightly concluded: 'In many respects economic growth has largely continued on lines set by the earlier colonial structure. Posts have been Africanized and there has been great expansion; but the structures which led to and have sustained inequality still remain: the centre still grows at the expense of the periphery and important parts of the economy are still controlled by expatriate interests.'[26]

The emergent social structure

All underdeveloped countries pursuing a capitalist economic strategy will share certain common features of social structure. In such countries one would expect to find a small native bourgeoisie, a small capitalist-farmer stratum or perhaps a landed oligarchy, a large salariat employed by the state, an external estate of representatives of international corporations (temporarily *in* society though not *of* it), a working class, a sub-proletariat of the unemployed and unproductively employed, and a large peasantry. But there are obviously immense variations among poor countries in the relative size of the various social strata, the degree of class consciousness, and the inter-relationships of the strata. Diversity also arises from the existence and intensity of different particularistic loyalties – to religion, language, race, region or ethnic group – which may or may not cut across class lines.

In Kenya people perceive much of the conflict in central arenas in ethnic or tribal terms. There are quite a number of self-identified 'tribes' in this country. According to its 1969 population census, the most numerous of these groupings are the following: the Kikuyu 2.2 million, the Luo 1.5 million, the Luhya 1.5 million, the Kamba 1.2 million, the coastal Mijikenda 0.5 million, and others 3.8 million, for a total African population of about 10.7 million. The figure of 2.2 million actually understates the numerical predominance of the Kikuyu, since its leaders can normally count upon the support of other culturally and linguistically similar peoples, notably the Meru and Embu, in conflict within central arenas. The Kikuyu along with these closely related peoples numbered about three million in 1969. One must immediately emphasize, however, that in conflicts *within* Kikuyu, Embu or Meru areas or involving mainly these groupings, the finer distinctions between groups become salient; in these situations, the line dividing Kikuyu and Meru or Kikuyu and Embu is usually of crucial importance.

Of course, the mere existence within a single state of ethnic groups with diverse cultural values does not imply the necessity of ethnic conflict. 'Tribe', as conceived here, is not a primordial loyalty causing political conflict, but is itself a dependent variable, a loyalty or identity which is politicized only under certain specifiable conditions. 'Tribalism', as ethnic conflict is commonly called, is generally the result of much more than simply cultural differences and traditional hostilities. In a new state composed of disparate peoples, solidarity on the basis of cultural–linguistic affinity becomes a reality only in the context of competition at the centre over the distribution of power, economic resources and jobs. A symbiotic relationship emerges between politicians, who wish to advance their own positions, and their 'people', who fear political domination and economic exploitation by a culturally distinct group allegedly organized for these ends. A politician thus gains a tribal power base by successfully manipulating the appropriate cultural symbols and by articulating and advancing his people's collective and individual aspirations (which he himself probably helped arouse).[27] An analysis along these lines has been used to explain the emergence in Kenya of 'tribal bosses' – such as Oginga Odinga (Luo), Daniel arap Moi (Kalenjin), Paul Ngei (Kamba) and Ronald Ngala (Mijikenda, especially the Giriama sub-tribe).[28] In fact, Kenyan political parties – including KANU, the governing party – have largely represented shifting coalitions of ethnic representatives and their followers and clients. Tribalism is a phenomenon to which I will return at several later points; my aim here is simply to suggest the nature and extent of ethnic cleavages in Kenya.

A fundamental determinant of the class structure is unquestionably the level of development of the capitalist economy. Although Kenya has a comparatively advanced industrial and commercial base in East African terms, it is still predominantly a peasant society. Almost nine-tenths of the population resides in the rural areas, and the bulk of this rural population is composed of peasants (i.e., smallholders who rely primarily upon family labour and simple technology to produce goods mainly for their own consumption, but also for the market). Indeed, one investigator has concluded that, contrary to what one might expect, the peasant farming sector is still expanding, as more white farmers are replaced by medium to high density African settlement. Whatever the legal form of land ownership, in practice the typical pattern of peasant economy emerges.[29] There is, of course, a certain amount of social differentiation in the countryside, from landless or nearly landless agricultural labourers at the bottom to emergent

African capitalist farmers (but not a landed aristocracy) at the top.[30] One consequence of the land consolidation programme initiated in Kikuyuland in the mid-1950s was the validation of the position of the larger African landholders, while leaving many peasants landless altogether.[31] Land reform after independence was also used to defuse rural unrest and to create conditions by which 'a middle-class of Africans would obtain rights and interests in the large-farm sector to politically and economically insure its continued functioning'.[32]

The unemployed and unproductively employed urban poor can usefully be considered an extension of peasant society, owing to the extensive interchanges of personnel and goods between these urban migrants and the countryside. It has been estimated that between 12 and 13 per cent of the potential work force in Nairobi is 'unemployed' (defined as adults seeking work and receiving zero income in the week previous to the survey). However, this figure reflects only part of the employment problem: an I.L.O. report on Kenya concludes that just over 20 per cent of adult males and just over 50 per cent of adult females in Nairobi are affected by the 'urban working problem' – that is, the lack of an opportunity to earn a reasonable minimum income.[33] Most of the working poor are employed in the 'informal' – i.e., the unenumerated, labour-intensive, small-scale service and manufacturing – sector.

Both the peasantry proper and the urban unemployed and underemployed manifest a very low degree of class consciousness. The hindrances to the development of a sense of common identity among peasants are well known.[34] Kenyan peasants have not been able to overcome on a sustained basis such divisive factors as their individualistic mode of production, the vertical barriers of clan, tribe and language, and the vagueness and diversity of political aims. Moreover, the absence of an indigenous landed aristocracy has denied these peasants even a conspicuous common focus of hostility. Only in Kikuyuland does one find an evidently class-conscious peasant segment, composed of the underprivileged former freedom fighters for whom *Uhuru* has meant very little. Some of the divisive factors already mentioned also go far to explain the low incidence of collective action by the amorphous urban migrants.[35] What class action there is on the part of these underlying strata is relatively spontaneous, irregular and localized, taking the form of riots, occasional assaults on government officials, and mass refusals to pay taxes or repay loans.

Consider next the privileged strata, those who have profited from *Uhuru*. It is difficult to know how best to characterize these; Marxist categories seem somewhat artificial, as the relationship between economic power (ownership of the means of production) and political power (control of the key state decision-making, implementation and enforcement positions) is quite different in underdeveloped African countries than it was in Marx's Europe.[36] In nineteenth-century Britain, for example, political authority was largely a function of social class and high social status. In newly independent African countries, however, political power is an independent variable shaping social stratification rather than simply a mainstay of a prevailing structure of inequality. Instead of high social status and the allied economic privilege leading to political power, the latter permits its holders to develop a class position and enhance their social status. Hence, the ruling groups in office can be accurately referred to as the 'political class'. 'The major activity of the ruling groups is an attempt to use the benefits of political power to redress the insecure position they find themselves in. This can be seen in more general terms as an "embourgeoisement" of the ruling elite.'[37] Wealth and business contacts acquired from the holding of political office are used to acquire property in the form of farms, houses, shares and interests in business enterprises.

The political class is composed of three frequently discordant sections: the politicians (M.P.s, cabinet ministers, county and municipal councillors), the top civil servants and heads of parastatal bodies, and the military and police officers. About the last section little at present is known, except that the regime has so far succeeded in placating most of the military elite by ensuring that it is accorded deference and opportunities for advancement. Of the two remaining sections, the bureaucrats are clearly the pre-eminent element. Since independence the central bureaucracy has accumulated resources and new functions at the expense of the local government system. Moreover, neither the National Assembly nor KANU, the moribund governing party, has emerged as an effective counterweight to the bureaucracy.[38] Indeed, the top political rulers have built their domination upon the bureaucracy rather than the party. The main aims of the executive and the civil service in the 'development' process are the provision of security throughout the country (thus maintaining a 'favourable climate of investment'), a basic infrastructure, and opportunities and incentives for enterprising individuals and firms.

Although the political class bases its privileged position in the first instance upon its control of the political apparatus, it has also linked its future to that of foreign capitalist interests. This class provides the investment climate within which the 'external estate' of international firms seeks to create further wealth and 'modernize' the economy. It is not only Marxists who suggest that the metropolis may now have more control over the Kenyan economy than in the colonial past, owing to the intertwining of the interests of the indigenous political class and big (i.e., foreign-controlled) business. The I.L.O. report previously cited asserts that, while before independence, 'such coalitions of interests were...conspicuous and racially vulnerable to nationalist challenges,...Kenyanization has significantly reduced this risk. Moreover, within the circle, the influence of foreign companies appears to be growing rapidly, certainly within the manufacturing sector but to some extent also in other parts of the economy.'[39] This congruence of interests is far from peculiar to Kenya.[40] One way in which this congruency is expressed in this country is in a common tendency on both sides to blame the unionized workers for economic and social problems. Representatives of both government and big business advocate a wages policy to restrict urban wages in order to alleviate inflationary tendencies, unemployment and the marked inequalities between the urban and rural areas.[41] By accusing the workers, the more privileged strata may perhaps divert public attention from their own conspicuous consumption.

The political class can also rely upon the support of two small emergent social forces with which it is partially fused – the urban bourgeoisie and the capitalist farmers. The embryonic bourgeoisie proper numbers no more than about 10,000, of whom the majority are still Europeans and Asians.[42] Not surprisingly, European immigrants who regarded Jomo Kenyatta as the 'leader unto darkness and death' during the Mau Mau rebellion, now evince deep admiration for the President. As one settler commented, doubtless mainly in jest, 'If ever there were a threat of a coup in Nairobi, we settlers would form a squadron and march down to protect the old man.'[43] Kenyatta will no doubt continue to receive such respect and support from the white community as long as he and his party stand for the preservation of free enterprise. The petty-bourgeoisie is a much more numerous and indigenous social formation, numbering in the tens of thousands and including Africans and Asians in trade, transport, construction, small-scale manufacturing and house rental.[44] This stratum is, as I mentioned earlier, dependent upon the political authorities in many ways. The other, rural-based stratum is composed of large African farmers; these, however, are generally also members of the political class and/or the indigenous bourgeoisie. The capitalist farmers are also dependent upon the state – often for their initial opportunity to purchase land ('Z' plots of 100 acres or so were allotted to 'community leaders' after 1964), and for credit and extension services.

What is the position of the unionizable wage-earners within this incipient class structure? One must first outline the dimensions and location of this social formation before discussing its consciousness and action. In 1969 wage-earners in all branches of activity numbered 1,072,300, or just under one-quarter of the work force.[45] Most of the remaining three-quarters of the labour force were self-employed on the land. Of those in wage employment, 445,100 or 41.5 per cent, were employed, either casually or full-time, outside of the enumerated or formal sector on smallholdings or settlement schemes or in rural non-agricultural activities. Almost all of these wage-earners also cultivate small plots of their own as a matter of necessity, as daily wages seldom exceed KSh3 on smallholdings or settlement schemes. Since these workers are generally only seasonally employed and, in any case, are scattered throughout the countryside and are too poor to pay dues, they are non-unionizable.

Only wage-earners employed in the formal sector of the economy belong to trade unions. This sector consists of urban firms, large-scale farms and plantations, mines and quarries and the public services. In 1969, 627,200 people, or 58.5 per cent of all wage-earners, were employed in this sector. Just over one half of these wage-earners belonged to one of the thirty-eight registered employees' trade unions in that year.[46] Agricultural workers on large farms were, not surprisingly, the most difficult to unionize, owing to ignorance and the often transitory nature of employment. In 1969, such agricultural employees in the 'modern' sector numbered about 170,000, or over one-quarter of those engaged in this sector. Many European employers allocate small plots of land to their farm labourers; these workers are thus as much peasants as wage-earners. Most of the remaining enumerated workers are employed in the urban areas by private enterprise (210,900) or in the public sector (237,600). Only 72,744 were employed in manufacturing and repairs in 1969.[47]

Most of this industrial employment, according to the industrial census of 1961, is concentrated in the vicinity of Nairobi, the capital city. Such industries as are located elsewhere are those that must be close to their sources of raw materials or that engage in the small-scale manufacture of goods for the local population. The Nairobi Extra-Provincial District accounted for 41 per cent of industrial employment in 1961; but if the surrounding areas such as Thika are included, the total is approximately 50 per cent. The next most important industrial centres are Mombasa on the coast and Nakuru in the Rift Valley, the capital of the former 'White Highlands'.[48]

In sum, only about one-quarter of the work force in Kenya are wage-earners at any one time, and only a fraction of wage-earners are unionized. The bulk of the work force is self-employed on the land. Of the wage-earners, a majority are employed in the rural areas, most of them on a casual or intermittent basis. Approximately 10 per cent of the work force are non-agricultural wage-earners; most of these are concentrated in three urban centres, about one half in the vicinity of the capital city alone.

To what extent can Kenyan wage-earners be regarded as a proletariat? A proletariat, in the full Marxian sense of the word, is composed of workers who, owning no means of production, have nothing to sell but their labour power. Proletarians are thus necessarily committed to wage-labour on a long-term basis. Most Kenyan workers retain some rights to land and, hence, are not entirely lacking in means of production. Yet these workers are now increasingly committed to long-term employment; to this extent they constitute an embryonic proletariat.

Until the end of the 1950s, the bulk of African workers were 'target workers' who entered the employment field outside their rural homes for comparatively short periods. The 'target' such workers seek is usually a sum large enough to obtain a permanently higher standard of living by means of the increased productivity of better equipped farms. Money earned in employment may thus be used to buy a waterproof roof for a house, storage sheds or a strong bicycle to carry crops to market, or to pay the bride price for wives who will be expected to work in the fields.[49] Another motivation for short-term labour migration is to earn funds to fulfil such personal oligations as taxes or school fees for one's children. The high incidence of target-working in Kenya in the 1950s is evidenced by a large-scale survey of turnover rates conducted in Nairobi in 1953. The survey showed that only 11 per cent of African employees interviewed had completed five years' service with their current employer.[50]

Since about 1960, however, Africans employed by the larger establishments have tended to remain in employment for longer periods. While there are few readily available statistics to document this tendency, it is attested to by both management and union representatives, confirmed by survey data and supported by fragmentary statistics on wastage rates. Agricultural enterprises, as one might expect, still register high turnover rates, though often lower than ten years ago. In urban enterprises, informal surveys undertaken by officials of the Federation of Kenya Employers have shown that the quit rate in the wealthiest expatriate companies is sometimes as low as 1 per cent per annum for African manual employees and slightly higher for clerical staff. The quit rate was thought to be considerably higher for smaller enterprises paying lower wages.[51] A survey conducted among a sample of 1,300 Kenyan and Ugandan industrial workers during 1965–6 found that 21 per cent of the workers had held their jobs for ten years or more; in 1953, by contrast, only 3 per cent of workers had held their jobs that long. Furthermore, 32 per cent of the workers interviewed had been employed in their current jobs for less than three years, whereas the corresponding figure in 1953 was 80 per cent. The absentee rates were also revealed to be considerably lower in 1966 than thirteen years previously. Bissman concludes from this evidence that 'the transition from migrant worker to permanent worker is being achieved'.[52] This conclusion is supported by the Rempel–Todaro survey carried out in eight Kenyan urban centres in December 1968. A total of 1,091 male Africans, who were between the ages of fifteen and fifty years and had migrated to a town in the last five years, completed questionnaires. One question asked how long the respondent intended to remain in, or looking for, urban employment; fully 59 per cent of those in the sample answered that they considered themselves a permanent part of the urban wage-earning force, while another 10 per cent were uncertain about their future migration plans. The remaining 31 per cent planned to leave town sometime in the future, though some intended to move to another town to obtain employment or a better job.[53]

The reasons for the decline of short-term employment in the larger urban enterprises are apparently threefold. One obvious factor is that recurrent expenditure has become a more important consideration for migrants than capital accumulation for specified purposes. With the development of the cult of education, pressure on parents to educate their children has increased. Keeping children in school necessitates the payment of school fees and the purchase of such items as clothes, books and perhaps shoes and cosmetics for older girls. These financial demands make it difficult for the working man to leave wage employment. Secondly, the rise in real urban wages since 1960 and the concomitant rising urban unemployment means that the opportunity costs of abandoning urban employment to return to the land have risen. Those who already hold jobs tend to keep them for fear that, if they leave to return home, they will be unable to find an opening in the future.[54] Thirdly, an increasing number of workers have no option but to remain in wage employment because they own no land as an alternative means of support. The scope of landlessness in Kenya is obviously difficult to gauge. However, a survey of middle income workers in Nairobi carried out in 1963 revealed that 54 per cent of the 342 respondents owned no land whatsoever.[55] Furthermore, about one-third of the 1,091 male Africans interviewed in the large-scale Rempel–Todaro survey reported that they had no rights to land. Although 66.1 per cent of the respondents claimed they owned no land, about one half of those who gave this answer could conceivably inherit land from their fathers, who did own land.[56]

But has the recent trend toward labour stability yet wrought widespread changes in the orientations of urban wage-earners? The evidence, though fragmentary, suggests that working-class consciousness is still embryonic in Kenya, that workers, though employed in the towns, retain a rural as much as an urban orientation. The attraction of the rural areas was indicated in an attitudinal survey conducted in Nairobi; only 23 per cent of the Africans questioned said they would prefer to remain in the city rather than return to their place of origin when they grew old.[57] Land is still seen as a form of insurance against unemployment and ill health, and as a place to which one can retire in dignity.

More problematic is the effect of the persistence of ethnic identities on the emergence of class loyalties. It is a fact, as Chapter 5 will substantiate, that most Kenyan unions draw their memberships from several cultural–linguistic groupings. Outside the Coast Province, the bulk of wage-earners in formal-sector employment are drawn from the four largest tribes, namely the Kikuyu, Luo, Luhya and Kamba. While the fact of ethnic heterogeneity is well established, its implications for class formation are less clear. The usual assumption is that ethnic and class identities are incompatible, so that once workers gain class-consciousness they no longer respond to ethnic appeals. However, two recent studies of cleavages in Nigerian politics have convincingly challenged this rather simplistic dichotomous conception.[58] Both of the writers were struck by the co-existence, or rather compartment-alization, of ethnic and class identities among Nigerian workers in the last half of 1964. During a two-week general strike all workers, regardless of tribal affiliations, had rallied behind their union leaders. Yet these same leaders, as soon as they championed a labour party in the general elections of December 1964, were deserted by the rank-and-file who continued to vote for the communal parties. The conclusion must be that Nigerian workers successfully compartmentalized their consciousness, i.e., they retained an ethnic consciousness in certain dimensions of action (e.g., political conflict) and a class-consciousness in others, most notably in employee–employer confrontations.

Although never as dramatically demonstrated, compartmentalization appears to characterize the consciousness of Kenyan workers too. The extent of Kenyan working-class consciousness may best be indicated by utilizing Lenin's distinction (in *What is to be Done?*) between 'trade-union' and 'political' (or social democratic) consciousness. As later chapters will show, formal-sector wage-earners often evince a considerable degree of trade-union consciousness, in that they clearly realize they share common economic aims that can be advanced through organization. Where such collective aims as improvements in wages and working conditions are at stake, wage-earners, irrespective of tribe, close ranks in opposition to the employers. But working-class consciousness does not often extend beyond the extraction of short-range economic gains from recalcitrant employers. There is little evidence that Kenyan workers have yet attained a political consciousness whereby they recognize, in Lenin's phrase, the 'irreconcilable antagonism of their interests to the whole of the modern political and social system'. In the political arenas, ethnic rather than working-class identities remain salient.[59] Given this situation where competition for resources at the centre (whether jobs, loans, development funds, etc.) generally occurs along ethnic lines, the degree of trade-union solidarity recently achieved by Luo, Kikuyu, Kamba, Luhya and other wage-earners is quite remarkable.

If the unionized workers do not possess a revolutionary consciousness, is it appropriate to conceive of them as belonging to a 'labour aristocracy'? The long-term urban African workers are, according to one well-known quasi-Fanonist formulation, aligned with the bureaucratic elites and sub-elites in a labour aristocracy. This social formation is conceived as a coalition of privileged groups who are dedicated to the preservation of the neo-colonial social order.[60] There are at least two serious flaws in the reasoning behind this formulation. In the first place, its adherents make the rather simplistic assumption that social groupings who benefit in absolute terms from a social order will act as mainstays of the *status quo*. In practice, however, what matters in explaining radical disaffection is not absolute but *relative* deprivation. It is thus quite conceivable, and indeed usual, that a particular social group may experience real gains in its living standards, and yet still feel impoverished relative to the disproportionately greater gains made by another social formation – perhaps, in this case, the political class.[61] In the second place, adherents of the 'labour aristocracy' thesis have offered no proof that the better-off workers are a support of the existing social order. The mere absence of organized, radical action by proletarians does not imply a recognition on their part of a mutuality of interests with the political class and external estate. Since no vanguardist groups are permitted to agitate and organize among the workers, one could hardly expect any sustained, oppositional activity sponsored by the proletarians on their own.

The actual relationship between unionized workers and the state is the subject of this book; I therefore need only observe at this juncture that the privileged position of these workers is more apparent than real, and that they as a group definitely do not regard their interests as congruent with those of the indigenous *nouveaux riches*.

The political system

The features of the socio-economic structure outlined above provide an environment in which a particular mode of political competition – what I call clientelism – can thrive. This mode of politics, I would maintain, is not peculiar to Kenya, but is characteristic of dependent capitalist societies in which the peasantry comprises the vast majority.[62] Many of the 'pitfalls of national consciousness' so aptly described by Frantz Fanon – the authoritarianism, venality, tribalism and factiousness of the 'national bourgeoisie' – are aspects of, or associated with, clientelism.[63] Since Chapter 6 discusses at some length the involvement of Kenyan unions in clientelist politics, I need here only sketch in the relationship between the socio-economic structure and the main features of clientelism.

A striking feature of the economy is the domination of the formal sector by technologically sophisticated international oligopolies. This fact accounts largely for the *political* basis of social stratification which I mentioned earlier. Since ambitious, enterpreneurial individuals cannot hope to compete with the expatriate controlled firms, they must develop opportunities for themselves through action in a political arena. These opportunities may take the form of access to a well remunerated office in the public sector or to a quasi-monopolistic position in business. When the drive for economic rewards and social status in poor countries necessarily leads individuals to seek political power or influence, one can begin to understand the authoritarianism and factiousness of the political class.[64] Whereas the new men of power are unwilling to contemplate the loss of their privileges owing to their removal from office, those presently denied sufficient political leverage to attain their ends manoeuvre for position.

Other significant elements of the social structure discussed above were the embryonic nature of class-consciousness and the cleavages along cultural–linguistic lines. Personalistic patron–clientship cannot thrive in a society characterized by inter-class hostility and class conflict. In Kenya, however, class conflict has not yet constituted a dominant motif in politics, though it may well become so in the future as the class structure ossifies and upward mobility is restricted. The vast peasantry in Kenya is internally divided, lacking in a class-wide organization and susceptible to particularistic appeals, in this case to tribal identity. These are the generic traits of peasant society which elsewhere have fostered the proliferation of patron–client ties;[65] one should therefore expect to find this characteristic form of organization in Kenya too. One of the few social classes with a resilient organizational web is the emergent proletariat, but this most conscious of classes is, as I have already suggested, restricted to a hardy trade-union consciousness. The weakness of class identifications is indicated by the sort of campaigns waged by the only manifestly socialist party – the Kenya Peoples' Union – which operated between 1966 and 1969. While the KPU leaders did make a class appeal to the dispossessed in Kikuyuland (and won only a single seat), Oginga Odinga, the party's President, appealed mainly to tribal solidarity in the KPU's Luo heartland. Furthermore, only some of Odinga's sub-leaders could be described as committed socialists.[66] Even Odinga had to come to terms with the predominant clientelist mode of politics.

Competition occurring along cultural–linguistic lines may sometimes simply mask a class struggle. This is however not the case in Kenya. Although the fruits of development in Kenya are inequitably distributed by region and tribe, one cannot discern a neat coincidence of class and ethnic boundaries. Ethnic consciousness, though undeniably a 'false' conscious-ness manipulated by the big men to advance themselves, is nonetheless a reality. This conjunction of pronounced ethnic cleavages and amorphous class identifications provides a structural situation in which patron–client-ship can flourish. Where ethnic groups must coexist in the absence of a value consensus, the ruling elite, who individually have exacerbated ethnic divi-sions, must rely on bargaining and compromise to maintain order. Integra-tion often depends on a series of personal bargains worked out at the highest political levels, whereby certain 'tribal bosses' are co-opted into the privi-leged sector while their peoples obtain a share of the national economic pie. Mutual self-interest is the one sure basis of inter-ethnic co-operation in a situation of minimal moral consensus.

This last point alludes to the final environmental feature which is closely interconnected with clientelism: the absence of a civic culture. Clientelism both reflects and produces loyalties based on self-interest and material incentives. In the absence of widely accepted normative rules defining the proper ends and means of political action, the dominant orientation of politicians is 'amoral pragmatism'.[67] In Kenya, the struggle for indepen-dence did not create a new, integrative normative order.[68] The colonial heritage is, of course, partly responsible for the feebleness of a civic culture emphasizing constitutionalism, popular representation and public-spirited activity (i.e., activity which benefits people other than one's kin). While colonialism disrupted traditional value systems, it did not replace these with a new ethos. The values of colonial society, as far as the African population was concerned, were autocratic, authoritarian and particularistic (since the settlers' interests were given precedence in administration). But colonialism is not wholly to blame for the prevailing political culture. The political class could have adopted an alternative strategy designed to suppress the practice of narrow self-interest and arbitrariness; this strategy, beset by a host of difficulties, would have required exemplary behaviour on the leaders' part and a socialist ideology of the collective good. One is probably of little use without the other. But both together would have allowed the leadership legitimately to employ coercion against those who exhibit an attitude of *enrichissez-vous*.

Having summarized the structural and ideological environment of clientelism, I must now elaborate upon its main features and relate these to the Kenyan context.

Patron–clientship is an interpersonal relationship with three fundamental characteristics.[69] It involves, in the first place, two persons unequal in status, wealth and influence, the archetype being the relationship between a landowner and a peasant working on his land. Second, it is a relationship whose formation and maintenance depends upon reciprocity in the exchange of goods and services: the patron offers economic benefits or protection, while the client reciprocates with more intangible assets, such as demonstrations of esteem, information on the machinations of a patron's enemies and political support (in elections or faction-fighting). Finally, patronage is a personal relationship, based on face-to-face contact.

While a patron–client linkage is a dyadic relationship, what characterizes many underdeveloped countries is patron–client *networks* – hierarchically ordered, linked series of patron–client relationships with little or no lateral contact between individuals at the same level in a network. These networks often extend from the 'big men' in the central political arena down into the peasant communities of the periphery. They also frequently cut across organizational as well as regional boundaries, as political rivals compete for new clients and access to new political resources. Hence, officers within the army, statutory corporations, the civil service, tribal unions, trade unions and co-operative societies sometimes operate as both patrons and clients within clientage networks.

Although these networks do permit some of the benefits of the underdeveloped economy to 'trickle down' the social pyramid, one must also recognize that they are part of the structure of domination in poor countries. Clientelism, emphasizing vertical, personal linkages, impedes the development of a consciousness of common interests on the part of the underlying strata. The underprivileged, who are nearly equally affected by a lack of opportunities, powerlessness and a lack of self-esteem, are unlikely to follow the onerous path of rebellion, a collective class-based act, when the possibility of individual advancement and protection still exists. Clientelism offers, or seems to offer, a personal solution to the generic problems of exploitation and oppression.[70] To the extent that clientelism vitiates class-consciousness among the underprivileged and promotes intra-class rather than inter-class conflict, it is a support of the inegalitarian *status quo*.

Factionalism is the main form of political conflict where patron–client networks pervade the political process. A faction may be defined very broadly as a segment of a clientage network organized to compete with a unit or units of similar type within one or more political arenas. It is a coalition of followers recruited on the basis of mercenary ties by or on behalf of a leader, who is in conflict with another leader or leaders. To the extent that the persons surrounding the leader feel bound to him by such moral ties as friendship, kinship or ideological commitment, rather than solely by mutual self-interest, they constitute a more stable clique. In central political arenas, each major faction will usually include leaders and sub-leaders of various ethnic groups; in the event of intense ethnic hostilities, however, factions will become more exclusive in tribal terms. Since factionalism is a dispute over the distribution of power, it frequently has only minor policy or ideological implications. Factional conflict at the centre involves efforts by patrons to advance their own followers, and to undermine or subvert those of their opponents, within strategic localities and organizations. In the course of their struggle, these 'big men' of the political class exacerbate factionalism at the local level and politicize many supposedly apolitical bodies. Yet factionalism at the local levels and in strategic organizations is seldom solely a function of conflict at the centre; local issues and conflicts intertwine with central ones to exacerbate conflict at all levels.

Kenyan politics adhere closely to this clientelist model, though an adequately detailed discussion must wait until Chapter 6. At this stage I will simply introduce the main actors and indicate the main antagonisms and arenas of conflict. Tom Mboya, until his assassination in 1969, was one of the major protagonists in factional conflicts at the centre. He had originally built his power on the basis of his control of the trade union movement, a control which he retained through clients after he relinquished formal leadership of the Kenya Federation of Labour (KFL) in 1962. Initially, Mboya's main opponent at the centre was another Luo politician, Oginga Odinga. After Odinga led a breakaway group out of KANU in 1966, the principal opposition to Mboya shifted to a coalition of Kikuyu and Kalenjin cabinet ministers. President Jomo Kenyatta remained neutral in many of these contests among his lieutenants, though he had intervened in the earlier period against Mboya, before switching in 1965–6 to back Mboya's coalition of 'conservatives' against Odinga's 'radicals'.[71] After the elimination of both Mboya and Odinga from the political scene (the former by death; the latter by preventive detention in 1969), the main clientage networks revolved around competing Kikuyu leaders with clients from other tribes.

In short, KANU existed largely as a congeries of competing clientage networks after independence in 1963. The general pattern has been one in which 'the groupings within the Cabinet influenced the groupings within the National Assembly. These in turn were paralleled at local levels by groupings within the [KANU] branch leadership that were determined by the association of branch officials with one or other of the national leadership groups.'[72] Factionalism at the centre thus spilled over to create or exacerbate factionalism in local political arenas throughout the country.[73] Patron–client networks also penetrated and created conflicts within organizations which were supposedly apolitical – including the civil service, agricultural co-operatives and, as we shall see, trade unions.[74]

This then is the political–economic context within which my study of organized labour is situated. I would expect my findings to be generally applicable to other predominantly peasant societies governed by an elite advocating a capitalist economic strategy, closely associated with an external estate, intertwined with local business interests, and deeply involved in clientelist politics. Although I refer to comparative material where this is available, the question of the generality of my conclusions can really only be resolved by the appearance of comparable studies.

Workers and the political class

Given the often repeated assertion that unionized workers in Kenya as elsewhere in Africa are a 'pampered' or privileged lot, one would expect them to comprise part of a 'labour aristocracy' devoted to the preservation of the *status quo*. Yet, as I previously indicated, this is a rather misleading formulation. Relations between the political class and proletarians are far from harmonious. Both the words and actions of urban workers reveal their hostility to the consumption-oriented and business-oriented ruling sectors, and their opinion of themselves as relatively impoverished.[75] Representatives of the political class, on the other hand, have frequently publicly rebuked workers and their unions. While prominent politicians, top civil servants and even businessmen refer glowingly to the brave role which the labour movement is supposed to have played in the liberation struggle, these same men also chide union leaders for failing to recognize the exigencies of the post-colonial era. Unions are portrayed as selfish, short-sighted organizations devoted to grasping higher wages and better working conditions for their already privileged members, without regard for the public interest in economic development, social justice and political stability.

The ruling elite, justifying its action in terms of the protection of this 'public interest', has sought to control the workers through their trade unions. Three important questions arise in this context: Why has the ruling elite felt it necessary to manipulate organized labour? What tactics has the government employed in order to bend trade unions to its designs? What has been the outcome of the regime's efforts at control? The first two questions are fairly straightforward; they will be considered in Chapter 2 and in Part II. The last question is more complex, requiring some elaboration.

Seldom have students of African unionism inquired into the question of how successfully governments have regulated the actions of unions and workers. One general assessment, supported by the meagre evidence available, is that 'even where the "take-over" has been maximal, unions have continued (frequently covertly) to function to protect the interests of workers.'[76] Such protection may operate more at the branch or shop levels of trade unionism than at the head office or trade union federation levels. In

Tanzania, one study reported that, though NUTA, the sole legal trade union, will not 'emerge as an open spokesman of workers' interests against the government', a 'quiet battle will be carried out day by day on many fronts, with little dramatic impact'.[77] In Zambia, an investigation of governmental efforts to constrain the behaviour of mineworkers found that 'rather than obtaining higher levels of discipline from the mass of copper miners, the government has been confronted with less willingness to work hard, greater insubordination, and increased propensities to strike', as well as continual high wage demands.[78]

In Kenya, the results of the ruling elite's labour policy have been mixed, as Part III will show. In the political sphere, the policy has been a success: though labour leaders have been deeply involved in factionalism within the political class, they have not seized a 'vanguardist' role to arouse workers against the prevailing political economy. Workers have in general been politically quiescent since independence. In the economic sphere, the government has been less successful. Militant economism persists despite governmental controls and exhortations to work in the public good, though union leaders have felt constrained to make some half-hearted concessions to the productionist function pressed upon them.

How have unions and workers managed to resist governmental demands and retain a capacity for autonomous action in the economic sphere? This is an important question, since too often the smallness of unions in African countries, together with their financial and sometimes organizational weaknesses, have led observers to conclude that these bodies are no match for a government determined to have its way. Yet these unions have frequently shown a remarkable obstinacy in pursuing traditional union aims in the face of governmental displeasure. Such resistance can only be understood in the context of the peculiar internal dynamics of trade unions. Governmental expectations of union behaviour are indeed a vital consideration for the full-time union officials who decide upon union actions. However, these expectations are not the only such consideration; union leaders must also take into account the often conflicting expectations held by ordinary union members and part-time officials. Whereas many previous studies of African labour tended to regard the latter as an essentially passive stratum responding to external commands (from political parties or union leaders, for example), this study emphasizes the active role of workers in defining and collectively pursuing their short-run interests.

To grasp how these conflicting pressures – from the government above and the members below – influence union leaders, one must examine the internal operation of unions, particularly the existence of mechanisms through which members can hold their leaders accountable for their actions. Few studies of African unions have actually delved deeply into their internal processes, though it is here that the success or failure of the ruling elite's strategy is largely determined. A notable exception is Robert Bates's analysis of the Zambian government's efforts to constrain the behaviour of the

African mineworkers. To explain the 'failure' of the Mineworkers' Union to transform itself into an agency dedicated to controlling and regulating the actions of its members, Bates investigated the power relations within the union.[79] Although this author's findings are provocative, their generality is unclear owing to the limitations inherent in analysing a single case. The present study sought to overcome this limitation by engaging in a comparative analysis of the internal dynamics of eleven existent Kenyan trade unions plus their predecessors, over the period 1960–72.

What, if any, resources can rank-and-file union members possess which provide them with leverage over their leaders? To answer this question, one must begin by explicitly distinguishing three levels of union leaders: the 'lower-level leaders' (shop stewards), 'middle-level leaders' (branch officials in industrial or general unions), and 'top leaders' (executive committee members of national unions). The lower-level leaders do not generally differ from the rank-and-file in terms of education, skill, and income or of interests and orientation. The question of responsiveness therefore relates mainly to the full-time top leaders and those among the middle leaders who are full-time union officials; these are the people who carry out the important negotiations with employers and the government. What power ordinary members have over these full-time leaders depends largely on their ability to affect adversely two sorts of goals shared by full-time officials but not shared by the rank-and-file.[80] One such goal is, of course, a leader's desire to further his own personal ambitions: after all, if a union leader is ousted from office, he may have no alternative employment, at least at the level of remuneration and prestige to which he has become accustomed. In principle, therefore, the rank-and-file's primary resource is the vote in union elections. The other personal goal of a top union leader is to advance the institutional interests of his union by safeguarding its security against internal and external enemies, and by providing a basis for growth in membership cohesion and power. A union leader's power and prestige is very closely linked to that of the organization he heads. Hence, another resource ordinary members often enjoy is the ability to undermine their institution's strength, either by ignoring the directives of unpopular leaders or by withdrawing from membership (if permitted by law), thus ceasing to contribute financially to the union.

My hypothesis is that full-time national and branch union leaders will, as long as they remain dependent upon those below for financial and personal support, cling tenaciously to traditional union goals (e.g., high wage demands, grievance-handling). The alternative, though not mutually exclusive, strategies open to the government in this situation are to repress any manifestations of independent union actions or to mould union behaviour in an acceptable direction by neutralizing the power of union members vis-à-vis their leaders. Outright repression of unions is an unlikely strategy in countries where political authority is fragile. Without labour organizations able to channel and resolve the tensions that inevitably arise in the production process, worker protest is likely to take the politically dangerous form of wildcat or general strikes or the economically detrimental forms of absenteeism and lower productivity. A less dangerous strategy for the ruling elite, though one which also has its pitfalls, is to transform the orientation of trade unionism by insulating union leaders from pressures from below. One means of achieving this end, for instance, is legislation that offers full-time union officials personal and institutional security in exchange for concessions in their interpretation of the formal goals of trade unions. Compulsory 'check-off' arrangements, 'union' or 'closed' shop regulations, training programmes for union officials, and pressure on employers to recognize the appropriate union will advance the union leaders' institutional interests. Both stringent legislation restricting the possibility of internal union opposition and state supervision of the internal processes of unions may be used to enhance the personal security of incumbent officials. If this strategy of isolating union leaders from rank-and-file pressures succeeds, it transforms leaders responsive to their members' aspirations into *de facto* public servants responsive to a 'public interest', as defined by the political authorities.

This model of union–government relations is applied here to the case of Kenya. In this country, where the political class has not succeeded in imposing many of its demands upon unionized workers, I argue that the persistence of traditional unionism owes much to the continued dependence of full-time leaders upon their lower leaderships and memberships. While the government has sought to augment the personal and institutional security of tractable union leaders, thus insulating them from pressures from below, certain contradictions in its labour policy have vitiated these efforts. Union leaders, whose primary interest is in maintaining their unions' strength and cohesion and their own positions, have thus reacted to the persistence of insecurity by militantly pressing workers' demands.

The generality of the contradictions I identify in the Kenyan case is difficult to gauge in the absence of comparable detailed studies of labour in other African countries. But my impression, based on the available comparative material cited in this book, is that some of these contradictions are of more general application. One contradiction, which is treated at some length in Part II, is between the formal rule that unions should be democratic in their internal procedures and the governmental expectation that a secure union leadership will accept responsibility for constraining their members' behaviour. Although the government has sought to make internal union opposition difficult, such opposition is not unfeasible. Internal union politics remain fluid and uncertain, with recurrent factional episodes often linked to struggles for control of the union movement. As long as union oppositionists are able to exploit the membership's dissatisfactions and tribal identity and to prevail upon their political contacts for campaign assistance in intra-union struggles, incumbent leaders are denied security and, hence, are driven towards assuming militant postures to ensure personal survival.

A second contradiction is between the informal rule that union leaders must be loyal to both the government and KANU and the practice that neither of these constitutes a cohesive entity. Since both of these bodies are faction-ridden, trade unionists can be subordinate to them, yet deeply involved in disruptive factional conflict. As I will show in Chapter 6, such political conflict invariably spills over to create or exacerbate factionalism within trade unions. The injunction that unions shall be politically loyal, therefore, does not enhance the security of union leaders. Again, the latter's personal and occasionally institutional insecurity pushes them towards militantly espousing traditional union aims in an effort to retain or capture their members' support.

The final contradiction, discussed at length in Chapter 9, is between the ruling elite's command that unions restrain wage and related demands in the public interest and its practice of self-enrichment and conspicuous consumption. Writers have often assumed that the new elite is committed, above all, to rapid economic development and social justice.[81] Hence, one general book on African trade unionism concluded with the injunction: 'Trade unions in the most advanced African countries must avoid becoming a radical opposition movement as their position is consolidated, since this could jeopardize the success of economic development policy.' The authors add, however, an important proviso: 'Opposition, even and especially political opposition, is only admissible when it is clear that the governing class is working for the consolidation of its own benefits rather than for the development of a progressive economy.'[82] Bates, in his study of the Zambian mineworkers, never considers the last possibility. 'It is,' he suggests, 'difficult to overemphasize the level of the government's commitment to rapid economic development.'[83]

The situation in Kenya is more akin to the danger foreseen by Ioan Davies in 1965, wherein the government, 'backed by a growing bureaucratic and commercial class, will deny increases in wages and services while at the same time swelling the power, privileges and earnings of the dominant economic groups'.[84] Owing to this growing contradiction, one can surmise that the government's present policy of wage restraint and union control is untenable in the long-run. The tension created by the disparity in wealth and the hypocrisy of the ideology of the public interest will likely become a major source of radicalization, where workers, perhaps allied with the urban unemployed, seize a political role independent of the party.[85]

2. Labour policy in Kenya

Why has the ruling elite of independent Kenya sought to control the emergent working class through its trade unions? Motives are, of course, always difficult to establish beyond dispute, given that one has to infer these from the public pronouncements of the political authorities and from the political and economic situation in which legislative or executive action against labour was initiated. In the literature on African unionism there is some disagreement over whether economic or political considerations constitute the foremost exigency determining post-colonial labour policies. The question often explicit or implicit in this literature is: do governments most fear that unions will provide a political base for opposition elements or an obstacle to economic growth? Some case studies of African trade unionism have simply listed both sets of considerations without assigning relative importance to them.[1] Other studies have assigned pre-eminence to the economic motive, in the belief that the political elite is wholeheartedly committed to economic development.[2] Yet other writers on the subject have concluded that the actual or potential political challenge posed by autonomous trade unionism was the most crucial factor.[3] Obviously, political and economic considerations cannot be neatly separated; economic actions by unions often have political implications. This must be the case since the government, as the largest single employer and the originator of legislation affecting labour's well-being, is often the immediate target of union-prompted industrial action. Beyond this, political implications of economic actions are ineluctable in a situation where the government has taken upon itself prime responsibility for economic development. Any major setbacks in economic growth occasioned by the demands and actions of organized labour redound upon the ruling elite's popularity and support.

While concern for economic growth is definitely important in understanding the Kenyan government's moves against organized labour, one can really only appreciate these within the context of the political economy adumbrated in the previous chapter. The political class, both as individuals and as a collectivity, is extremely insecure. Although the political class established its domination at independence with its inheritance of the state machinery, it has yet to secure its hegemony.[4] The new rulers, that is to say, have normally been able to obtain the assent of the ruled through the use or threat of use of varo sanctions – whether negative (in the form of coercion or penalties) or positive (in the form of material rewards). But it is doubtful whether they have managed to move beyond 'assent', which is coerced or bought, to 'consent', which is based upon conviction. The political class has not created a new political culture which legitimates its right to command; it simply shelters behind the popular image of Jomo Kenyatta, the hero of *Uhuru*, and of KANU.[5] Further, even the domination of this ruling group is insecure. Lacking a firm socio-economic base, the members of the ruling elite must rely for their positions upon the uncertain loyalty of clients, personal ethnic followings and the military.

Owing to this hegemonic crisis the government is suspicious of any organized social force outside its control. In Kenya (as elsewhere in Africa) the workers are one of the few organized social classes or class segments. Trade unions are, moreover, in a relatively powerful position, as they possess the finances, the prestige and the national importance to project their leaders as widely known personalities, as their members are strategically concentrated close to the centres of governmental power in the cities, and as they have the demonstrated capacity to articulate and activate the grievances not only of their own members, but of the entire wage-earning force and unemployed in the urban areas.[6] Hence, unionized workers constitute one of the few social forces capable of championing the ideal of social equality. Although the workers and unions are thoroughly 'economist' rather than radical, they can still play a decisive political role in a situation of hegemonic crisis. 'The "egotistic" oppositional action of urban wage-workers (and peripheral semi-employed) can', according to one astute analyst, 'debouch onto a genuine critique of the power system of postcolonial clientage – if the confrontation is sufficiently *sharp* and *sustained* and if it is relayed by groups with a wider social vision and programme...'.[7] Given this possibility, an insecure ruling group will direct its attention to the control of the emergent proletariat.

This chapter seeks to establish the inferential basis for the preceding assertions and to describe the main tactics employed by the state to regulate the behaviour of unions and their members. To demonstrate the continuity in Kenyan labour policy, I begin with a brief discussion of its development during the colonial period. Colonial regimes also sought to prevent unions from pursuing 'unacceptable' political and economic aims or employing 'irresponsible' tactics, and they also utilized coercion as well as rewards to elicit the compliance of trade unionists with their conception of organized labour's proper role. I do not, however, provide an historical account of the first stirrings of working-class consciousness and action and of the colonial regime's initial responses to this development; this task is left to other capable writers.[8]

The colonial period

Before the Second World War the Kenya government, like most other colonial governments, was openly antagonistic to the development of trade unions. Both the influential European community and the government were agreed that the necessary conditions for the emergence of unions were lacking, and that such organizations would be used for political agitation. However, organizations calling themselves trade unions and articulating the workers' grievances did emerge. In April 1935, Makhan Singh formed the non-racial Labour Trade Union of Kenya from the Indian Labour Trade Union. This union, which later changed its name to the Labour Trade Union of East Africa, initiated strike action against Nairobi Asian and European builders and contractors in April and May 1937. 'To prevent all irresponsible agitators from causing trouble among labour in the Colony', the Legislative Council passed the Trade Unions Ordinance in August 1937.[9] This ordinance merely required the compulsory registration of all trade unions; it neither legalized peaceful picketing nor protected unions from actions of tort. These two legal immunities were eventually granted in legislation passed in 1939 and 1943, respectively, largely in response to pressure from the Colonial Office.[10]

After the war, official policy in Kenya, as in all British colonies in Africa, shifted towards the fostering of trade unionism. While there were misgivings as to the appropriateness of the policy on the part of those responsible for implementing it, the Kenyan government nevertheless became formally committed to it after the arrival of a British Trade Union Labour Officer in April 1947 to advise trade unionists. The new policy, prompted by an awareness that Kenyan unionism was a permanent feature and pressure from the new British Labour government, had two aspects. The first was the belief that the state should protect the interests of the basically honest and loyal, though illiterate, members from actions of their allegedly 'unscrupulous' and 'semi-educated' leaders. This trusteeship role implied that the state, through the Registrar of Trade Unions, was obliged to supervise the internal administration of all unions. The second aspect of the policy was that the state should guide the development of trade unionism into solely economic channels. Unions were to pursue no political activities, apart from making representations to the government on matters concerning the terms and conditions of employment of their members. Moreover, the industrial relations activity of trade unions was to be conducted (if not *now*, at least in the *future*) in accordance with the British practice of free collective bargaining, through voluntary negotiating machinery.

Trade unions were to be guided towards 'proper' (i.e., honest and democratic) internal administration and 'responsible' industrial activities by means of regulation and supervision carried out by the Registrar of Trade Unions and advice and training schemes offered by the Labour Department.

Regulatory and supervisory roles of the state

The early post-war period demonstrated that the policy of restricting trade unions to solely economic goals would not succeed without further legislation. A Mombasa general strike of 15,000 African workers in January 1947 was the first incident to suggest that opponents of colonial rule could exploit the grievances of urban workers for their own political ends. Labour unrest, instigated by Chege Kibachia and his newly formed African Workers' Federation (AWF), spread upcountry from Mombasa in 1947. According to the Labour Department's *Annual Report*, 1947, a general strike in Kisumu in April was 'a reflection of the Mombasa general strike engendered by political elements desirous of making the Mombasa strike Colony-wide and having little or nothing to do with an industrial dispute'. The government's immediate reaction was to deport Kibachia to the northern part of the colony on the grounds that his activities were subversive to law and order. The AWF soon withered.[11]

The East African Trades Union Congress (EATUC), formed by Makhan Singh in May 1949, was primarily concerned with political goals. Some of its most prominent leaders, such as Fred Kubai and Bildad Kaggia, were also members of the radical wing of the Kenya African Union (KAU). Moreover, its constitution committed its members to ameliorate the 'social and political' conditions of the working class as well as its economic conditions. Predictably, the body was refused registration on the grounds that it was not a trade union as defined by the relevant ordinance.

This action did not deter the EATUC; it continued to function, arguing that, as a federation of trade unions, it was not legally a trade union but a society. As such, registration was not required. In early 1950, the Congress boycotted the celebrations accompanying the granting of the Royal Charter to Nairobi to protest against the 'racial and anti-trade union policies of the Government'. Attempts were made during the protest to assassinate two moderate African leaders – the KAU Vice President, Tom Mbotela, and the Nairobi Councillor, Muchohi Gikonyo. The next political action by the EATUC occurred on May Day, 1950. After the authorities refused to permit the organization to hold a procession and rally, trade union representatives, pledged, *inter alia*, that 'our unions and the EATUC would do their utmost for the achievement of workers' demands, complete freedom and independence of the East African territories and lasting peace of the world as a final solution to the problem of the workers in East Africa.' This call for independence echoed the policy announced a few days earlier by Kenyatta's KAU.[12]

The immediate reaction of the authorities was to arrest Makhan Singh and Kubai, charging them with being officers of an illegal trade union. To protest against the arrests, the EATUC then called a general strike in Nairobi. This was defeated only by a massive show of force in which the army as well as the police were employed, and some 300 strikers were arrested.

The reaction of the Labour Department to the political activities of the AWF and the EATUC was twofold. Following British practice elsewhere in the African colonies, this Department began in 1949 to encourage the formation of staff associations and works' committees as alternative forms of employee representation to trade unions. Staff associations, restricted to individual companies, employing no full-time officials and enjoying few legal immunities, were considerably easier to control than trade unions. Union leaders, realizing that these associations were an alternative to trade unionism, unreservedly opposed their establishment. Employees, too, apparently recognized that negotiations, with no legal recourse to the strike weapon, meant relying largely on the benevolence of employers. This, many workers were unwilling to do, provided there was an alternative. Hence, after 1950 a number of staff associations were converted into trade unions by their most active participants.

The second response to the failure of unions to develop as they were intended was increasingly restrictive legislation. Amendments to the Trade Unions and Trade Disputes Ordinance were passed in 1949; this Ordinance was replaced in 1952 by a new Trade Unions Ordinance. By March 1952, the Legislative Council had delegated such important supervisory powers as the following to the Registrar of Trade Unions: he could inspect the books of accounts, lists of members and other documents of registered unions at any time. He was given discretion either to register a trade union immediately on application or to place the prospective union on probation. Alternatively, he could refuse to register a new union or could cancel or suspend a union's registration once it had been granted, and the grounds on which he could exercise both these powers were progressively broadened. Needless to say, this power of registration is an important means of control, since an unregistered union is an illegal body whose leaders are liable to a fine or imprisonment.

Essential services legislation was another means by which the government attempted to regulate trade union activities. All governments, of course, must legislate to ensure that the public is protected from the dangerous consequences of stoppages in such public services as light, power, water, hospitals and sanitation. But when essential services legislation is extended to include almost all major industries, one has grounds for claiming that the authorities are reluctant to accept, in practice, their pronounced policy of encouraging free collective bargaining through voluntary machinery. This charge can be laid against the Kenya government during the 1950s. The original Essential Services Ordinance included the usual six services (the five listed above, plus the transport facilities necessary to the operation of them); three more were added in 1950, and a further four in 1954. Thus, by the latter date, the principle of compulsory arbitration had been extended to almost all major industries. It was not until 1958 that the Essential Services Ordinance was again amended, reducing the number of services in the schedule to ten.

The proclamation of a State of Emergency in connection with the Mau Mau rebellion in October 1952 led to more restrictions on trade unions. All meetings now required licences. Members of the Kikuyu, Embu or Meru tribes needed permits to travel or reside outside of their home areas. Moreover, members of these three tribes could no longer be employed as collectors of union subscriptions. During the first two years of the Emergency, the bulk of the Kikuyu, Embu and Meru union leaders were either repatriated or detained; those who remained usually avoided any active association with unions. Even trade unionists from other tribes were closely watched by the police, and occasionally interrogated.

Yet it was at this low point in trade union development that the contemporary structure of unionism was decided. With the advice of Jim Bury, the International Confederation of Free Trade Unions' adviser in East Africa in 1953–4, Tom Mboya, then head of the Kenya Federation of Registered Trade Unions, prevailed on the Labour Department to accept the principle that the appropriate basis of trade unions should be industrial (as in the United States and Canada), rather than craft (as in Britain). The aim was to avoid the proliferation of small, weak unions, a goal that was substantially achieved. The first few African unions organized after the Second World War had catered mainly for such occupational categories as printers, tailors, clerks and drivers, and had thus been restricted in the number of members they could recruit. However, the formation of industrial unions, to which all except executive and administrative grades could belong, greatly increased the scope of trade unionism after 1955. By 1960–1, the basic structure of the union movement was completed with the addition of unions catering for the various agricultural workers.

How successful was the government after 1952 in ensuring that only 'responsible' persons gained union office and pursued only narrowly defined economic goals? Emergency regulations effectively reduced the handful of new unions to mere shells, with few members weakly led; they revived fully only in the late 1950s. However, financial backing from the International Confederation of Free Trade Unions allowed the Kenya Federation of Registered Trade Unions, formed in June 1952, to survive and play a moderate political role. As no national African political organization was permitted after the Proclamation of the Emergency, it was not surprising that the KFRTU and its successor, the Kenya Federation of Labour, began to articulate the political as well as the economic grievances of Africans.[13] During the height of the Emergency in 1953–4, the Federation was cautious in its representations. It protested such things as the arrest of Kikuyu union leaders and members during the various sweeps in Nairobi and elsewhere. It urged the government to guarantee that all detainees with long service records, who were cleared of suspicion, would be reinstated with their former terms of service and privileges. It demanded that the government ensure decent housing for those arrested, and provide for their dependents. It protested to the Labour Department over the cancellation of the History of Employment Cards (the so-called 'Green Cards' that all Kikuyu, Embu and Meru workers were required to carry) belonging to various union members. Finally, it called for the removal of the restrictions on the movement of workers from these three tribes. In pursuit of these demands, Mboya and other Federation officials often successfully enlisted the support of the

British Trades Union Congress, British Labour Party backbenchers and the ICFTU.[14]

As long as the Federation restricted itself to private or public demands on issues directly affecting the interests of workers, its actions were defended by the government. But when it began to issue statements on broader political issues, the government reacted antagonistically. The first action of the KFL to arouse the ire of the authorities and the European community was its dispatch of a series of resolutions, passed at its May 1955 Annual Conference, to the Third World Congress of the ICFTU in Vienna. These resolutions demanded an inquiry into the injustices of 'forced labour' and 'imprisonment without trial' in Kenya, and suggested a number of measures (such as the granting of voting rights to Africans) to terminate the Emergency.[15] Further public statements and resolutions commenting on political issues or denouncing the colonial government were issued by KFL bodies or officials in 1956. In February 1956, following a particularly critical press conference held by Tom Mboya in London,[16] the Registrar of Societies was prompted to notify the Federation that it had one month within which to show cause why its registration should not be cancelled. He claimed that the organization had 'assumed the character of a political association', thus pursuing objectives undeclared in its application for registration.

Mboya and the KFL were able, at this juncture, to mobilize influential defenders in Britain, particularly Sir Vincent Tewson, Secretary General of the Trades Union Congress, and a large number of Labour Party M.P.s and officials.[17] The pressure from abroad apparently had some effect, for the Registrar of Societies eventually declined to cancel the registration of the KFL. Instead, he insisted that the association provide him with an undertaking not to participate in politics, other than to make representations on labour legislation, trade disputes and 'matters arising directly from the employer–employee relationships'.[18]

Although the KFL provided such assurances, the impunity with which these were ignored and repudiated suggests that the confrontation between the government and trade union federation was really won by the latter. For example, the list of resolutions submitted by the Federation to the Fifth World Congress of the ICFTU in July 1957 were as politically contentious as those submitted to the two previous world congresses. Demands for universal adult suffrage, an end to racial discrimination and the removal of the undertaking the KFL had been forced to sign were amongst the resolutions. Then, in October 1957, the Federation submitted a memorandum to the Colonial Secretary entitled 'The Functioning of Trade Unions in Kenya'. This document demanded, among other things, that the Kenya government be instructed to nullify the KFL's 'assurances', since these 'directly contravened the United Nations Declaration of Human Rights and the I.L.O. Conventions on Freedom of Association and the Right to Organize and Bargain Collectively'. It also requested the Colonial Secretary to press the Kenyan government to terminate the Emergency, ban European immigration to Kenya and set aside a part of the 'White Highlands' for African Settlement. Furthermore, Tom Mboya, reporting to the KFL's Annual Conference in September 1958, gave notice that the Federation would not abide by the 1956 ruling that it should not mix trade unionism with politics. He later vehemently condemned the provisions for a qualitative franchise under the Coutts recommendations and revealed that the KFL had requested the ICFTU to examine Kenyan legislation which seemed to sanction forced labour.[19]

The union movement's effective contribution to the nationalist struggle was, in fact, limited to the articulation of political grievances of Africans. Although political strikes were proposed on two occasions prior to independence, both attempts failed. In early April 1960, Joseph Mathenge, the General Secretary of Mboya's political party, the Nairobi Peoples' Convention Party, announced that the party would organize a 'Stay-at-Home' strike and a large procession to present a petition to the Governor demanding the release from detention of Jomo Kenyatta. Both of these ventures were to take place on Good Friday, 15 April, which was to be recognized as 'Kenyatta Day'. In the event, both the proposed procession and strike failed to materialize, owing to the firm stand adopted by the authorities.[20] It appeared that no union leader was willing to risk the de-registration of his union by publicly exhorting his membership to participate in what was patently a political strike. Without strong leadership from the top, the strike was doomed to failure. Mboya himself was away on one of his foreign trips during most of this time. But, as the Federation of Kenya Employers' paper on trade unions and politics noted, 'What would have happened if Tom Mboya had been in the country seems more doubtful.'[21]

The second attempt at a political strike also miscarried, this time largely because of political differences among African politicians and trade unionists. On 20 January 1961, the Governing Council of the newly formed Kenya African National Union (KANU), of which Mboya was Secretary-General, decided to call a three-day strike, beginning on 1 February, to obtain the release of Kenyatta from detention. Two days later, when revealing the party's plan at a public rally in Mombasa, Mboya asserted he would 'actively help to organize it'. It is likely that the KFL leader felt constrained to provide strong backing for the strike since Oginga Odinga and others had publicly blamed James Gichuru and Mboya for the delay in releasing Kenyatta.[22] In any event, the proposed strike failed to materialize; the leaders of several unions affiliated with the KFL rejected it. Once again, it was clear that few union leaders were willing to risk their unions' registration or their own positions for purely political objectives.

Less dangerous demonstrations of union support for KANU were, however, quite acceptable to union leaders. For instance, the Labour Day celebrations of 20 October 1961 were really a KANU affair. Organized by the KFL, the gathering of workers was addressed by both Kenyatta and Mboya, sang the KANU song, and displayed placards asserting allegiance to the party. The obvious preference of most union leaders for KANU occasionally led its opponent, the Kenya African Democratic Union, to propose establishing its own unions. Nothing followed from these proposals, probably because the bulk of workers came from tribes favouring KANU.

Three factors largely explain the KFL's success in asserting its right to play a moderate political role in the late 1950s. First, since Mau Mau had effectively been defeated by 1957, both the government and the settler community had less fear of trade unions becoming subversive and were less hostile to the idea of the trade union federation pronouncing on political matters. Second, Tom Mboya successfully capitalized on liberal opinion in Britain, and to a lesser extent in the United States, in defence of the KFL's right to take political stands. Third, Mboya became an increasingly powerful person once he entered the Legislative Council in 1957. Parliament provided Mboya with another public platform from which to defend organized labour against restrictions.

Advisory role of the state

The Colonial Office evidently felt that supervision and coercion were insufficient means of guiding trade unionism into 'responsible' economic bargaining activities. In 1942, it began to experiment with attaching experienced British trade unionists to colonial labour departments. Their job was to advise and train local union leaders on how best to organize and administer their organizations and establish mutually beneficial relations with employers. In West Africa and the West Indies, the experiment was largely successful. 'Trade Union Labour Officers' began to arrive in the less economically developed East African territories in 1947, after Major St J. Orde Browne had recommended such appointments in his report to the Colonial Office on labour conditions in that part of Africa.[23]

James Patrick, the first such labour officer in Kenya, arrived in April 1947, at a time when only three miniscule African unions had been registered. He soon encountered European hostility to union organisation. Shortly after his arrival, Patrick made the mistake of advocating the policy of encouraging trade unionism in a speech to a meeting of employers. Their reaction was to pass a virtually unanimous resolution suggesting that the British trade unionist return to Kenya in twenty years, at which time the conditions for trade unionism might be favourable. When Patrick reported this resolution to his Labour Commissioner, he was surprised to discover that his superior agreed with it![24]

The employers need not have worried about Patrick or his successor after 1955, R. A. J. Damerell. Both officers clearly saw their job as encouraging only a very restricted and apolitical form of labour organization. In pursuit of this end, they advised groups of employees on the procedures for registering a union, and often virtually drafted the prospective unions' constitutions. They spoke at innumerable union meetings on such topics as the following: 'Trade Unions and the Government' (unions were legal and no one would be arrested for being a member or an official), 'Trade Unions and Politics' (there should not be any in trade unionism), 'Central Office Set-up and Branch Set-up' (union leaders were not the 'bosses' – the members were), 'Shop Stewards and Their Functions', 'Procedures in Handling Grievances', 'History of Trade Unionism in Britain', etc. The Labour Department also distributed literature in English and Swahili to unions, including reprints of relevant labour legislation and commentaries on the rights and obligations of union leaders under this legislation. A pamphlet written by Patrick in 1949 entitled 'What a Trade Union Is' illustrates the kind of advice offered to neophytes in Kenyan trade unions. 'A trade union', he held, contrary to British practice, 'is not an organization with political aims, it is an association which has as its main object the regulation of relations between workers and their employers.' Furthermore, 'trade unions are formed so that strikes can be avoided. Trade unions try to make sure that workers and employers understand one another.' On the virtues of hard work and increased production, Patrick advised that 'the value of a worker to his employer depends on the kind of work he does and how he does it. Good, hard work is of more value than bad, lazy work. Good workers who work hard can expect to get better wages and conditions than bad, lazy workers.'

Labour Department officials also constantly advised trade unionists on how best to negotiate with employers. Since most of the correspondence between unions and employers was copied to the Labour Department, officials kept a paternal eye open for any statements which seemed unnecessarily provocative. Not infrequently, the following or similar notation appears in the correspondence files of the Labour Department, directed to the Labour Officer (Industrial Relations): 'use next opportunity to tell Mr. X that this sort of provocation of employers is bringing his union into disrepute.' The object of all such advice was clearly to demonstrate to union leaders that they could gain more by following established collective bargaining machinery than by threatening employers. On occasion, when a union leader was particularly 'responsible' in his approach to a dispute, a labour officer would try to persuade the relevant management to reward such behaviour with concessions.

It is easy to criticize the trade union advisers in Kenya and many other British colonies for being too pro-employer and pro-government. Indeed, both Patrick and Damerell operated under an onerous conflict of interests since, on the one hand, they were employed by the Labour Department and, on the other, their job was to advise and assist union leaders. For Patrick this conflict of loyalties was especially agonizing, as several of his superiors and most of his European social contacts were bitterly hostile to trade unionism. At a time when many employers believed that the best way to handle labour problems was by calling the police or dismissing some workers, Patrick's views were progressive. By 1952, he had abandoned his short-lived efforts to encourage the formation of works committees rather than trade unions and had accepted the desirability or perhaps inevitability of strong trade unionism.

Trade union advisers could, of course, only be effective if union leaders were willing to consult them. During the difficult times occasioned by the Emergency regulations, Tom Mboya accepted assistance from any quarter in his organizational efforts. He thus advocated 'friendly understanding' with the Labour Department from the beginning of his union career in 1953. In the atmosphere thus created, Patrick and Damerell were successful in gaining the respect of prominent union leaders. Owing partly to their advice and training schemes, unions had acquired enough expertise by 1958 or shortly thereafter to enter into direct negotiations with employers.

To sum up, the Labour Department in colonial Kenya was quite success-ful in its policy of guiding unionism into economic channels. The first bodies calling themselves trade unions had capitalized on the political as well as economic grievances of Africans to foment strikes and disturbances against the colonial regime. The government had responded with severe sanctions against the leaders of these ephemeral unions and with more stringent union legislation. These actions successfully intimidated most union leaders so that, after 1953, politics really only preoccupied the Kenya Federation of Labour, not its affiliates. Since the KFL was the only African association permitted to exist on a territory-wide basis between 1952 and 1960, its insistence on articulating the political grievances of Africans is understandable. Indeed, any other course would have branded the Federa-tion's officials as the puppets of the colonial establishment. To the extent that Kenyan trade unions devoted themselves largely to economic and bargaining activities in the 1950s, leaving politics to the trade union federa-tion, the Kenyan pattern of union development was similar to that elsewhere on the continent.[25]

The independence period

After national independence in 1963, Kenyatta's KANU government soon showed itself to be just as concerned to control organized labour as the colonial regime had been. This concern, I earlier argued, was a consequence of certain economic and political exigencies which bear a resemblance to those operative during the colonial period. The ruling elite demanded both political subordination and economic responsibility on the part of unions, and it wielded a number of sanctions to obtain the acquiescence of workers' leaders.

Political subordination

Both colonial and nationalist regimes have been suspicious of union de-mands for political autonomy. But while the response of the colonial regime was to try to insulate the organized workers from politics and the struggle for independence, the nationalist regime has instead demanded the unswerving loyalty of unions to both the government and the governing party.

As soon as it became clear in 1960 that independence was in the offing, the KFL enunciated a policy on the proper political role of the labour movement in the post-colonial situation. This was contained in a mature and well-written policy statement entitled 'This Is Our Stand'. In a section headed 'Trade Unions and Politics Before and After Independence', the statement asserted that the union movement had an important political role to play. 'If the movement must be free and independent of the Government and Employers, it must be capable of formulating its own policies on those problems which affect the workers either as employees or as a certain class that lives and occupies a position in the Society and Community in which it exists.' Trade unionism must not limit itself strictly to matters concerning the terms and conditions of employment, but must also concern itself with such other questions as 'human rights legislation, matters of economic policy, housing policy, education and welfare policy, social security and old age pensions and many others'. After independence the union movement would become 'more and more interested in the national economic policies of the government, it will be interested in the defence and promotion of workers' interests and, generally it will have interests and face problems identical to those of the government....But its own existence as a free and independent movement will continue to be a principle that must be maintained.'

Ironically, the first African cabinet minister to threaten trade-union political autonomy was Tom Mboya, the very man who, as General Secretary of the KFL, had earlier drafted the above policy statement. The circumstances leading up to this threat require some adumbration. Towards the end of 1962, the top KFL leaders began to assume a position of independence from both Mboya (who at this time was both Labour Minister in a coalition government and formal head of the KFL) and his party, KANU. The union leaders sought independence partly because of their personal estrangement from their erstwhile patron, Tom Mboya, and partly because they feared that an independent KANU government would follow Tanganyika's example of reducing the autonomy of trade unionism. KFL bodies consequently adopted resolutions criticizing politicians for their 'petty insinuations' and infighting, and demanded that the government announce its plans for economic development, which should include the nationalization of key industries and the creation of collective farms.[26] Most dramatically, the Federation's Executive Committee decided in February 1963 that it should sponsor its own independent labour candidates in the forthcoming general elections. Mboya, to preserve his own position and ensure that valuable urban KANU votes were not siphoned away by labour independents, acted quickly to bring the Federation back into line. At a public meeting in Mombasa on 10 February, he warned the unionists that 'politics is not a joke. If trade union leaders oppose us now, we shall have to deal with them if we come to power.'[27] The KFL's capitulation to Mboya's threats and personal pressure tactics was signified on 1 March by a joint press statement issued by the KFL's President and Acting General Secretary and the Labour Minister (Mboya). This announced that the Federation would not sponsor its own candidates, but would support any labour candidates sponsored by a political party.

Kenyan trade unionism never again sought to exert itself as an independent force in politics. Union leaders continued to take part in politics, but they participated, as Chapter 6 reveals, as individuals in the complex factionalism which has characterized Kenyan politics since independence. While KANU leaders have always disagreed on which faction should hold pre-eminent influence in trade unions, they have been united in the view that union leaders should take no actions which weaken the position of the ruling elite as a whole. Since no opposition party existed between November 1964 and April 1966, no problem about the political loyalty of trade unionists arose. However, this question was acutely posed in 1966 when dissident KANU leaders broke away to form a new opposition – the Kenya Peoples' Union. At this point a firm informal rule was introduced: all officials of the trade union federation must be loyal to the ruling party as well as more generally to the government. This rule was affirmed by the Central Organization of Trade Unions (Kenya) in April 1966 when its Executive Committee dismissed four of that body's members for leaving KANU to join the KPU. It was later confirmed in policy statements issued by COTU's two secretaries-general, both of whom either were at the time, or soon became, KANU M.P.s.[28] Interviews with some prominent political leaders revealed the reason for this informal injunction: they suspected that a supporter of the opposition party would inevitably use his COTU position to embarrass the government. However, KPU members were, before the banning of that party in October 1969, not excluded from leading individual unions, though they had to take care to demonstrate their 'responsibility' in industrial relations. In any case, only two of the thirty Kenyan general secretaries were known KPU supporters in 1969.

The ruling elite has also gradually increased its own direct control over the decision-making apparatus within the union movement. Most of these governmental initiatives were undertaken while union leaders were split in factional rivalries. Hence, when intra-union conflict led to three deaths in Mombasa in June 1965, President Kenyatta appointed a Ministerial Committee to suggest how labour unity could be restored. This committee was composed of Mboya plus two allies, two 'progressive' ministers (Joseph Murumbi and R. Achieng-Oneko), and three who were close to Kenyatta (Charles Njonjo, J. G. Kiano and James Gichuru). Their compromise proposals to end disunity involved closer governmental supervision in the union's sphere.[29] The KFL and the Congress were both to be deregistered immediately, and a new federation, the Central Organization of Trade Unions, established. All affiliations with organisations outside Kenya were to be cancelled. Government-supervised elections were to be held in all unions, starting at the branch level. Finally, the Attorney-General's Department was to prepare COTU's constitution, incorporating a number of the Committee's recommendations.

COTU's Constitution, completed in January 1966, entrenched state super-vision of that federation's internal affairs. Its Governing Council, Executive Board and Finance Committee include a governmental representative. Elections are held triennially, under government supervision. The President of the Republic appoints the secretary-general, deputy secretary-general and assistant secretary-general from a panel of names submitted to him by the Governing Council after the triennial conference. At any time the Labour Minister desires, the conduct of these three officials may be investigated. In addition, the President of the Republic may revoke the appointments of any or all of the three principal officials.[30]

The government has sought increasing control over COTU's internal affairs since 1966. For instance, the Registrar of Trade Unions' office assumed in 1967 the task of examining COTU's expenditures each year to ensure that these are not only licit and constitutional, but also 'valid' or well-balanced. (COTU leaders would be reprimanded if it were discovered, for example, that 60 per cent of the budget was spent on wages, or 30 per cent of the budget on transportation, even though such expenditure is legal and constitutional.) Then, on 14 December 1968, C. K. Lubembe, then Secretary-General of COTU, received a confidential letter from the Per-manent Secretary, Ministry of Labour, asserting that the government had decided to introduce, with effect from 1 January, some changes in COTU's structure and organization. These changes were to form part of the official policy on trade unions. The most significant items were the following: an economy measure reducing both the salaries of COTU officials and the number of full-time staff members; the termination of teachers' and civil servants' unions' membership in COTU; the stipulations that no quorum on the Governing Council or the Executive Board of COTU would be complete without government representation, and that the government representative would have a veto on all financial matters; the requirement that all external affiliations or financial assistance for either COTU or its affiliates gain the approval of the Minister for Labour; and the rule that the failure of a national union to gain COTU's sanction for strike action would constitute an offence. Clearly, these changes, taken together, represent a significant increment in centralized, government control. The object seemed to be to obtain a strong voice in COTU for public officials, and then to provide COTU with more authority over its supposedly autonomous affiliates. The proposed rule requiring unions to obtain COTU's permission before under-taking strike action is a case in point.

COTU officials were at first obdurate. Lubembe secured the backing of both his Executive Board and the Governing Council to reject the government's paper. The government, far from united on the issue, decided not to press the matter until after COTU's triennial elections, scheduled for early February. Later on, the Labour Ministry sent the same list of demands to Denis Akumu, who had defeated Lubembe for COTU's top post. Akumu, fearing that recalcitrance would provoke even more restrictive measures in the form of a new trade unions act, decided not to confront the government publicly over its paper. The demands, in any case, would not have any legal effect. Thus, in October 1969, the Minister of Labour announced some of the changes as part of the government's policy on trade unions. Others were never made public.

By 1972, in short, the scope for independent political action by unions was negligible. It was, in fact, far more confined than it had been between 1958 and 1962. COTU leaders were permitted, apart from pledging 'unflinching' loyalty to the President and KANU, to submit petitions to, and lobby with, government officials on policies or laws affecting the immediate economic interests of working people or the institutional interests of trade unions. How trade unionists have actually operated in the political sphere is the subject of Chapter 6.

Economic responsibility

In the economic sphere, both colonial and post-colonial regimes have sought to prevent the emergence of workers' organizations which might provoke industrial unrest, make 'unreasonable' demands and lower production. In addition, the independence regime has enunciated a more positive productionist role for unions. In doing so, the governing party amended its earlier commitment to a high-wage economy.

Miserable terms and conditions of service for African workers provided the context in which African unions emerged. The Carpenter Commission, established to investigate minimum wage policy in 1954, claimed that African wages had barely kept pace with increases in the cost of living between 1945 and 1954.[31] During this period, minimum wages were predicated on the supposed needs of a bachelor occupying a single-bed space. It is doubtful, however, that these wages were even adequate to provide for a bachelor's barest needs. A survey carried out in 1950 revealed that a large proportion of the workers had little or nothing to eat during the last few days of each month.[32] Moreover, inquiries into the Mombasa labour disturbances of 1939, 1944 and 1947 reported that their basic causes were low wages and appalling living conditions.[33] Employers apparently allowed these conditions to persist because of their evaluation of the short-run effects of higher wages. Disbelieving that the purchasing power of Africans could ever be significant, they tended to view African workers as 'lazy, undependable, irrevocably unskilled and likely to respond to higher wages by lower productivity'.[34] Not surprisingly, therefore, the Carpenter Commission was moved in making its recommendations by 'a growing recognition of social evils (overcrowding, malnutrition, venereal disease, juvenile delinquency, etc.) which are seen to result from the employment of migrant labour in towns'.

The government's acceptance of the main principles of the Carpenter Commission in 1954 marked the beginning of the end of a cheap labour supply. To encourage the formation of a permanent wage-earning force and thus increase labour productivity, the Committee advocated the payment of a wage sufficient to provide for the needs of the worker *and* his family. It suggested a dual minimum wage system: one for married workers and the other for bachelors. In its own white paper, the government accepted this idea, but decided to use age rather than marital status as the criterion. It thus established 'adult' and 'youth' minimum wages. In the same year, the government also accepted the principle that salary scales in the public service should be set up without distinction as to race. Both policies tended to encourage wage increases for Africans.

Political pressure on firms to grant high wage increases in order to become known as a 'progressive' employer was heightened after 1960 when the newly-formed Kenya African National Union endorsed a high wage economy. In August 1962, the Labour Ministers of Kenya, Uganda and Tanganyika jointly declared that: 'Having reviewed all the economic arguments and possible implications, [they] agreed that the future policy must be based on a high wage economy and that each East African Government should review its wage structure aiming at a minimum wage that would provide a worker and his family with a reasonable standard of living.'[35] On the same theme, KANU's 1963 Election Manifesto asserted: 'We have clearly stated our belief in a high wage economy and the steps we intend to take to improve the lot of the workers.'

KANU's pronouncements on the economic role of trade unions changed after independence. Exhortations directed at union leaders to discipline their members, restrain their wage demands and refrain from strike action posed dilemmas for these leaders in defining the proper activities of their organisations. Tom Mboya, the Minister most closely associated with organized labour, very clearly articulated the government's expectations in a 1964 paper entitled 'Trade Unions and Development'.[36] Since Mboya here raised arguments which have since been endlessly repeated by other officials, it is worthwhile to quote the article at some length.

On the question of discipline, Mboya maintained that trade unions must insist upon hard work and obedience to instructions on the part of their members. Union leaders would have to 're-educate' the workers so as to change their attitudes toward employers and the government. Workers must realize that employers, who yesterday were 'the arch-supporters of the colonial regime', are now the colleagues of their nationalist government. Trade unions must therefore 'persuade the workers that if we are to progress, they must put greater effort into their work'.

With respect to wage increases, Mboya called upon unions to recognize the public interest in capital formation and social equality which might conflict with the immediate economic interests of workers. 'If unions concentrate too much upon the wage interest, they may end up by producing a new elite of paid workers, as against the poorer self-employed peasant farmers.' Instead, the primary objective of union leaders should be to increase the size of the total economic pie, rather than to seek a larger slice of the existing pie for its members. Unions should adopt other useful goals to retain their members' interest once unions restrain their wage demands in the public interest. Unions could make an important contribution to their members' well-being in the fields of vocational and adult education, health insurance schemes and clinics and workers' co-operatives in retail and wholesale trade and housing.

Finally, Mboya appealed to unions to desist from strike action and instead dedicate themselves to increasing production for the good of all. He hinted that if the unions did not co-operate voluntarily with the government's pleas, they might be forced to do so. 'I would not be happy to see the curtailment of trade union rights in my own country. But the guarantee of the continuance of those rights will rest upon the recognition by the unions of the responsible role they must play in building prosperity.'

That legislation curtailing trade-union powers would be necessary was suggested in Sessional Paper No. 10 of 1965. After enumerating the detrimental economic effects of strikes and high wages, the white paper went on to advocate legislation providing for the 'compulsory arbitration of major issues not resolved through the regular bargaining process'. As well, 'special legislation may be needed in sensitive industries to avoid the economic paralysis that could result from work stoppages in these areas.'

The legislation directly bearing on the economic role of unions includes the Trade Disputes Act, 1964 setting up the Industrial Court, the Trade Disputes Act, 1965 and the amendment to this Act in 1971. While I do not intend to summarize the evolution of the industrial relations system in Kenya, a few key features of this legislation are worth mentioning.[37]

Guided by the Minister for Labour, E. N. Mwendwa, the second Trade Disputes Act received the sanction of the National Assembly in June 1965. Speeches made by the Minister and others in support of the bill suggest that they felt its restrictive provisions were required to prevent unions from calling 'unnecessary' strikes and causing labour unrest.[38] One of its provisions extended the list of essential services by five, and provided that the Labour Minister could refer a trade dispute in any essential service to arbitration by the Industrial Court. The Act also stipulated rigorous procedures to be followed in reporting and resolving trade disputes. Most importantly, the Minister of Labour was empowered to declare strikes (or lock-outs) illegal. He may declare an actual or threatened strike unlawful where the parties have not yet exhausted their voluntary disputes-settlement machinery (sec. 19), or where there is an agreement or award regulating the matters under dispute (sec. 20), or where the action is sympathetic and not related to a dispute within the employee's own industry (sec. 21). In practice, the requirement that a union must exhaust the voluntary disputes-settlement machinery has been interpreted very broadly. The Industrial Court, a permanent arbitration tribunal, has been considered by the Minister of Labour as part of the voluntary machinery within each industry. Hence, the only conceivable occasion on which a strike can be lawful is when the union is willing to take a trade dispute to the Industrial Court but the employer refuses.

The government, apparently feeling that these powers were insufficient, introduced a further rule restricting the right to strike in 1969. This was established in June 1969 after a large number of unions served strike notice on employers and several unions organized work stoppages. Discussions were held between the Ministry of Labour and COTU, at which the Secretary-General was informed that the government was considering legislation to ban strikes entirely. After consultation with affiliated unions, COTU negotiated an informal agreement whereby unions would only call strikes with its approval.[39] Thus, the right to strike was preserved in principle, but unions were obliged not only to exhaust all voluntary disputes machinery, but also to secure COTU's endorsement for strike action. In October 1969, the Labour Minister announced this as a formal commitment, warning that failure by unions to comply with this agreement would be considered an offence. COTU has, not surprisingly, been unwilling to sanction a strike unless there has been an extremely clear-cut case for one.

The Trade Disputes (Amendment) Act, passed in July 1971, contained further restrictions on the right to strike, though its real significance lay elsewhere. This bill was introduced just before the expiry of the second Tripartite Agreement for the Immediate Relief of Unemployment (discussed in Chapter 8), which committed the trade unions to a year-long wage freeze. According to Peter Kibisu, the Assistant Minister for Labour who introduced the bill, the amendments were necessary to prevent high wage demands at the expiry of the agreement from crippling the economy.[40] One of the amendments expanded the definition of 'strike' to include 'go-slows', while another narrowed the definition of what were acceptable trade disputes. Also, the 'cooling off' period of strike notice was extended.

The potentially most important part of the Act is that dealing with the implementation of an incomes policy. In its *Development Plan, 1970–1974*, the government had announced its intention to secure a 'just distribution of national income' through the regulation of urban wages. This was to be accomplished by requiring that all collective bargaining agreements be approved and registered by a reconstituted Industrial Court. This body was to decide whether increases in wages and fringe benefits were justified on the basis of guidelines established by a committee of the cabinet. Little more was heard about this proposed incomes policy between the publication of the development plan in November 1969 and the introduction of the Trade

Disputes (Amendment) Act in June 1971. This Act followed the proposals contained in the *Development Plan, 1970–1974*, except that the guidelines for the new Industrial Court were to be issued by the Minister of Finance instead of a cabinet committee.

Two years after the passing of this bill into law, its provisions dealing with the incomes policy had still not come into operation. The delay is partly a result of the complexity of machinery for fixing wages and prices: expert staff have to be recruited to advise the Industrial Court; the rent control board and costs and prices committee have to be given more authority and expertise; and realistic guidelines on wage increases have to be formulated. All these changes take time. Apart from this, top political leaders feel that an incomes policy, which is bound to be unpopular with a large section of the urban population, should not be initiated until after KANU completes its elections at all levels. These were not finished by the end of 1973.

By 1973, therefore, the unions' freedom to bargain collectively and press their members' individual and collective demands had been limited but not eliminated. At the same time, however, politicians and officials of the Ministry of Labour constantly exhorted union leaders to exercise restraint, follow orderly (and time-consuming) procedures and counsel hard work and obedience. How unions have adapted to this situation and the dynamics of the process of adaptation are treated in Chapters 7 and 8. What remains to be considered here are the *tactics* employed by the government to secure the compliance of trade unionists with its conception of proper union behaviour.

The use of sanctions

How did political leaders prevail on union leaders to accept severe limitations on their independence of action? It is notable, in the first place, that the government has always introduced restrictive legislation when the union movement has been badly split. With top union leaders bitterly opposed, there was little prospect of them uniting in opposition to the new controls. Furthermore, the contending factions of union leaders were usually partially dependent on prominent political leaders for resources; hence, Tom Mboya, when he backed the introduction of labour legislation in 1964 and 1965, could rely upon the support of the KFL leadership. True, the anti-KFL leadership and its political allies were bound to object, but this group did not carry enough influence to block the legislation. Union leaders' reliance on KANU factions for resources and support continued even after the KPU breakaway in April 1966. This dependence has meant that few union leaders have been willing to antagonize their patrons in the government by taking an irrevocable stand against further state encroachment on union autonomy.

A closely related point is that many union leaders view trade unionism less as a vocation than as a convenient 'step-ladder' (to use the colloquial phrase) into politics. Hence, trade unionists are frequently disinclined to jeopardize their political ambitions by publicly opposing the wishes of powerful politicians.

The government has also operated on the principle that if trade unionists are allowed to share in the confraternity of power, they are less likely to regard themselves as having distinctive interests conflicting with those of the political elite. Union leaders have been co-opted to a number of governmental boards and committees, where they participate together with members of the political and economic elites.[41] Moreover, the Minister of Labour is easily accessible to any union leader with a particular grievance. With the same aim of increasing the feeling of participation in policy-making, KANU's second election manifesto of November 1969 contained the assurance that consultations would be held with COTU on all matters affecting economic development – particularly wages policy.

It is probably not accidental that restrictive labour legislation usually also contains some benefit for trade union organization. As a *quid pro quo* for limitation of the right to strike in the Trade Disputes Act, 1965, for example, trade unionists were granted a voluntary 'check-off' system.[42] Employers with more than four union members in their employ were made legally responsible for remitting monthly union dues directly to trade unions. This system provided many trade unions with financial security for the first time. Similarly, the Trade Disputes (Amendment) Act of 1971 contained, along with provisions restricting the strike weapon and laying the groundwork for an incomes policy, a boon for trade unions. One of the amendments empowered the Industrial Court to consider dismissals and to order employers to reinstate employees who had been wrongfully dismissed. This change represented a considerable advance for unions since, prior to August 1971, the Industrial Court could merely recommend that a particular employee be reinstated. That this provision was conceived as a *quid pro quo* by the government was implied by the assistant minister who seconded the Trade Disputes (Amendment) Act. He observed that 'a go slow will have to be replaced by the fact that any member [sic] who is sacked will be taken to the highest Industrial Court in the country and, therefore, an employer will not be sacking anybody with [out] good reasons and on the other hand, there will be no go slow strikes.'[43]

Finally, the government controls a number of coercive powers that can be used to gain the compliance of recalcitrant union leaders. All the labour legislation passed in 1964, 1965 and 1971 stipulated severe penalties for any infractions of the rules. In Kenya, as in many African countries, the state, besides defining the scope of union economic action, decrees the structure of trade unionism, specifies the general content of the union's constitutional rules, including the qualifications for candidates for top union office, supervises union elections at all levels, and requires the submission of periodic reports on finances and the election of office-holders. Moreover, the 'Presidential Declaration' of policy on trade unions of September 1965 empowered the President of the Republic to remove any or all of the three principal officers of COTU. If these powers are not enough, the Preservation of Public Security Act, 1966 allows the President to detain without trial any union leader (or anyone else) whom he suspects of subversive activities. By 1972, six union leaders had been detained under this Act.

These are impressive powers, but I suggested in Chapter 1 that union leaders will only become fully amenable to governmental demands when they feel secure in their positions and are isolated from rank-and-file pressures. To a large extent, the exigencies of internal union politics determine the behaviour of union leaders in all spheres of activity. It is to these exigencies which I now turn.

PART II

The state and the internal organization of unions

3. The tendency toward oligarchy

What sort of organization is a trade union? To recapitulate briefly, I have contended that union leaders are normally quite responsive to the desires of their rank-and-file. This is the case not because unions are 'democratic' in the full sense of the word, but because the unions' institutional interests (i.e. their strength and financial viability) and the union leaders' personal interest (i.e. in maintaining their positions of power) together ensure that union decisions are congruent with the members' interests. As long as unions remain voluntary associations in which oppositions can operate and from which members can withdraw, union officials have limited room for man-oeuvre. In an underdeveloped country, 'free trade unionism', as one authority has remarked 'must ordinarily appeal to the worker on an all-out consumption platform.' There is no other choice because new workers have 'an urgent and insatiable demand for the consumer goods which have just been revealed to them. Trade unions must therefore be militantly pro-consumption at the risk of alienating their constituents.'[1]

How then can governments transform trade unions into instruments for controlling the workers' demands and actions? In the absence of overwhelming coercion such as that wielded by Stalin, the political authorities must offer organizational and personal security to union leaders in exchange for concessions in their interpretation of the role of trade unionism. Although this strategy may succeed (from the viewpoint of the ruling elite) in subduing the unions, it may well not solve the problem of worker alienation and protest. Workers are not automatically responsive to their union leaders' exhortations.

What has been the situation in Kenya? This chapter seeks to demonstrate that Kenyan unions have constituted no exception to Robert Michels' famous 'Iron Law of Oligarchy'. But, at the same time, members have retained means of holding their leaders responsive to their desires. The following two chapters deal with how and why internal factionalism persists, in spite of legislation designed to discourage opposition. Internal union politics still remain lively; this ensures that union leaders seek to fulfil their members' expectations before those of the state.

The power-holders

Authority in most Kenyan unions is highly personalistic. Although the unions' constitutions divide authority between various offices and bodies, many unions are dominated by one or two 'strong-man' leaders who run their organizations regardless of the niceties of these constitutions. Who are the power-holders and to what do they aspire?

The number of elected national officers in unions ranges from six to ten. All unions elect a president, general secretary and treasurer, plus assistants to these posts; a few have, in addition, a second or third assistant to the positions of president and secretary and, occasionally, an elected auditor. There are generally six offices in each branch, comprising a chairman, secretary and treasurer and assistants to these positions. In a couple of unions, a single individual fills the combined post of branch secretary–treasurer. The number of full-time national officers ranges from one to six, depending on a union's size. In most branches all officials are part-time, though the larger ones are run by a full-time branch secretary. The smaller unions have no full-time branch officials at all while the larger ones have up to fifteen.

Most union constitutions are unclear as to whether the president or the general secretary should be pre-eminent. The result has been frequent rivalries between the persons holding these two positions. While the president is usually empowered to 'preside at all conferences and meetings, enforce observation of the Constitution and Rules of the Union and perform such duties as by usage and custom pertain to his office', the general secretary is to 'be responsible to the Central Council [or Executive Committee] for all Union activities'.

In practice, the general secretary is in a more favourable position to resolve the constitutional ambiguity in his own favour than is the president. In nearly all cases, the former is a full-time official whereas the latter is only part-time, employed on a full-time basis elsewhere. The general secretary normally has the advantage therefore of being able to channel all his time and energy into union activities, while the president has commitments elsewhere. Consequently, the general secretary can more easily build up a personal following among the branch officials and members, often with the aid of one or more 'organizing secretaries' whom he has hired. Not surprisingly, then, the president has managed to assert his paramountcy in only three of the fifteen unions studied, and in each of these cases a general secretary eventually managed to oust the president.

Why do people struggle to become union officials? This was a question I directed at all union officers with whom I came into contact. The most frequent response was that men sought office in order to advance their own careers in some respect or to gain certain material benefits. Politically ambitious people were attracted to full-time union posts, many suggested, because of the opportunity it offered them to learn such crucial political skills as effective speech-making and organizing supporters, to obtain publicity and to use the union's resources to win political office. The following was a typical comment: 'Being an official means that you can get ahead. You meet important people and become widely known. If a person is politically ambitious, trade unions provide a good launching pad. A union leader has the opportunity to meet important political leaders who may want to sponsor him in politics.'

Union leadership can also be useful in gaining promotions for a part-time official within his firm. Shop stewards and branch and national officials have a chance to bring themselves to the attention of their superiors and to demonstrate their leadership abilities. Moreover, an effective or militant union official can often count on his employer promoting him as a means of winning his compliance and silence.[2] During the process of Africanization, branch and national officials have gained many important positions, especially in the personnel departments. Of course, most of the promotions have not been as dramatic as the jump from clerk or carpenter to administrative, executive or managerial positions. Many involved a transition from typist to accounts clerk after learning bookkeeping, or from office messenger to trainee clerk through on-the-job instruction. Such upgrading is much sought after; involvement in trade unionism usually helps a person's chances of obtaining it, given management's desire to appease union officials. The high turnover rate of union officials is partly a consequence of their loss of interest in union affairs upon promotion. For instance, the Petroleum Oil Workers' Union had forty-six national officials in eleven years (some of whom held more than one post at different times), or almost four new officials per year.

Union leaders also often mentioned the importance of material benefits in explaining why people aspire to full-time union office. One general secretary claimed that people saw that union leaders, who had formerly been clerks, were now living well and were looked up to. Their example interested a lot of people in trade unionism. Another mentioned that being a full-time branch official was better than having no job at all, and jobs were scarce. One typically frank answer was the following:

Some union leaders feel that, if elected a national official, he will get certain privileges that he would not be able to get by working in industry. He may be given scholarships and allowances. If he is in an important union position, he might hope to get aid from sponsors in Eastern Europe [he is here apparently alluding to his arch-opponent at the time]. If the union has a car, people may think that they can become a big man by driving the car. Also, the union has many parties, and people enjoy being invited to them.

Quite substantial material benefits can, in fact, be derived from trade unionism, especially since the 'check-off' system was legislated in 1965. Salaries for a full-time general secretary range from K£60 to K£200 per month, depending on the size and financial resources of the union.[3] Where the deputy or assistant general secretary is a full-time official, he will usually make between K£50 and K£75 per month. Other full-time officials get lesser amounts. A full-time branch secretary will usually only receive between K£10 and K£25 per month, depending on the union and the location of the branch. Even this position, however, is apparently coveted; apart from the salary, there is the prestige of a white-collar occupation, the chance of moving up in the union hierarchy or into politics, and the opportunity to make other money on the side (since supervision from head office is not generally very stringent). Relative to their training and the wage structure of the society, most full-time trade union officers are thus well-paid. Part-time national and branch officials also get material rewards in the form of general and sitting allowances. In the Commercial, Food and Allied Workers, for example, the president received K£30 per month, the vice-president K£15, an assistant secretary-general K£20, and two trustees K£9 per month in 1966–8. Apart from the salaries and monthly or sitting allowances, top full-time national officials (and some full-time branch officials) generally receive a number of other benefits, such as the use of an automobile and driver, an expense account and a travel allowance. Since these national officials may also hold paid positions in the national union federation, and be appointed to public or private boards, the material rewards can be high indeed.

The psychological rewards are also important. Next to the advancement of personal ambitions, the most frequently mentioned reason why people aspire to become union officials was to attain enhanced prestige. An official of a large union remarked that 'shop stewards, branch officials and national officials are important people within their own area who get their names in the paper and associate with important people – such as big employers and politicians.' Similarly, a general secretary claimed: 'At the branch level, many people feel a sense of pride to be able to represent "their" people in grievances against employers. Many people like to be a big fish in a small pond.' Almost every respondent commented that union office – even as a shop steward – was a step upwards and that union officials were 'looked up to' by their fellow workers. Full-time officers apparently gain prestige from their 'executive' life-style: they wear business suits, work at desks in their own offices and often interact with important personages. Their style of life is thus far removed from that of the mass of union members, who are usually manual workers.

Union officials at all levels have, in short, a lot to lose by exclusion from their offices. A later chapter will investigate the sources of opposition to the incumbents' positions. At this point one must merely assert that union officials – especially full-time ones who have staked their immediate futures on trade unionism – live in great insecurity, surrounded by ambitious individuals who covet their posts. It is hardly surprising in these circumstances that union leaders seek to consolidate their power, often in the process disregarding their unions' constitutions and some of the rules of fair play. One means of consolidation is for leaders to monopolize information and knowledge about their unions' affairs. Another is to build up a personal machine.

Leadership control of communications channels

Control of communications channels permits office-holders to determine, in varying degrees, the information and knowledge that their members have about the union.[4] Free publicity in the local press, the distribution of newsletters under his signature and finances to visit the branches enable the pre-eminent leader and his followers to justify official policy and discredit opposing proposals. Denied access to such channels, a challenger's organizational activities are usually severely circumscribed.

The significance of control of formal communications channels depends on the size and dispersion of a union's membership. Where members are scattered in various enterprises all over the country, such control obviously gives office-holders a tremendous advantage over any challengers. Where, on the other hand, the membership is concentrated in one location, or where interaction among members is high even though the membership is dispersed, then such control is much less effective. In the latter case, opposition leaders can circumvent the incumbents' monopoly of the formal channels by recourse to such informal means as word of mouth and the distribution of leaflets. The existence of informal channels thus reduces members' reliance on 'official' information.[5]

Consider first unions with a concentrated membership or a high incidence of interaction between union members. The Dockworkers' Union (DWU) and the Railway African Union (RAU) are the foremost examples. In the former case, all 6,700 members work in the Kilindini docks at Mombasa.[6] In contrast, the 13,393 members of the RAU in December 1968 were dispersed in twenty branches located along the railway line, though Nairobi branch alone accounted for 4,891 members, Mombasa 2,860 and Nakuru 900. However, communication among the active minority in this union is facilitated by a small number of employees whose jobs require constant movement along the line (either to repair the line or to run the trains) and by the high rate of transfer of middle-level employees from one station to another. There are several other unions, such as the Petroleum Oil Workers' Union and Quarry and Mine Workers' Union, in which the majority of members are located in one or two areas. But there is little evidence of contact between members who are employed in different enterprises within the same area. Informal communications between members in the DWU and RAU are enhanced by the fact that all members in each union work for the same employer.

In the DWU, there are many opportunities for opposition leaders or their agents to communicate with members and for members to exchange information. Since the exits by which dockers must leave the port are few, distribution of leaflets poses no problem. In addition the nature of work on the docks dictates frequent pauses in the routine during which workers can discuss, among other things, union politics. During several months of the year, rain frequently forces a short cessation of work. Cranes often break down. For stevedores, the system of 'spelling-off' means that, at any one time, one gang is working and one resting. Shore-handling crews, for their part, get to rest during the time it takes a crane to move a cargo up to the hold and return for another load. These opportunities for discussions on the job do not occur in most other occupations, such as factory or construction employment. It is little wonder, therefore, that rumours sweep through the docks in an amazingly short time. Indeed, false or inaccurate rumours have led to work stoppages on several occasions over the years.

In addition, dockers comprise the closest thing to an 'occupational community' in Kenya.[7] Since dockers live mainly in four residential areas and belong to their own club, they interact off as well as on the job. It is not surprising, therefore, that for all their apparent internal divisions and rivalries, dockworkers have a reputation for being a tight-knit group.

Since there are many informal communication channels open to opposition factions, dock union leaders go to great lengths to ensure that they, too, get their message across to the workers. Communication between the union and its members is the most impressive in Kenya. Each section has its own shop steward and there is, in addition, a chief shop steward; grievances may be directed to either of these stewards at any time. As well, there are opportunities for members to engage in informal discussions with office-bearers. Occasionally, the latter congregate outside the port gates when a shift finishes work. More frequently, a particular section or category of members (e.g., clerks) is invited to visit union headquarters at a stated time for special discussions. The union also holds many general meetings (usually in the Baggage Hall in the Port) at which the general secretary explains recent developments and members ask questions. These meetings have often been held as frequently as once a week during such crises as a factional encounter or a threatened strike.

Finally, the union has always distributed mimeographed Swahili leaflets to members. Now called 'Mwandishi Mkuu Asema' ('The General Secretary Speaks'), they are normally issued at weekly intervals, though one a day is not unusual during a strike, a 'go-slow', a factional encounter or before an election. Approximately 3,000 at each publication were distributed during the early 1960s; the number has since risen to 6,000.[8] Analysis of the thirteen leaflets issued between early September and mid-November 1968, which the author managed to collect, gives an impression of some of the topics dealt with. Five of the leaflets advertised forthcoming meetings, either of the membership as a whole or of a particular segment, and four dealt primarily with industrial relations matters. Two requested members not to engage in a 'go-slow' over the employer's refusal to grant all the union's demands 'so that the Employer should not find an excuse for creating a conflict between us and our government'. A further two commented on the progress of negotiations with the corporation, and claimed that the union was trying to defeat a 'diabolical plan' whereby employees of the East African Railways were taking over executive and clerical jobs in the East African Cargo

Handling Services. Two further leaflets dealt primarily with the union's plans for the celebrations accompanying the opening of the union's new headquarters. The final two were purely political in content. One explained why a central council member was suspended; he had apparently 'uttered obscene words in a bar and insulted committee members in public'! The last one featured a retraction of an allegedly slanderous statement about Juma Boy made by the leader of the current opposition faction in one of his own leaflets.

Work on the railway does not provide the same opportunities as that on the docks for the circulation of information outside of the formal union channels. However, as already mentioned, opposition groups establish contact by means of their supporters who travel along the line. Moreover, thousands of railway employees live in railway housing estates where their proximity facilitates informal communication of information and the organization of a faction.

Formal channels of communication are not as highly developed in the RAU as in the dockers' union. For example, national officials seldom toured the branches between 1966 and 1969, with the result that they grew increasingly cut off from the rank-and-file outside Nairobi. One explanation for the poorer communications is the less important position of the individual union member in RAU politics relative to the DWU. Whereas dockers directly elect their national officials, railway workers merely choose their branch officials who, in turn, elect the national officials. This system encourages contenders at the head office level to concentrate on cultivating the small group of branch delegates rather than the mass of the members. As well, there is not the same pressure to develop effective formal communication channels with members as informal communications are not as effective as in the Kilindini docks.

In contrast to other predominantly manual-worker unions, the RAU's Swahili newsletter is particularly impressive. Approximately 6,000 copies per publication were distributed in 1969.[9] In the early 1960s, the newsletter changed its name to 'RAU Yasema' ('The RAU Speaks'), and became increasingly militant and propagandistic, reflecting the strong views of the then General Secretary, Walter Ottenyo, who was also the editor. When Ottenyo was ousted from office in February 1966, the newsletter tended to become less virulent and partisan. Yet the incumbent group still frequently used it as a campaign weapon to discredit opponents as 'tribalists', 'deceivers', 'self-seekers', 'cowards' and 'failures'.

Consider next those unions characterized by widely scattered memberships and a low level of interaction between members and branch officials employed in the various enterprises and areas of the country. In this situation, it is difficult for an opposition group to organize beyond a single branch or enterprise. It can neither rely on word of mouth to counteract the propaganda dispensed by the established leaders, nor does it usually have the funds or the organization to permit adherents to tour the various work-places or distribute leaflets. Normally, of course, challengers will not aim at winning over the passive and dispersed membership, but will concentrate on recruiting disaffected branch officials. The incumbent group, however, attempt to prevent the coalescence of a broadly-based opposition faction by ensuring that branch officials only interact with each other through or under the supervision of head office. Only a couple of times a year do branch officials assemble together – at central council meetings and triennial or annual conferences – and then only for a day or two. A few unions even go so far as to include a provision in their constitutions forbidding any contact between the officials of different branches, except through headquarters. Under these conditions, control of such formal channels of communication as newsletters and direct contact with branches by established leaders and their agents is a major advantage.

The foremost examples of unions with widely dispersed memberships are the Plantation and Agricultural Workers' Union, Local Government Workers' Union (KLGWU), Commercial, Food and Allied Workers' Union (KUCFAW), Building and Construction Workers' Union and the Chemical Workers' Union (KCWU). Catering for workers employed in the tea, coffee, sisal and mixed farming industries, the agricultural union grouped its 1968 membership of 40,275 into twenty-two branches all over Kenya. The KLGWU's membership of 20,812 was dispersed in forty branches in 1968, though the largest number (4,076) was centred in two Nairobi branches. Since this union represents employees of local authorities, it draws members from every tribe and section of the country. The KUCFAW, represents employees in a wide array of enterprises. Rule 3 of its constitution authorizes the union to recruit members from the following industries:

(i) *Distributive and Commercial Group*: which shall embrace employees engaged in Warehouses and Merchandise, Flour, Coffee, Spice Mills, Food Processing, Banks, Insurances, Offices, Cinemas, Showgrounds, Shopworkers, Wholesale and Retails, Watchmen organizations, Distributive Dairy Workers and Co-operative societies.

(ii) *Laundry Cleaners and Dyers Group*: which shall embrace all employees engaged in Dyers, Dry Cleaners and Laundry Industries.

(iii) *Tobacco Trade Group*: which shall embrace all employees engaged in Tobacco Industries.

(iv) *Bottling and Brewing Group*: which shall embrace all employees in bottling and brewing industries.

Even if one considers only the firms, co-operative unions and marketing bodies which have joined the Federation of Kenya Employers, one arrives at a total of 202 enterprises employing 30,602 people that fell into the above categories in 1967.[10] The KUCFAW claimed 19,650 members scattered in twenty branches in 1968, though approximately one half of its membership was located in Nairobi. As one would expect, the membership of the construction workers' union is dispersed in construction sites around the country. There are frequent oscillations in the various branches' membership figures, depending on the extent of construction currently in progress.

The union's 7,015 members in 1968 were spread over ten branches, though, again, the Nairobi branch alone boasted 4,283 members. Finally, the 3,251 members of the KCWU were distributed among eleven branches. About 40 per cent of this number were employed in Nairobi chemical firms.

None of these five unions presently utilize a newsletter as a channel of communication with members. However, the KUCFAW, formerly issued one, in English. Called first the 'Umoja-Unity Newsletter' and later the 'KUCFAW Newsletter', it was published irregularly between late 1964 and early 1967.[11] As it was printed only in English, its readership was necessarily restricted primarily to clerks. Between 1,000 and 2,000 copies were sent to the branches for distribution.[12] The newsletter's aims were clearly and colourfully stated by the editor in the first edition (26 September 1964):

The tasks ahead for Umoja are numerous and terrible. First, it has to advocate the whole policy of the Union and know it full well and must see that no one else misinterprets it. Secondly, and perhaps most important, it has to educate the grown, the young and yet unborn among the working community regardless of colour, religion and political affiliation.

This is the biggest challenge of all to any organization manned by man and it is in this context that we welcome this foresightedness the Patron of Umoja Newsletter and the General Secretary of the Union to have made it possible for the launching of this Mouth Organ that will freely, help advocate the most delicate issues of the Union and if possible expose enemies of progress standing in the way of the working community.

A perusal of the issues of this newsletter reveal that it never deviated from lauding the incumbent regime's achievements, deriding opponents and championing increased unity. Typical is the following assessment of the General Secretary's abilities:

If there is any honest Union Leader in Kenya today, Sammy is perhaps one that very many people agree to have known. His human character is second to none and really behaves like a good and sensible Father. His directives to many of his aides are law...

This man Muhanji is really a Kenyan who is devoted to serve the people at all times. For the many years I have known him, I have satisfied myself that if there is any able negotiator, administrator and pen-pusher, Sammy ranks high as far as trade union affairs are concerned and there is no exaggeration or favouritism and painting in this case. He smokes just for fun and he drinks just for a pass-time. His actual hobby is unknown to many except to his dear wife. He imitates nobody but admires and adores the qualities of the President of Kenya Mzee Jomo Kenyatta in whom he has much good faith and love. Next week you will read Muhanji at the Industrial Court. ('KUCFAW Newsletter', 5 May 1966.)

A forerunner of the Plantation and Agricultural Workers' Union, the General Agricultural Workers' Union, also attempted to distribute a newsletter. Ambitiously conceived, the Swahili 'Macho ya Mashamba' ('Farm-Guard') was designed to be a weekly publication, several pages in length. Its failure exemplifies the difficulties of distributing a newsletter to a largely illiterate membership. As a 1961 report by the union's general secretary observed:

It did really surprise me to find that in all the branch offices except at Naivasha, piles and piles of these valuable and useful newspapers seemed 'stock of a warehouse'. Some Branch Secretaries did not even open some consignments. Out of 19,898 copies published only 7,333 were sold at the branches.[13]

The most crucial advantage that office-holders in dispersed unions now hold over challengers is the funds to permit personal contact with branch officials and members. Not only can they hire full-time organizers to guard their interests, but the general secretary now has an expense account allowing him to visit the branches. Oppositionists rarely have similar freedom of movement, especially since they are often in full-time employment themselves.

Four of the five unions with the most widely dispersed memberships employ full-time organizers. The Local Government Union, for example, has utilized four organizing secretaries since 1963. Since the centralization policy of 1966, these appointees have, in effect, been dependent upon the general secretary for their jobs. They can, therefore, be assumed to be the eyes of the secretary in the branches. In common with many unions, the KLGWU's largest expenditures, after wages, go for travel and organizational activities.[14] The Commercial, Food and Allied Workers employs one director of organization, an occasional organizing secretary, several elected national officials and the branch secretaries of the largest four branches. Similarly, two national officials, several branch secretaries and the occasional organizing secretary are full-time in the Building and Construction Union. The Plantation and Agricultural Union is an organizer's nightmare, owing to the large number of small farms and plantations spread across the countryside. On paper, the union boasts an impressive bureaucracy of full-time officers. At head office, there is an elected general secretary and deputy general secretary and an appointed director of organization. Next in the hierarchy are four elected provincial secretaries, who are supposed to be responsible for all administration in their Provinces. Their job, among other things, is to co-ordinate branch activities within the Province and to ensure that all union staff and officials fulfil their duties. In addition, provincial organizers are often appointed. At the bottom are the full-time branch secretary/treasurers and branch organizers. Although duties are clearly demarcated on paper, in practice lines of authority are often ignored. The general secretary, for example, has occasionally intervened to dismiss a branch secretary/treasurer who seemed unreliable.

Employing organizers certainly has its advantages, but it can also be risky. Organizing secretaries frequently interact more with branch officials and members than the general secretary does. Furthermore, their duties permit them to gain knowledge about the operation of the union and to develop such necessary political skills as speech-making, organizing group activities and negotiation techniques. This combination of knowledge, political skills and the opportunity to build up personal followings renders them formidable opponents, should they decide to strike out on their own.

Table 1. *Total expenditure on organization, travelling allowances and accommodation, various unions, 1958–68 (KShs)*

Union	1958 or 1959	1960 or 1961	1962 or 1963	1964 or 1965	1966 or 1967	1968
RAU(K)	2,925	5,641	No information	36,121	No information	—
DWU	11,222	20,772	56,717	53,539	65,920	—
KPOWU	—	—	9,283	27,985	28,529	—
KUSPW	—	7,184	35,237	44,087	No information	40,010
KPAWU	—	—	—	35,743	60,420	148,058
EAFBCWU	—	—	—	—	27,434	56,454
KUCFAW	—	—	—	—	23,085	29,298*

SOURCES: Compiled from the audited annual accounts submitted by each union to the Registrar of Trade Unions, and from financial reports given to various annual or triennial conferences of unions.
NOTE: There is no standard format for presentation of a union's income and expenditure in the annual accounts. Most unions do not itemize their expenditures. Figures in the above table were arrived at by adding all expenditures relating to travel and organisation.
* This is the total for the first nine months of the year.

Therefore, if a general secretary is not extremely careful in choosing his organizing secretaries, he may find himself organized out of a job.

In historical terms, finally, it is important to realize that the established leaders' advantage over challengers in terms of organizational resources developed relatively recently. During the Emergency period, the membership of most unions was limited to Nairobi, with perhaps a few members in Mombasa and Nakuru. Unions expanded rapidly after the termination of Emergency regulations in 1960. Yet most unions lacked sufficient funds for organizational purposes until the 'check-off' system was either negotiated by the union or imposed by the government. As the fragmentary evidence in Table 1 reveals, there is a significant increase over time in the amount of money spent by unions on organizational activities, travel and accommodation.[15] Of course, one reason for this increase is the tendency for more general secretaries to have their own vehicles and drivers. None the less, office-holders now clearly command the resources to finance frequent contact with the branches. Whereas challengers might have managed to compete with incumbents by visiting the few branches in the early 1960s, they are now in a more difficult position. Unless they can find external patrons to finance their organizational activities, there is little likelihood of ousting established leaders in a widely dispersed union.

The construction of personal machines

Most pre-eminent union leaders feel they need, besides organizing secretaries, a personal following who will back them in confrontations with opponents. As a general rule the size of such personal teams will vary directly with the strength of the opposition within a union. A team, at one extreme, may consist only of a leader plus one or two of the other national officials (usually the treasurer or president) and the leaders of one or more strategic branches. At the other extreme, a team may be composed of all the national officials plus most of the more powerful branch officials. In either case, however, the team is an informal grouping of individuals who are willing to work in the interests of a particular leader in the competition for power.

People follow a leader because either they are morally committed to him or they expect to receive some material reward in exchange for their support.[16] One type of tie is thus moral: men follow because they are personally committed to a leader owing to kinship ties, friendship or belief in his extraordinary powers or because they are committed to an ideology articulated by the leader. Alternatively, followers are attracted to a leader by calculations of personal advantage. Those held by mercenary ties alone are obviously less reliable supporters than those with some moral relationship. While the former followers may be won over by promises of material gain, such promises are insufficient lure for the morally committed.

There are few morally based teams within Kenyan trade unions. A common commitment to a socialist ideology is one possible moral tie, but there is little evidence that it has been significant in Kenyan unions. While several intra-union conflicts have ostensibly been fought over the question of the KFL's disaffiliation from the 'imperialist-dominated' International Confederation of Free Trade Unions, subsequent inconsistencies on the issue by the main proponents throw doubt on their commitment. The most common moral tie utilized in building up a core group is ethnicity. Relying too much on one's tribesman is a risky tactic, however, as there is an unwritten rule labelling such action improper.

Since most leaders' teams are largely composed of followers held by calculations of material advantages, these may be called 'personal machines'. The nature and magnitude of the resources which union leaders can allocate to followers must now be assessed.

Money

As previously mentioned, few unions enjoyed substantial or dependable incomes before the establishment of the 'check-off' system in the early 1960s. Since members had seldom paid their dues regularly, most unions had been dependent on external sources for funds – either a KFL subsidy or contributions from International Trade Secretariats[17] or other overseas bodies. The KFL, for its part, also drew the bulk of its income from overseas sources (especially the International Confederation of Free Trade Unions). During the era of the 'Cold War', foreign countries and agencies willingly supplied funds and scholarships in an effort to influence the ideological orientation of emergent labour movements. The difficulty for union incumbents was that such subsidies and contributions were uncertain and irregular. Moreover, an opposition faction could often gain access to significant funds from an Eastern-supported Kenyan national union federation, in the event that the incumbent group was committed to the Western-financed KFL. The Presidential Declaration on Trade Union Policy of September 1965 sought to end this reliance on foreign sources by demanding the immediate severance of all international ties.

Table 2 reveals a remarkable recent increase in the annual incomes of most unions. Apart from the establishment of the 'check-off' system, this growth in income is due to two factors: the expansion in the membership of most unions during the 1960s; and the increase in membership dues since 1960. While most unions required a monthly subscription of only KSh1 in the early 1960s, all unions, with the exception of the Sugar Plantation Union, have since raised this to at least KSh2, and in many cases to KSh3 or 4. There are several cases in which union income has temporarily declined but these can generally be traced to the disruption of the normal functioning of the union, brought about by internal struggles for control.

This augmentation of union funds has had a significant impact on union politics. As already suggested, the larger incomes have permitted estab-

Table 2. *Total annual income of various unions, 1953–68 (in KShs)*

Union	1953 or 1954	1955 or 1956	1957 or 1958	1959 or 1960	1961 or 1962	1963 or 1964	1965 or 1966	1967 or 1968
KDCWU–KUCFAW	6,366	6,630	23,886	96,355	216,667	273,143	350,309	744,869
EAFBCWU	1,269	8,034	16,170	54,835	2,717	51,788	122,698	314,430
KLGWU	7,031	15,031	13,248	42,740	108,737	37,165	301,936	624,011
RAU(K)	6,958	23,359	15,188	No return	19,402	180,220	375,427	347,717
DWU	—	8,954	31,994	51,023	72,221	156,454	211,831	487,322
KCWU	—	—	—	18,643	48,831	84,085	84,353	168,403
KPOWU	—	—	—	12,696	60,594	107,424	86,916	87,454
KUSPW	—	—	—	—	11,695	84,048	89,738	118,600
KQMWU	—	—	—	—	916	11,668	29,850	44,699
CSACSU(K)	—	—	—	—	—	5,931	25,217	21,301
KPAWU	—	—	—	—	—	265,927	423,609	744,301

SOURCE: Annual audited accounts submitted by the various unions to the Registrar of Trade Unions.

lished leaders to increase organizational and travel expenditures. As well, unions can now afford to employ more people, thus providing jobs for personal followers. Established leaders now also have the funds to engage in fairly lavish campaigning before the branch and head office elections. As the unions' audited annual accounts are usually not itemized,[18] it is difficult to estimate the money expended on entertaining or rewarding potential supporters and financing followers in the branch elections. A few unions, however, do periodically specify expenditure on such items as 'entertainment', 'sundries', 'miscellaneous expenses' and 'general expenses'. The amounts involved can be relatively substantial in terms of the unions' total incomes and members' small wages. One union, for example spent over K£1,300 on 'entertainment and food' during the 1965 union elections year. Another spent over K£1,000 on the same item during the year of the following triennial elections, 1968. A third union expended K£500 on 'entertaining' and over K£2,100 on 'sundry', in 1967. A fourth, smaller union contracted a deficit of over K£2,000 during 1968. Although the evidence is scant, it is clear that the significant increases in union incomes over the past few years have given office-holders an important financial advantage over challengers.

To overcome this disadvantage, oppositionists seek to undermine the unity of the incumbent office-holders and to gain access to external resources. The latter strategy is discussed in the next chapter.

Scholarships

Access to foreign scholarships and travel grants is another important resource. These benefits are donated by such bodies as the International Labour Organization (ILO), the ICFTU, International Trade Secretariats, the national union federation or affiliated unions of various countries, and foreign governments.[19] Although the usual recipient in Kenya has been a national federation, specific union leaders or contenders have occasionally received direct aid. In principle, the national union federation, individual leader or trade union was to apportion scholarships on the basis of merit; in practice – and this was frequently the unstated intention of the donor – these benefits were distributed on a patronage basis.

Trade union federations in Kenya have frequently allocated scholarships to trade unions or individual union leaders on the basis of either personal or organizational loyalty. For instance, a KFL Executive Committee meeting in 1962 voted to rescind a scholarship it had granted because one of its members believed the recipient was opposed to the KFL.[20] In his campaign to win election as general secretary of the KFL in August 1963, Clement Lubembe, the Chairman of the Federation's Education Committee, used the lure of foreign scholarships to build up support. He told the delegates to the KFL's Biennial Conference that he had arranged for a number of foreign study tours and hoped 'that many of you will benefit from them'.[21] As well, one of the criticisms raised by the oppositionist 'Action Group' against the operations of the Central Organization of Trade Unions, in 1967, was that scholarships were distributed on a patronage basis. This group went so far as to demand that the Minister of Labour require COTU to make a public statement on the allocation of its scholarships since 1965.

Trade unions and individuals, for their part, also frequently dispensed their scholarships or travel grants with the aim of creating personal followings. Especially numerous are the travel grants awarded by many communist countries to enable Kenyan union observers to attend such ceremonies as May Day celebrations and the opening of trade union congresses. In addition, Eastern European countries before 1966, frequently provided trade unionist protégés in Kenya with an allotment of scholarships to distribute to prospective followers. In the absence of records, it is impossible to estimate how many scholarships and travel grants have been made available to the various national union federations and trade unions in Kenya. Impressionistic evidence suggests, however, that the number was high during the period 1959–65. Local Kenyan newspapers, KFL and union newsletters, and the minutes of union meetings continually refer to trade unionists leaving to attend all manner of foreign conferences, celebrations and study courses. In addition, it is clear that Labour Department officials believed that the number of foreign scholarships was high. They had difficulty, on several occasions, in persuading the KFL to nominate candidates for trade union courses in Britain. Moreover, in December 1961 the Permanent Secretary of the Department had to inform the African Field Officer, ILO, that 'difficulty is being experienced in Kenya in finding sufficient candidates from the trade union movement for over-seas study,... in view of the large numbers of other opportunities currently offered.'[22]

This bonanza ended with the 'Presidential Declaration' of September 1965. Stipulating that the Ministry of Labour be notified of all offers of foreign assistance, this declaration was interpreted to mean that all foreign scholarships must be approved by the Ministry's permanent secretary. In practice, this approval has nearly always been forthcoming. The decline in the number of scholarships offered actually owes more to the disillusionment of both East and West with the effects of their assistance programme than to the 'Presidential Declaration' as such. Experience has shown that the views of union leaders are not as easily moulded as both sides seemed, at one time, to believe. But established leaders still usually have access to enough scholarships and travel grants to make demonstrable loyalty profitable.

Jobs and promotions

Union leaders are sometimes in a position to select people for government statutory boards, to influence decisions about who shall receive promotions or demotions within certain enterprises and to grant followers paid union positions. Access to the latter two resources has grown increasingly significant over the past few years.

Controlling appointments to governmental boards has constituted a minimal resource. Registered national union federations have recommended 'employees' representatives' on such boards as the Labour Advisory Board (LAB), the General Wages Advisory Board, the Agricultural Wages Advisory Board, the Industrial Court (until August 1971), the Apprenticeships Board, the Advisory Committee on Training, the Factories Committee, the National Wages Policy Advisory Committee (in 1964–5) and the National Social Security Fund Council. Individual unions select the ten to fourteen employees' representatives on wages councils established for the trade or industries from which they draw their members.[23] However, with the possible exception of the Industrial Court, none of these positions was very lucrative. There are no sitting allowances – only travelling expenses – provided for such boards as the LAB, the General Wages Advisory Board and the Agricultural Wages Advisory Board. Employees' representatives on wages councils receive either a sitting allowance of KSh15 per day or a maximum travelling allowance of second-class transport plus KSh25 for accommodation and food. On the other hand, members of the Industrial Court used to get a sitting allowance of KSh50 per day. But members seldom sat on these bodies for longer than one to four days per year. Thus, all a general secretary really has to offer in the case of wages councils, for example, is a free trip to Nairobi for a few of his branch supporters once a year.

It is obviously difficult to determine the extent to which certain union leaders informally influence promotions, demotions and dismissals within industry.[24] There is certainly a widespread belief that several established leaders are listened to in such matters. Management is sometimes willing to indulge a general secretary either because of a collusive relationship working to their mutual benefit or a concern to 'keep on the right side' of a powerful union leader. Two present and former personnel managers of large companies, who admitted occasional informal consultations with general secretaries over promotions, both gave this latter reason. They claimed, however, that they had not been bound by any advice received. Clearly, many employees are promoted after they become union officers. But such promotions may be the result of capable individuals being given an opportunity to demonstrate their abilities to management or of the latter's desire to quiet noisy critics, rather than a consequence of union pressure. Finally, established leaders in several unions have threatened strikes to obtain the dismissal of opponents. This is obviously an effective means of discouraging opposition elements.

In large American unions, the leaders' control over lucrative positions in the unions' hierarchy is apparently one of the most important means of building up a personal machine.[25] In Kenya, the number of people on the payrolls of the larger unions, though still small, has certainly expanded over the past few years as a result of enlarged union incomes. The increased amounts spent on wages and allowances since 1965 are evidenced by the following statistics, drawn from the union's audited annual accounts. The Sugar Plantation Union spent KSh1,519 on wages in 1961, KSh26,267 in 1965 and KSh67,457 in 1968. Formed in August 1963, the Plantation and Agricultural Workers' Union expended KSh135,076 on salaries in 1964, over twice that amount two years later (KSh274,129) and KSh393,632 in 1968. Figures for only two years are available for the Building and Construction Workers Union: in 1966, the total for head office wages and allowances was KSh33,181; this figure had almost doubled, to KSh63,655, two years later. In the Dockworkers' Union KSh25,365 was spent on the same items in 1961, and over four times that amount, KSh111,130, a mere seven years later. Finally, the Commercial, Food and Allied Union expended the large sum of KSh200,310 in 1967 and KSh223,765 in the first nine months of 1968 on salaries and allowances.

Office-holders in most unions have thus gained access to an increasing range of resources with which to buttress their positions. The result, as the next chapter will disclose, is that factional conflict within trade unions has tended to decline. But, for reasons soon to be revealed, such conflict is unlikely to decrease to the point where it ceases to represent a danger for union leaders.

Tactics of control

Consider next the manoeuvres employed by leaders in unions where the style of leadership is oriented toward extensive control. While not all union leaders follow the tactics described below, they are of wide enough currency to warrant mention.

Controlling the branches

In all unions except the Dockworkers' Union, the branch officials dominate the national conferences and select the national officials. This is seldom a constitutional requirement; most constitutions merely state the number of delegates to which each branch is entitled, usually calculated on the basis of the branch's membership. In practice, the branch officials select themselves as the delegates to the centre.

Full-time leaders must thus pay close attention to the grievances and loyalties of the branch officials – particularly the most powerful of these, the secretaries, chairmen and treasurers. The frequency with which national officials or their agents visit the various branches varies widely from union to union. General secretaries usually claim that they tour the branches 'as the need arises', rather than according to a set schedule. The frequency depends on a number of factors, one of which is obviously the existence of some pressing grievance or industrial dispute requiring the intervention of the head office. Another is the emergence of a factional dispute in a branch. In such a case, national leaders or their agents usually try to mediate or arbitrate in the dispute, the tactics adopted depending on the loyalties of the various contenders within the branch. A final factor is the size and spread of the union. The sole full-time leader of one of the smaller unions with a widely-dispersed membership will obviously be unable to make the national office's presence felt to the same extent as the leader of a large union with several paid officials and organizers and a more concentrated membership.

While a few branch officials complain of never seeing their general secretaries, few of these officials can be accused of sitting in their Nairobi, Kisumu or Nakuru offices ignoring their branches. Of course, their self-interest dictates travelling around the country, since their positions depend on the local union officials. Moreover, the concentration of industry in Kenya is such that a general secretary in Nairobi need not expend much effort in visiting the larger branches. As the work force in non-agricultural pursuits is mainly concentrated in five urban centres on an accessible 700-mile road-rail line between Mombasa on the Indian Ocean and Kisumu on Lake Victoria, a general secretary is seldom more than 300 miles away from his larger branches.

In those few unions in which an honorary (i.e. part-time) president is pre-eminent, attempts have been made to *limit* the general secretary's access to the branches. This happened in the Railway African Union (Kenya) in 1966, for instance. After struggles for control between the president and various general secretaries had disrupted the union's operation on several occasions, the National Executive Committee, at the urging of the president, passed a rule that no national officer was permitted to visit a branch without presenting a valid reason to the Committee. The implicit purpose of this rule was to prevent the newly-appointed General Secretary, Johnstone Mwandawiro, from developing his own alliances at the branch level, as his predecessors had done. Although the new rule did help to prevent competition for support between national officials, it meant that the head office regime, as a whole, grew increasingly cut off from the branches and membership. This situation encouraged a more militant faction outside the regime to confront the established leadership in 1969. This challenge was defeated only through the expenditure of considerable resources by the incumbent group. A similar challenge in early 1972, however, was successful.

Branch elections are one occasion on which full-time national officials normally visit the branches. Normatively, their role is to ensure that their union's constitution is complied with; pragmatically, they often attempt to ensure that their own supporters win.

Prior to the Trade Unions (Amendment) Act, 1964, and the Presidential Declaration on trade union policy in 1965, the formal procedures for the election of branch officials were often ignored. The branch secretary frequently failed to give the requisite two weeks' notice to all paid-up members before the convening of an annual or triennial branch general meeting. Instead, only selected members were notified. In addition, the branch secretary and national officials frequently ignored the stipulation governing the quorum for a branch general meeting. And often some of the people present at the meeting were not paid-up members; as such, they were not constitutionally entitled to a vote. In fact, it frequently happened that the opposed factions at the head office level each held their own set of branch elections, and each claimed that their own slate of branch officials was the only valid one.

Confusion over who were the accredited branch officials was somewhat alleviated by the 1964 Trade Unions Act requiring general secretaries to register all branches of their union and the names of all branch officials with the Registrar of Trade Unions. This new legal stipulation immensely enhanced the position of those already in office, since incumbent leaders in some unions simply refused to apply for registration of smaller branches controlled by their union opponents or to register the names of branch officials whose loyalty was suspect.

Irregularities in branch (as well as national) elections grew less flagrant and prevalent after the promulgation of the Presidential Declaration of September 1965. One object of this declaration of policy was to obviate intra-union factionalism by ensuring that union members had the opportunity to elect the leaders they wanted without interference and in accordance with democratic procedures.[26] To this end, all union elections were to be supervised by supposedly impartial officials from the Ministry of Labour. These supervisors were supposed to submit a report on the branch and national elections to the Registrar of Trade Unions so that, in the event of a dispute over leadership, that official would have a basis on which to make a ruling.

This system of state supervision worked quite well in practice, though shortcomings have been apparent. For example, a comparison of the reported numbers attending branch elections in 1965 and 1968 with the number of paid-up members for the same branches reveals that few branches attained the requisite turnout to constitute a quorum.[27] If government officials wished to enforce this formal requirement, most elections would have had to be declared invalid. In practice, however, this provision seems only to have been enforced in contested elections in the larger branches. The number of members attending branch elections (according to the reports submitted by Ministry of Labour officials) ranged from one-twelfth of the eligible members to over twice the number who were eligible! One branch election was attended by only fourteen members, eleven of whom were elected to some office or the branch committee. At the other extreme was the attendance of 'approximately 200' members at a branch election when the branch's total reported membership was eighty. Not surprisingly, the agricultural unions and others with rapidly changing memberships (such as the Building and Construction Union and the Quarry and Mineworkers'

Union) usually had the smallest proportion of members attending branch elections.

Union officials made several criticisms of the supervision carried out by the Ministry of Labour. One common allegation was that a supervisor was biased in favour of one candidate. Upon investigation of several of these charges by the Ministry of Labour, only one was found to have any substance.[28] Another common allegation was that the labour officer presiding did not follow constitutional procedures. The reports submitted to the Registrar of Trade Unions clearly indicate that officials have not always insisted on the secret ballot, instead allowing members to line up behind candidates or vote by show of hands. These elections were often declared invalid by the Registrar. Labour Department officials in the field, who often had to supervise a large number of branch elections in a few days, sometimes were not conversant with a union's constitution, with the result that they were forced to rely on the national officials' interpretation of the rules. This gave national officials an important advantage over opponents, especially regarding the question of who was eligible to vote and to contest office. The labour officer was also often too hurried to check whether the people who were present at the general meeting were all paid-up members. Moreover, he often supported a general secretary's ruling that particular people present were not union members and should be excluded from the meeting.[29] Thus, it is still possible for a union leader to 'pack' a branch meeting with some of his own supporters.

National union leaders continue to influence branch elections in most unions. The philosophy 'if you are not with us, you are against us' is often adopted.[30] General secretaries continue to channel money and organizational assistance to their adherents within the principal branches, and to provide preferential treatment to their allies in arranging the branch election.[31] If a general secretary is very prestigious or popular, of course, an indication from him that he does not favour a particular candidate may be enough to ensure that person's defeat. Control of the largest and most strategically located branches is crucial, so most effort is normally focused there. As one general secretary remarked, 'Nairobi and Mombasa are the hottest, but the other places are very easy. We need to spend much money in Nairobi and Mombasa.' In his particular union, the opposing factions in the Nairobi and Mombasa branch elections had tried to out-do each other in lavish entertaining of union members.

Swaying national conferences

The constitutions of all unions provide for the convening of annual, biennial or triennial conferences at such times and places as the central council (or executive committee) shall decide, provided that the general secretary shall give six weeks' written notice to each branch.[32] All national officers, trustees, executive committee members and a specified number of branch delegates have the right to attend.

Varying widely among unions, the number of branch delegates permitted to attend depends on such factors as the size of the union and the distribution of support for incumbent leaders among various branches. Each branch usually holds the right to send one delegate for every 100, 200, 500, or 2,000 paid-up members (depending on the union's size), provided that no single branch is entitled to more than a maximum number of delegates, ranging from two to ten. A few unions have adopted an alternative formula: all branches are permitted to send an equal number of delegates, regardless of variations in branch membership. Obviously, the effect of stipulating either a low maximum number of delegates or an equal number of representatives from each branch is effectively to lessen the influence of the larger branches on the selection of national officials. Where established leaders are faced with opposition within the largest branch or branches – a common occurrence – such discrimination clearly works in their favour. In the Plantation and Agricultural Union, for example, there were twenty-two branches prior to the 1968 Triennial Conference, and branches varied widely in their membership figures. Of the union's total membership, 20 per cent were located in Kericho, the largest branch, and the centre of opposition to the union's leadership in 1964–5. Moreover, above 35 per cent of the membership belonged to the three branches in which most tea plantation workers were concentrated – Kericho, Nandi Hills and Sotik. This union's constitution was amended in October 1968 providing for each branch to send its four elected officials to annual and triennial conferences. This change worked to the advantage of the predominantly Kikuyu leadership group since the tea workers were largely Luo, Kipsigis, Kisii and Luhya, while the Kikuyu predominated in at least eleven of the small and medium-sized branches.

The annual or triennial conference, formally the 'supreme authority in the union', is empowered to establish the union's policy, to give directions regarding organization and to elect national officials and members of the central council. The general secretary is supposed to prepare the conference's agenda. All matters for discussion and nominations for office usually must be sent to head office from two to four weeks prior to the date of the conference. A quorum is normally two-thirds of the members entitled to attend and vote.

Owing to the Registrar's concern that union members should be enabled to call their leaders to account in the period between national conferences, nearly all constitutions provide for 'special conferences'. While commendable in principle, such meetings are impractical as a means of membership control. A special conference must normally be convened by the general secretary either on the directions of the executive committee or at the written request of a specified proportion of the union's paid-up membership, varying from one-tenth to two-thirds. Obviously, to obtain the signatures of one-tenth of a union's membership is an immense task, but to gain the written assent of two-thirds of a union with, say, 14,000 members is practically impossible. Moreover, a general secretary need not convene a special conference, in any case, until the requisitioners deposit a large sum, ranging from KSh1,000 to KSh2,000, with the union's treasurer. These stipulations clearly ensure that the convening of a constitutional special conference against the wishes of the established leaders is only a theoretical possibility.

Before 1965, many of the constitutional provisions were ignored in a number of unions.[33] Annual conferences were sometimes simply postponed. When they were held the general secretary often invited only friendly delegates. Occasionally, 'delegates' were simply picked up off the street and paid to attend a conference while branch officials might not even know that an election was being held. Oppositionists frequently called 'special conferences', neglecting the complex constitutional requirements.

Such flagrant stratagems were less effective once the Registrar of Trade Unions was empowered to investigate the validity of any change of officers and government officials began to supervise elections in 1965. However, some questionable tactics, a few of which directly contravened the formal rules, were still employed. The fact, for instance, that supervising Labour Ministry officials were frequently uncertain who the accredited delegates were provided the incumbent union leaders with the opportunity to exclude legitimate opponents from national conferences.

Contenders for national union office continued to cultivate branch officials prior to elections. In principle, campaigning was to take place solely at the two- or three-day conference itself. In practice, incumbents, and opponents, if sufficiently affluent, toured the branches prior to the conference to entertain and perhaps distribute gifts to the branch officials. This entertaining of delegates continued at the triennial conference. As there were only between thirty and ninety delegates at union conferences (usually between thirty-five and sixty-five), it was sometimes possible for a determined leader with a supply of funds to maintain control of a union, even if he was none too popular.[34]

To consolidate control over their teams, a few union leaders have adopted a 'bloc' election strategy. In most unions each post is elected separately. It is generally obvious to delegates, in the event of factionalism, to which team a particular candidate belongs; sometimes the various factions adopt distinctive symbols. Yet it is still possible that members of rival factions can be elected to different posts. The bloc election system eliminates this possibility. Delegates vote for either one complete slate of officials or the other. Adopted initially in the Railway African Union and the Dockworkers' Union, the system was intended to consolidate a team of officials behind a leader. Proponents claim that there will be fewer leadership rivalries among the national officials if all are elected under the banner of the general secretary or president, as the case may be. Thus, the other officials derive their authority from the general secretary, rather than the vote of the delegates. The main shortcoming of this system is that a leader is tempted to choose his running mates on the basis of personal loyalty rather than merit.

A popular leader can thus carry to office with him several incompetents. Moreover, if a leader has dictatorial proclivities, he may purposely pick weak or illiterate people for the other offices trusting they will be dependent upon him. He can then entirely control the union and its finances. While these tendencies never emerged in the dock union, they allegedly did in the railway union with the result that 'bloc' voting was abolished by the RAU Executive Committee in 1961, after the offending general secretary had been ousted.

Another likely consequence of the 'bloc' system is the encouragement of factionalism. Enhancing 'team spirit', the system forces opposition groups to achieve a high degree of organization and to formulate consistent stands on issues. A team such as this is unlikely to dissolve after a defeat, but tends to remain as a critical opposition within the union. To increase its popularity, the opposition will probably try to exploit any necessary compromises which incumbents must make in negotiations, and dispute the necessity for the workers to fulfil certain onerous contractual obligations. This, for better or for worse, was the result of bloc voting in the Dockworkers' Union in the 1960s.

There is a trend toward the unanimous election of national officials (as well as branch officials). In most of the unions, at least four national officials and often all of them were elected unopposed in the 1968 and 1971 elections. The opposition faction was successfully excluded from the meeting place on several occasions, while the incumbent group was returned unanimously. This trend toward unopposed elections is but another indicator of the 'settling down' of union politics into an oligarchical pattern.

Bypassing union committees

All union constitutions prescribe the composition, frequency of meetings and powers of certain committees. The central council (or governing council) usually consists of the national officers, trustees and representatives from each branch elected at a union's conference. As the maximum number of representatives from each branch varies from one to five, a union with between ten and forty branches may have at least forty or fifty members on its council. The executive committee is a smaller body, composed of the national officers, trustees and between three and eighteen members elected by the central council from amongst its membership. While the larger body should meet two, three or six times a year (depending on the union), the smaller committee is generally supposed to meet once per month. In principle, the central council is next in authority after the conference, and the executive committee is 'the supreme authority in the periods in between the meetings of the Central Council'. The role of both bodies is 'to supervise and direct' the national officers, to whom the daily management of the union is committed.

In practice, the full-time officials often seek either to capture control of these committees (by ensuring that they are dominated by allies) or to ignore and bypass them. It is not unusual for a general secretary to fail to convene the committees within the constitutional periods of time. The Ministry of Labour files record many instances of visits by delegations from various unions, especially rural ones, complaining that a full-time general secretary refused to convene a council meeting or to attend one called by the president. Prior to the 1964 legislation, the Ministry could only advise such delegations that the government could not interfere in the internal affairs of trade unions, but that the union's central council had the power to suspend or dismiss any officer. There are other instances where the general secretary usurped the powers of the committees. For example, full-time officials have occasionally dismissed or suspended other officers or ordinary members without bothering to gain the approval of the relevant committee. In short, the committees have seldom been used as a forum for investigation of union leaders' actions.

Members and the 'power of the purse'

One might expect, given the resources disposed of by union leaders and the stratagems of control to which they have recourse, that leaders need not be particularly responsive to their members' desires. Such, however, is not the case. Union leaders continue to live in an insecure world. As the next chapter shows, they remain personally insecure owing to the persistence of internal conflict. As well, their unions' viability as institutions remains vulnerable to membership alienation. Although leaders can dominate the formal machinery, they cannot yet prevent members from 'voting with their feet'. The rank-and-file's most effective weapon in holding leaders responsible for their actions is the right to withdraw from membership, thus ceasing to pay subscriptions. Since the first 'check-off' agreement was negotiated by the Petroleum Oil Workers' Union in 1960, every such agreement has safeguarded the right of union members to revoke their monthly deduction of union dues at any time. An employee has merely to inform his employer in writing that he has ceased to be a member of the union. The Trade Disputes Act, 1965, empowering the Labour Minister to oblige employers to deduct union dues each month, still protected the right of a member to withdraw.

In practice, it may require some courage on the part of a union member to exercise his right of revocation, particularly if the timekeeper or section clerk responsible for dealing with revocations is himself a union official or avid union supporter. Such employees may have, or be thought to have, considerable influence over the length and course of a labourer's career. None the less, there are still many cases of members withdrawing from their unions.

The reasons for members' dissatisfaction with their union's performance or leadership are diverse. A defeated opponent will sometimes try to demonstrate his strength by urging his supporters to terminate their membership in the union. On other occasions, disaffected shop stewards may lead the campaign for revocation. In one union, for example, several ex-shop stewards in a number of Nairobi firms persuaded union members to withdraw from membership after the triennial conference had returned the same old group to power. One of these ex-shop stewards explained he had participated in the campaign for revocation because 'we are not allowed to elect our representatives both in the factory and the union officials...The corruption within the union have [sic] caused some of our accreditable shop stewards to resign themselves and some have been expelled unconstitutionally, both in our factory and other industries too.'[35] But the more usual basis of dissatisfaction is the national officials' alleged neglect of their members' interests. In January 1971, for instance, four shop stewards, employed in two firms catered for by the Commercial, Food and Allied Workers' Union, prevailed on a total of 838 union members to sign letters of revocation in protest against the headquarters' ineffectiveness in dealing with several grievances.[36] Predictably, national officials immediately gave the issues involved their full attention.

It is likely that trade union legislation to be presented in the future will contain a provision for a 'closed shop' or 'union shop' in Kenya. Under either system, once 50 per cent of the workers in any firm voluntarily agree to join the relevant union, employers must deduct union subscriptions from the monthly wages of *all* their employees. Union members, denied the right to withdraw their financial contribution, would thereby lose an important source of power vis-à-vis their leaders. Aside from the displeasure of a prominent political leader, nothing throws as much fear into the hearts of union leaders as threats of mass resignations by their members.

In sum, even though leaders have centralized control of their unions into their own hands, they are still sensitive to their members' desires and take these into account when making decisions. Rank-and-file wishes are made known to leaders in at least three ways. First, branch executive committees occasionally send resolutions to head office calling upon the union to take certain action in regard to a dispute or grievance. The general secretary cannot ignore these requests without angering branch supporters. Second, individual members and groups of members sometimes bypass the branch executive in order to correspond directly with the general secretary. He can refuse to take note of their complaints, but only at the risk of losing members. A good leader will respond.

But the most effective forum in which members can, and do, express their grievances is the branch general meeting. A general meeting called by a general secretary either just after work or during a lunch break generally draws a large crowd. In fact, if the general secretary is a well-known public figure, workers from enterprises not catered for by the union in question will also attend. After the general secretary outlines his efforts and achievements on behalf of the members, he asks for questions. There is usually no shortage of these. Question periods involving dockers, railwaymen or workers in the oil and chemical industries are particularly lively affairs. Members appear quite sure of themselves as they rise to address a question in Swahili. They make it quite clear that they regard themselves as the employer of the general secretary, and that he had better give a good account of himself. Frequently raised are searching questions about why headquarters has not vigorously pressed management on some currently contentious dispute or demand. The general secretary must respond, though sometimes he is at somewhat of a loss for an explanation. Trade unionism in Kenya is strong at the grass roots.

4. The persistence of internal conflict

A career in trade unionism in Kenya today is only for the forceful and daring, only for those who can operate in a situation of uncertainty in which routines have only just been established and imaginative innovation wins the day. Conflict within trade unions has not disappeared. It continues, even though incumbents have centralized control of decision-making and even though recent legislation has made opposition more difficult. As long as internal challenges by militant opponents persist, union leaders are unlikely to give precedence to the ruling elite's injunctions to practise wage restraint, counsel hard work and follow procedures for peaceful settlement. It is thus important to assess both the extent and patterns of intra-union conflict and the impact of the state's intervention into internal union affairs.

The striking variety of modes of conflict in trade unions can be reduced to three types, which together exhaust the main tendencies. The political process in unions may be characterized either by contests for the main posts on an individual basis, or by the absence of overt competition owing to the monopolization of offices and resources by a personal machine, or finally, by conflict between organized teams for control. Each of these types will be considered in turn.

Individual competition

'Individual competition' characterizes the political process in unions in which contests for office take place between individuals rather than teams.[1] There may be a rapid turnover of all office-holders except the general secretary (or president, depending on who is pre-eminent), but the defeat of incumbents does not reflect on the position of this leader, because he remains neutral in all elections. In public statements, the leader portrays himself as the defender of the right of delegates to choose freely their officers, and of the normative rule best expressed by the phrase 'let the best man win'.

In actual practice, the leader's exemplary behaviour is neither always consistent nor disinterested. Few general secretaries remain neutral in *all* contests for office; they will frequently try to influence the selection of at least the treasurer, perhaps the president and often the secretaries of the largest branches. These, of course, comprise the most powerful offices within the unions. In addition, union leaders do not necessarily adopt the 'individual competition' strategy because they are more committed to democratic norms than others; rather this strategy promises high returns at low cost. Where there is no apparent opposition to a particular leader, he is under no pressure to control who is selected for the other union posts. Acquiring and keeping such control is, in any case, an expensive and enervating process, especially where a union's membership is dispersed in a large number of branches all over the country. Moreover, permitting freedom of selection legitimizes a leader's own position among his members and branch officials. He will, of course, be compelled to change his *laissez-faire* strategy at the first sign of organized opposition, and begin to organize his own supporters into a team.

Of the fifteen unions under study, individual competition has most clearly and consistently characterized the history of only two – the Local Government Workers' Union and the Chemical Workers' Union. The records of the two unions reveal a high turnover of national officials, other than the general secretary, though the only instances of team competition occurred in the chemical union before the triennial elections in 1965 and 1971, and in the local government union in 1971. The present general secretaries of both unions acknowledged that delegates at national conferences often asked their opinions of various candidates; however both claimed, and other sources concurred with their opinion, that they generally refused to back any particular candidates. Informal bargaining among the delegates apparently characterized the election of national officials at triennial (and formerly annual) conferences, especially in the KLGWU. Usually if the president is chosen from one tribe, it is deemed proper that the vice-president should come from another tribe, and so on. In this way, all the larger tribes gain representation among the national officers. Before 1965, moreover, it was uncommon to have national officials, other than the general secretary, elected unopposed.[2] Delegates were allowed to nominate candidates from the floor, and the absence of any control is evidenced by the fact that members of the executive committee nominated various candidates for the same post. Some of these, obviously, were defeated.[3]

The 'individual competition' model does not imply the absence of internal disputes, but only that disagreements do not escalate into factional struggles for control. Although the KCWU has experienced only two instances of factionalism, there have been many other cases of disputes which did not result in team conflict. In the early 1960s, for example, there were numerous acrimonious exchanges between the union's full-time General Secretary, Were Ogutu (centred in Nairobi) and officials of the union's second largest branch, located at a Bamburi cement factory (near Mombasa). The main antagonist at Bamburi was the Branch Chairman (who was also the Union's President for a few years). Voiced at conferences, central council meetings and in correspondence, the main charges against Ogutu were that he failed to keep the President informed of developments at headquarters and neglected to attend to union business at Bamburi.[4] Bamburi delegates felt that the General Secretary stayed in his Nairobi head office too much. But the point is that these, and other disputes, were resolved (or, at least, aired) *within* the union's committees and conferences, and did not escalate into struggles for control. Votes of confidence in the General Secretary were taken, in accordance with the rule laid down by the union's Central Committee meeting of 20 February 1960: '...if there is any misunderstanding or a disagreement between two officials of the Union, the matter must be dealt with by the Union...but the two persons involved should not try to struggle to settle the matter privately.'

The Local Government Workers' Union has only experienced one factional struggle. There have, however, been squabbles at the branch level in which the general secretary took sides, and attempts by branches to operate independently of head office. These branch disputes arose in 1963–4 owing to the general secretary's inability to cope with the tremendous expansion of the union in the early 1960s. While the union had a total of twelve branches when the State of Emergency ended in 1960, this number had risen to twenty-eight by the beginning of 1961. To assist the chief officer in organizing the union, the executive committee appointed regional organizing secretaries for five regions. The problem was that these regional organizers began to regard themselves as sovereign within their own regions, often ignoring instructions from headquarters. Confusion was compounded in 1964 when factionalism emerged in a couple of branches on the basis of the struggle to control the national union federation. The situation was only righted after a former National Treasurer of the Union was appointed Acting General Secretary in late 1964. His solution was to centralize decision-making and financial power.[5] Regional offices were abolished in favour of centralized administration. Four organizing secretaries were appointed, but they were all to operate from head office under the General Secretary's direction, and were not confined to organizing in any particular area of the country. The head office also made itself responsible for allocating funds to the branches.

Non-competitive oligarchy

Many American trade unions, dominated by entrenched and stable oligarchies, manifest this type of internal politics.[6] It is the type in which ambitious trade unionists prefer to 'wait their turn' until a vacancy occurs in the union hierarchy, rather than to engage in hopeless contests against prestigious and powerful incumbents. These office-holders, for their part, are anxious to forestall cleavages within their union; they are, therefore, prepared to co-opt ambitious people into the union's hierarchy when positions become available. A union official so co-opted can hope to advance up the ladder as vacancies arise and his talents are recognized. Although there is thus an absence of overt opposition, this is not necessarily a permanent feature of a union's political life. An important issue or an organizational crisis (such as the death or retirement of the pre-eminent leader) may suddenly provoke team conflict.

Few Kenyan trade unions resemble this model. As Kenyan unions are a relatively new phenomenon, they are only just beginning to manifest stable and entrenched oligarchies. Moreover, there is little or no bureaucracy in Kenyan trade unions into which ambitious contenders can be co-opted, and up which they can hope to climb. In the smallest unions, the general secretary is usually the only full-time official, though he may occasionally use the services of an appointed organizing secretary. In larger unions, there are three or more full-time national officials, plus several full-time branch secretaries. Even in these cases, however, there is often little division of labour among the full-time officers. Regardless of whether a document exists clearly demarcating the various offices, the general secretary usually intervenes in all aspects of his union's activities, and the various other full-time officers assume diverse and often overlapping responsibilities. In short, there is no clear union hierarchy within which an ambitious person can hope to progress. Instead, a general secretary or president dominates the whole union; he is rarely sufficiently foolhardy to co-opt into a post next to him an ambitious and able person who will then be in a position to undermine him.

Having said all this, however, one must still note a trend toward the non-competitive oligarchical situation in many Kenyan unions. One reason for this is the tendency, already noted, for incumbent leaders to gain access to increased resources over the past few years, owing largely to the 'check-off' system. Established leaders have thus become more formidable opponents. As well, legislation passed in 1964 and 1965 – particularly relating to the role of the Registrar of Trade Unions in intra-union conflict – has strengthened the position of those in office vis-à-vis challengers.

Although nearly all unions experienced a decline in overt competition until the pervasive factional conflicts of 1970–1, three unions – the Building and Construction Workers, the Plantation and Agricultural Workers and the Commercial, Food and Allied – most nearly approximated the non-competitive type. In all three unions, there was an attempt to ensure that only members of the oligarchy were elected to national and branch posts. The incidence of uncontested posts at both levels is very high; in fact, every branch and national official of the Building and Construction Workers' Union was returned unopposed in the 1968 triennial elections. To maintain cohesion, the leaders of these unions constantly emphasize to the oligarchy the dangers of internal division. Consider, for example, the kind of imagery employed in the following address by a general secretary to his union's final central committee meeting before the impending elections:

Beloved Brothers, you know that a divided kingdom cannot last for long. If we want to preserve the unity and strength of this union, for the benefit of the workers, we must remember that Unity is the very foundation of the well-being of the Union. We are all aware of the difficulties we got into during the time of 'Splinter Groups' which did not only delay the payment of wages of the workers but spent all the Union money and incurred great debts that became a disgrace in the whole country. Pray God that we don't go back to such a situation in this year...

Remember that, in this year, there are various types of battles to be fought: you know that the General Elections for Union branches and the national office-bearers will be held this year. From Branches to the Head Office, we are surrounded by enemies who wait to take over our leadership. Branches like Nakuru, Nyeri, Kisumu and Kisii have already experienced this struggle sometime last year but we fought bravely and evicted all the enemies.

Don't you deceive yourself that these people have been quietened, they will try very hard and in every way possible to spoil our names. Let us agree among ourselves that we shall all fight together under one General and in this way we shall succeed – many times.

I don't think there is anyone of us here who would not like to see every one of us returned back in the Committee at the end of the year and if my assumption is true, then I don't see why each of us should not fight hard for his comrade without looking at what tribe he belongs, religion, rich or poor.

When the battle for election nears, the Executive Council of the Union will be called upon to make proper arrangements which will destroy our enemies completely. Remember, that if we lose any one of our Committee members we shall have lost one important soldier in our Company.[7]

Team competition

During the period 1960 to 1972, factionalism was the most common form of union politics in Kenya. A faction, as earlier defined, is a coalition of followers recruited on the basis of mercenary ties by or on behalf of a leader, who is in conflict with another leader or leaders. If an opposition team manages to persist for a long time, thus gaining legitimacy in the view of many union members and leaders, a 'party system' emerges.[8] Drawing this distinction, Lipset, Trow and Coleman admit, however, that their case which exhibits a party system – the International Typographical Union – is 'unique'.[9] There is certainly no example of a party system in Kenyan trade unions. Opposition groups are pejoratively referred to as 'splinter groups', out to wreck the 'workers' unity' to advance the 'selfish interests' of certain 'power-hungry individuals'. Labelled as 'anti-union', oppositionists are often expelled from union membership. Even the most apparently progressive of the union leaders interviewed would not agree that an opposition faction should be permitted to organize support or criticize incumbents on a long-term basis. In short, established leaders are not dissuaded from using unfair tactics to eliminate opposition elements by any widespread belief in the legitimacy of opposition.

Factionalism may arise either in the form of the 'ins' against the 'outs' or from a split among the elected officials. Often, factionalism emerges when a cabal within a union's executive tries to oust the general secretary (or president) and his closest supporters. A 'palace coup' normally leads to factionalism, because the allegedly ousted leader or leaders seldom concede defeat without a fight. Usually, each side claims to have dismissed or suspended the other from office. Since the passage of the 1964 Trade Unions (Amendment) Act, procedures exist for resolving these disputes over who are the valid officials; these solutions will be discussed shortly.

One can distinguish between two types of factions – 'majority-bent' and 'separatist' – on the basis of the goals that they pursue.[10] The former type aspires to capture or maintain control of the union as a whole; the latter seeks to split off a section of a registered union in order to form a separate organization under its leaders' control. Which goal a faction leader adopts depends on his estimate of his team's potential strength vis-à-vis the incumbent's machine, together with the scope of the union's membership. Of the fifteen unions under study, only five have experienced separatist factionalism and fourteen the majority-bent variety. The same union frequently undergoes both types, sometimes a single leader shifting from one strategy to the other as his estimate of relative strengths shift.

Separatist factions tend to emerge in general unions, that is, those unions that cater for the employees of more than one industry. Four of the five unions in the present sample which have experienced separatist factionalism are, or were at the time, general unions. There is a good reason for this. Since Kenyan government policy has long been to encourage the formation of clearly demarcated industrial unions, a separatist faction can only hope to persuade the Registrar of Trade Unions to grant legal recognition to a new union if it represents a separate industry. And general unions are, by definition, the only unions that currently represent the interests of more than one industry.

Although their goals differ, the two types of factions employ similar tactics. The leaders of both types seek to demonstrate their support among the branch officials and union members. In the case of separatist factionalism, of course, the arena of competition is not the union as a whole, but the particular firm or industry whose employees the opposition faction claims to represent. Both types of factionalism may lead to industrial unrest and strikes as one side or the other extends the struggle to the work place. Moreover, in both cases, established leaders try to manipulate to their own advantage the rules governing the convening, composition and powers of the various bodies. Lastly, the Registrar of Trade Unions is now the final arbiter in both kinds of disputes; it is he who must decide whether to accept a change of officers or to register a 'breakaway' union. He is thus an important person to impress.

The incidence of factionalism in the various unions can be compared in terms of the number of 'factional encounters' experienced. A factional encounter is a show-down between factions in which their conflicting claims to support are put to some appropriate test. It continues until the competing teams, as well as interested outsiders, are forced to agree on a version of the opponents' relative strength.[11] In other words, one faction or the other wins, an outcome evident to both contenders and bystanders. Although the losing faction need not necessarily dissolve upon defeat, this is frequently the case in unions.

An encounter may begin with a vote to oust (i.e., dismiss or suspend) opponents at an allegedly constitutionally convened annual or triennial conference, special conference, central council or executive committee meeting. Alternatively, it may commence with the submission to the Registrar of Trade Unions of an application for the registration of a separate union. Such an action constitutes an encounter, as the Registrar then calls upon the established leadership to show that it represents a 'substantial proportion' of the employees for whom the proposed union claims to speak.

Encounters are terminated in several ways. They may be ended by the initial vote, ousting one of the contending groups, provided the verdict is accepted. More usually, further votes are taken by various union bodies convened by the various contenders. One of the factions may successfully impress its opponent with its power by effectively excluding all known supporters of its opponent from a conference, and electing all officials unopposed. Often, a dispute can only be ended by a conference supervised (or at least attended) by some neutral outsider. Since the legislation of 1964, the most frequent conclusion to a factional struggle is the Registrar of Trade Union's decision whether to register a particular Notice of Change of Officers or a new 'splinter' union.

Most factional encounters have occurred since 1960, when the Emergency regulations were lifted. During the Mau Mau Emergency most unions were little more than shells, owing to restrictions on the holding of public meetings, the collection of money and travel.[12] Moreover, as workers feared association with unions, these bodies were impoverished. Although the colonial government was officially committed to the policy of fostering trade unions, many members of the settler community and the police force clearly believed that trade unionists were actually or potentially subversive. Hence, Africans found with union membership cards during the periodical police sweeps of Nairobi and other urban areas were subjected to rougher treatment than others. Many workers obviously concluded that union membership was grounds for detention or ill-treatment, no matter what the Labour Department officials said. In this situation, there was an understandable dearth, rather than an abundance, of people competing for union leadership posts. Union office, below the post of general secretary, was not a coveted prize before 1960; indeed, the problem for many unions was not one of internal struggles, but of finding enough educated people who would consent to hold office. Only after the Emergency regulations were lifted did branch and national office become highly prized.

Most unions which existed for at least three years between January 1960 and January 1970 experienced three or more factional episodes (See Table 3). The only ones not manifesting this high incidence of organized encounters were the Local Government Workers, the Chemical Workers, the Tea Union, the Coffee Union and the General Agricultural Workers' Union. The

Table 3. Number of factional encounters at national level, 1960–70

Union	Length of existence	2 year periods beginning:					Total
		Jan. 1960	Jan. 1962	Jan. 1964	Jan. 1966	Jan. 1968	
EAFBCWU	May 1952–	2	1	3	0	0	6
KDCWU–KUCFAW	June 1952–	1	3	3	0	0	7
KLGWU	Sept. 1953–	0	0	0	0	0	0
RAU(K)	Oct. 1953–	2	0	1	1	1	5
DWU	Oct. 1954–	2	1	1	2	1	7
KPOWU	Aug. 1958–	0	0	2	2	0	4
KCWU	Aug. 1958–	0	0	1	0	0	1
TPWU	Sept. 1959–Aug. 1963	0	1	Defunct			1
CPWU	Nov. 1959–Dec. 1961	1	Defunct				1
KUSPW	Nov. 1960–	0	1	2	2	1	6
GAWU	Feb. 1961–Aug. 1963	0	0	Defunct			0
KQMWU	Sept. 1961–	0	0	3	0	2	5
S&CPWU	Aug. 1962–Aug. 1963		3	Defunct			3
CSACSU(K)	Sept. 1962–		1	0	1	1	3
KPAWU	Aug. 1963–		1	3	1	1	6
Total		8	12	19	9	7	55

SOURCES: The files of individual unions, the KFL and the Ministry of Labour, together with interviews with participants.

Table 4. *Frequency of defeat of top two incumbent officials*

Union	No. of majority-bent encounters, Jan. 1960 to Jan. 1970	Max. no. of incumbents who could have lost	No. who were defeated	Frequency of defeat (%) $\left(\dfrac{\text{Actual no.} \times 100}{\text{possible no.}}\right)$
EAFBCWU	4	8	2	25
KDCWU–KUCFAW	2	4	1	25
KLGWU	0	Not relevant	Not relevant	
RAU(K)	3	6	3	50
DWU	7	14	4	29
KPOWU	4	8	0	0
KCWU	1	2	0	0
TPWU	1	2	2	100
CPWU	1	2	0	0
KUSPW	6	12	7	58
GAWU	0	Not relevant	Not relevant	
KQMWU	5	10	2	20
S&CPWU	1	2	1	50
CSACSU(K)	3	6	3	50
KPAWU	4	8	2	25
Mean average	2.8	6.5	2.1	33.2

SOURCE: compiled from the files of the Registrar of Trade Unions.

last three, however, did not persist long enough for one to judge their long-term prospects, while the first two were characterized by the 'individual competition' pattern.

Table 3 also indicates that the total incidence of factionalism increased to a peak in the period of January 1964 to December 1965. The struggle for supremacy between the KFL and the Kenya African Workers' Congress between April 1964 and August 1965 was largely responsible for this trend, whereas the decline in factionalism after 1965 was due mainly to the termination of this struggle and new union legislation. However, the period 1970–1, not covered in the table, saw a resurgence of factionalism. While I did not collect detailed information on all eleven extant unions in my sample upon returning to the field in 1972, my impression was that every one of these unions had undergone internal conflict in the previous two years. Intra-union factionalism was again the result of a struggle to control the national union federation, in this case COTU. One of the COTU factions had access to a vast amount of money, which it employed in fighting for power in unions aligned with the opposing group within COTU. Further discussion of this conflict is contained in Chapter 6.

The principal shortcoming of Table 3 is its failure to indicate whether factionalism posed any real threat to incumbent leaders. If, for example, opposition was merely nominal and easily defeated, then the incidence of factionalism is almost irrelevant. Table 4 seeks roughly to measure the significance of factional struggles by reference to the frequency of defeat of the two top union officials – the general secretary and president. Assuming that both these officials are on the same team, each majority-bent factional encounter could lead to the defeat of both of them. In other words, the maximum possible number of defeats is twice the number of majority-bent encounters in a particular union. In practice, the assumption of unity between the president and general secretary is false in approximately 25 per cent of the encounters. Thus, the high frequency of defeat of incumbent officials – which in several cases is at least 50 per cent – actually understates the significance of factionalism for leadership change. Where the general secretary and the president lead rival factions, only one of them can lose office. Factional opposition has been merely nominal in several unions (e.g., the Petroleum Oil Workers' Union) and crucial in others (e.g., the Tea Plantation Workers' Union). Finally, it should be noted that most of the successful defeats of established leaders eventuated in the earlier part of the decade, indicating somewhat of a decline in effective opposition over time. This trend too was reversed in 1970–1, but is probably true in the long-term.

Table 5 suggests that a separatist faction's likelihood of success is slim indeed. Of the fourteen instances of separatist factionalism, only one 'breakaway' union – the Quarry and Mineworkers' Union – achieved registration.

Table 5. *Success of separatist factions, 1960–70*

Union	No. of separatist encounters, Jan. 1960 to Jan. 1970	No. of 'breakaway' unions actually registered
EAFBCWU	2	1
KDCWU	6	0
RAU(K)	2	0
S&CPWU	2	0
KPAWU	2	0
Total	14	1

SOURCES: various files and interviews.

State agencies as regulators of conflict

It is in the government's interests to regulate these factional struggles within unions. At the least, intra-union conflict pushes union leaders toward assuming militant positions in an effort to outflank opponents. At the worst, factionalism can lead to costly industrial unrest and violence. In Kenya, legislation has authorized the state to penetrate deeply into the union's internal affairs in order to ensure the observance of proper procedures. What has been the effect of such efforts in obtaining a more predictable and secure world for trade unionists?

The officer charged with the main responsibility in regulating internal union conflict is the Registrar of Trade Unions. The present incumbent, a European, has held the post since the late 1950s, though his African assistant now attends to all routine matters. Being a European has, para-doxically, been advantageous to the Registrar in fulfilling his duties as arbiter. He personally handles only politically sensitive or complicated intra-union disputes, and the fact that he is not a tribesman of any of the disputants helps allay suspicions as to his impartiality.

The Registrar's authority as arbitrator within unions stems mainly from his discretionary powers regarding registration. Since the first ordinance in 1937, Kenya's trade union legislation has always stipulated the compulsory registration of unions. A union, without registration, could have no legal existence and, hence, no legal immunities. The grounds on which the Registrar could cancel a union's registration have broadened over time. Registration could be cancelled, according to the 1937 ordinance, only if the Registrar was satisfied that registration had been obtained 'by fraud, or mistake, or that such trade union has wilfully, and after notice from the Registrar, violated any of the provisions of this Ordinance, or of any rules made thereunder, or has ceased to exist'. Replacing all previous ordinances, the 1952 Trade Unions Ordinance empowered the Registrar to suspend as well as cancel a union's registration. He could take either of these steps if he was satisfied *inter alia* that: registration was obtained by fraud or mistake; any of the union's aims was unlawful; the constitution of the trade union or of its executive was unlawful; the trade union was being used for an unlawful purpose; the trade union had wilfully and, after notice from the Registrar, contravened any provisions of the Ordinance; or the union's funds were expended in an unlawful manner, or on an unlawful object or on an object not authorized by the ordinance.

The Registrar's role as umpire was considerably augmented by the Trade Unions (Amendment) Act, 1964. In addition to the grounds mentioned in the Trade Unions Ordinance, 1952, he was authorized to suspend or cancel a union's registration if a union 'wilfully and after notice from the Registrar' contravened any of its *own* rules (Sec. 17(2)(e)). The Registrar of Trade Unions was thus placed in a position to enforce not only the *legal* rules regulating intra-union conflict, but also the union's own constitutional rules.

How has the Registrar used his power to cancel or suspend registration? Since the official aim of Labour Department policy after the Second World War was to foster the growth of trade unionism, he has generally been reluctant to deregister unions. To bring recalcitrant unions back into line, the Registrar has usually confined himself to requesting the union to 'show cause why its registration should not be cancelled'. The idea was to apply 'shock tactics' (as officials of the Colonial Labour Department liked to call it), in order to convince a union to right its own affairs.[13] Thus, although five of the fifteen unions under study have at some point been threatened with deregistration, only one of these – the Coffee Plantation Workers' Union – actually had its registration cancelled.[14]

The Registrar of Trade Unions has used to full advantage his authority to enforce a union's own rules since October 1964. The depth of the Registrar's involvement in the political process of unions can be gauged from a letter written by the Assistant Registrar of Trade Unions to the Acting General Secretary of the Dockworkers' Union in March 1966.[15] In the Assistant Registrar's words, the union was experiencing at this time 'a great deal of uneasiness regarding the union's leadership. It would appear that a good section of your union would like a Special Conference convened in terms of Rule 6(a) of the registered Rules of your Union to thrash out the issues involved.' He suggested, therefore, that 'if a proper requisition has been made by at least 24 paid up members of your union', the Acting General Secretary was bound to convene a Special Conference. Noting that such a requisition had apparently already been made, the Assistant Registrar warned that he would consider cancelling the union's registration if its constitution was not followed. Under this threat, the union soon held a Special Conference, supervised by the Senior Labour Officer (Coast). The leadership issue was thus resolved – for a short time.

Separatist factionalism

Separatist factions have always been at a disadvantage vis-à-vis incumbent groups because government policy has been to discourage the proliferation of small, weak unions. Of the dozens of 'breakaway' unions that have applied for registration over the years, only a handful have actually been granted it. Most of these, moreover, were registered in the late 1950s. In this early period, the Federation of Kenya Employers, the Kenya Federation of Labour and the Labour Department were together still carving out a rational demarcation of union boundaries.

The Trade Unions Ordinance of 1952 empowered the Registrar of Trade Unions to refuse to register a new union if any previously registered union is 'sufficiently representative of the whole or of a substantial proportion of the interests in respect of which the applicants seek registration'. In practice, the Registrar has cited this grounds for refusing registration to a separatist faction even when the relevant registered union represented less than ten per cent of the workers in the contested firm or industry.[16] His decision may be appealed to the Supreme Court. Yet appeals have been infrequent, probably owing to the expense involved and unfamiliarity with the law or the court system.

In 1964, the Tripartite Agreement on Measures for the Immediate Relief of Unemployment and the Trade Unions (Amendment) Act further encumbered the formation of a separatist faction. The former agreement, recognizing that unions 'must be able to maintain their authority during the wage pause', recommended legislation designed, *inter alia*, 'to discourage the formation of splinter unions'. Passed a few months later, the Act fulfilled this recommendation. It decreased from three months to twenty-eight days the period within which a proposed union could function without being legally recognized. All penalties for infringing sections of the ordinance were stiffened. In addition, the fee payable upon application for registration was increased from KSh2/50 to KSh100 in order to discourage frivolous applications.

The effect of the policy expressed in the Tripartite Agreement was virtually to remove the possibility that a separatist faction might gain registration. A month after the signing of the agreement the Chief Industrial Relations Officer advised the Assistant Registrar of Trade Unions not to register a new union 'unless it is clearly established that a *vast majority* of the employees concerned are in support of the proposed organization. Any other course would bring strong opposition from the KFL and a possible collapse of the Tripartite Agreement.'[17] A separatist faction's problem arises from the normal apathy of workers; seldom can the bulk of the workers be aroused to the point where they are willing to demonstrate their support for a separatist group, even if they are dissatisfied with the established union. As a separatist faction will almost inevitably be unable to convince the Registrar that it fulfils the 'vast majority' requirement, he will generally arbitrate in favour of the incumbent group. Not surprisingly, therefore, applications for registration of 'breakaway' unions have declined drastically since the early 1960s.

Majority-bent factionalism

Recent legislation has also worked to the advantage of established union leaders in regard to majority-bent factionalism. Under the 1952 Ordinance, the Registrar of Trade Unions had no discretion to question whether a particular change of officials was carried out according to constitutional procedures. The Ordinance merely stated that 'notice of all changes of officers...shall, within seven days of such change, be sent to the Registrar by the trade union together with the prescribed fee, and the Registrar shall thereupon correct the register accordingly' (Sec. 38(2)). Where a change of officers was arrived at by means of a particularly blatant disregard of a union's constitution, the Registrar would sometimes refuse to register the names of the new officers on the grounds that the executive was 'unlawfully constituted'. The legality of such a refusal is questionable, though the intentions behind the act are not. In any event, the point is that nearly any faction within a union could, with considerable ease, get its leaders registered as the legally-recognized union executive. It had merely to state on the appropriate form that elections had been held, to name the new office-bearers, and to submit the form, together with the requisite fee of KSh10, to the Registrar's Office. The ease of registration of new officers led to so-called 'Ten Shilling Wars', where leaders of warring factions would arrive, sometimes almost hourly, at the Registrar's Office to submit their Notices of Change of Officers. At the height of factional struggles, the legally recognized office-holders might change as often as ten times within the space of a single month.

The Trade Unions (Amendment) Act ended these practices. Designed 'to ensure that the unions are run properly in the interests of members and in accordance with their own constitutions',[18] the legislation assigned to the Registrar of Trade Unions the role of referee in intra-union conflicts. It authorized that official not only to enforce the unions' own constitutions (a point discussed earlier), but also, more specifically, to investigate the 'validity or propriety' of any Notice of Change of Officers submitted to him. If such inquiry failed to satisfy the Registrar as to the validity of any appointment, he could refer the matter to a 'Trade Unions Tribunal'. This Tribunal, composed of one or more independent persons appointed by the Labour Minister, is empowered to decide on the basis of an inquiry who are the recognized officials.[19] There exists the usual provision for an appeal to the Supreme Court in a case where the Registrar refuses to register a change of officials; however, an appellant is unlikely to obtain a favourable verdict if the Tribunal has already adjudicated.

Between 1964 and early 1970, the Tribunal had adjudicated in thirteen cases: one case originated in September 1965, ten cases in 1966 and two cases in 1967. In 1967, the Registrar-General's Department, together with the Chairman of the Tribunal, decided that the Act authorized the Registrar to reject Notices of Change without a reference to the Tribunal. Only Notices whose validity still appeared debatable after investigation were to be submitted to the Tribunal. However, it is likely that the paucity of cases heard by that body since 1967 is only an indirect consequence of this interpretation of the Act. No less than ten of the thirteen cases submitted to the Tribunal by early 1970 involved unions led by men identified with Oginga Odinga and the Kenya Peoples' Union (KPU). During the period of intense political struggle in 1965–6 when KANU leaders were trying to oust Odinga's adherents from all positions of influence, decisions on the registration of changes of union officials were politically contentious. The Registrar may, therefore, have felt that such decisions were best taken by the Tribunal, so that both factions would have an opportunity to state their cases publicly. Between 1967 and 1970, no further KANU–KPU conflicts were fought out within particular unions, which may partly explain why the Tribunal was not used so frequently in this period. It was busy again in 1970–2, as another phase of politically-inspired factionalism convulsed trade unionism.

Since 1964, the enhanced supervisory and arbitratory roles of the Registrar and the Tribunal have operated to the detriment of opposition factions. Before the Trade Unions (Amendment) Act, a faction could always aspire to legal recognition, if only for an hour or two at a time, but now the Registrar frequently rejects Notices of Change of Officers. To oust the established leaders, oppositionists must follow the constitutional procedures; yet these are controlled by the incumbents. Union conferences, aside from the special conference, and committee meetings must be convened by the general secretary and chaired by the president. As long as these two officers remain united, an opposition faction will experience considerable difficulty convening a constitutional executive committee or central council meeting to dismiss the incumbents. Moreover, the convening of a constitutional special conference against the wishes of the general secretary requires much more effective organization than most factions possess. Finally, the Registrar's duty to enforce the unions' rules and to decide the validity of changes of officials means that the administration and police now stand ready to enforce expulsions or suspensions decided upon by established leaders. An expelled oppositionist can now be entirely excluded from contention.

To the extent that intra-union conflict has declined somewhat, the ruling elite's policy has succeeded. But if one of its goals was to create an entrenched, stable union leadership who would feel sufficiently secure to renounce belligerence for moderation and pliancy in the use of union power, then this aim has been only partially achieved. Internal union politics remain fluid and uncertain. While the potential for intra-union conflict is high, full-time union leaders must respond to pressures from within their unions as well as to pressure from the political class. These internal pressures, I have suggested, push union leaders towards aggressive economic demands and militant tactics in defence of the collective and individual interests of wage-earners. That, after all, is what union members pay for.

5. The bases of cleavage

Why has conflict in trade unions persisted? One would have thought that union officials, with the impressive resources under their control and the benefit of legislation making opposition more difficult, would have successfully entrenched their positions, thus becoming stable and irremovable. Yet factionalism and insecurity have continued. An examination of the bases of cleavage in unions will perhaps throw light on this phenomenon.

Two sources of cleavage stand out in studies of trade unionism: occupational status and ethnicity. Occupational status may become a salient principle of solidarity if union members believe that their office-holders are advancing the interests of a particular occupational category at the expense of others. Ethnicity may be politicized if workers perceive that one ethnic group is seeking to monopolize jobs and power at the expense of others. Needless to say, occupational and ethnic lines may sometimes coincide.

Studies of African trade unions have arrived at somewhat divergent conclusions regarding the salience of the two sorts of cleavages. Consider first Smock's study of the Nigerian Coal Miners' Union (NCMU). Unskilled labourers in this union composed only 22 per cent of its Executive Council, though they formed over one-half of the mines' work force, whereas clerical employees and foremen constituted 50 per cent of the Executive Council's membership but under 5 per cent of the work force. Smock concluded in this case that occupation represented a significant line of cleavage since manual workers resented their union leaders' propensity to concentrate on winning benefits for a small group.[1] At the same time, 'ethnic factionalism' was a key aspect of intra-union disputes, even though 99 per cent of the union's membership was Ibo. The principal basis of cleavage was between the less advanced Abajo-Ngwo Ibo, whose home area surrounds the coal mines near Enugu, and those Ibo who migrated to the mines from other areas. This cleavage, which persisted for a long period, was articulated in terms of the 'local people' against the 'strangers'. In Smock's words, 'this division within the Ibo group is so sharp that Ibo strangers welcome non-Ibos into their groups and even give them positions of leadership. They are drawn together by a common opponent – the local people, who are more numerous. Control of the NCMU has passed back and forth between the local people and the strangers, and whichever group is in control of the Union keeps the other group from exerting significant influence and from winning many of its demands.'[2]

Grillo carried out a similar study of the internal politics of the Kampala branch of the Railway African Union (Uganda). He discovered that thirty-one of the thirty-five persons who held or competed for branch office in 1963–5 were clerical, skilled or technical Group 'B' employees, even though the unskilled or semi-skilled Group 'C' workers constituted about five-sixths of the union's membership. He also noted the excessive concern of some leaders of the RAU(U) with their own promotions: but he did not consider occupational status to be a source of cleavage in the union. He reported that neither team in a 1963–4 factional encounter represented an occupational interest, as thirteen of the eighteen core leaders of the factions were Group 'B' workers, mostly clerical employees. This led him to conclude that 'occupation and grade do not provide frames of reference which clearly distinguish one competitor from another', though tribe did, under certain conditions.[3]

Scott, in his study of Ugandan trade unions, was in agreement with this last statement. He observed that office-holders in tribal associations – especially the Baluhya and Luo – were quite often union leaders as well. He found, moreover, that the bulk of union members perceived many intra-union conflicts in terms of tribal affiliations, though, in fact, the basis of conflict was often economic interest rather than traditional animosities *per se*.[4]

Epstein, while finding that conflict within the African Mineworkers' Union on the Copperbelt occurred along tribal lines, argued that this masked struggles between groups of different occupational status. As the educational system in Nyasaland was established earlier than in Northern Rhodesia, and as Nyasas frequently gained mining experience in Southern Rhodesian mines, they tended to monopolize posts in Copperbelt mines open to educated Africans during the early period. The Bembas, nearest rivals to the Nyasas, filled only minor posts. Thus, the conflict between the Nyasas and the Bembas, both within and outside the union, was based primarily on a clash of economic interest rather than on any traditional hostility.[5]

It is this tendency for ethnic boundaries to overlap with occupational divisions that sometimes accounts for discrepancies between the findings of various researchers. In Kenya, however, it is unusual to find one tribe monopolizing the higher positions while other groups are relegated to subordinate grades. Members of the four largest tribes – Kikuyu, Luo, Luhya and Kamba – are usually represented in the top positions, though admittedly often not proportionately to their strength in the wage-earning force.

Of the fifteen Kenyan unions whose internal politics over the decade 1960–70 I studied, only one, the Railway African Union (Kenya), has exhibited occupational cleavages cutting across tribal lines. Factionalism is often ethnically based; even the most powerful union leader may be vulnerable to opponents relying on a tribal appeal. Why this should be so is the question this chapter seeks to answer.

Occupational status as a frame of reference

Why has occupation not constituted a more salient frame of reference in internal politics? There is, in Kenya as in most developing countries, a wide gap between trade union officials and their rank-and-file in terms of occupational background and average monthly earnings. But this gap, documented by the figures below, has not apparently prompted many internal struggles for power.

The leadership–membership gap

In 1967 the Ministry of Labour collected data on employment by broad occupational categories for the first time.[6] The fact that this information refers only to employees of urban firms, large farms and plantations, mines and quarries, other rural non-agricultural enterprises and the public services is no limitation for our purposes, since Kenyan unions cater almost exclusively for wage-earners in this 'modern' sector. This information reveals that 53 per cent of all employees were unskilled labourers, while 23.7 per cent were skilled wage or salary earners, 9.1 per cent were clerical, 2.4 per cent were employed in sales, 5.7 per cent were teachers and the remaining 6.1 per cent were classified as professional, technical, administrative and managerial. Of course, unskilled labourers comprised far more than 53 per cent of most unions.[7] Teachers, for example, were concentrated in their own trade union, and those in professional, technical, administrative and managerial positions were disproportionately non-African and were, in any case, often ineligible for union membership owing to the confidential or responsible nature of their work. As well, many of the semi-skilled manual workers, such as production process employees, have more in common with unskilled labourers than they do with the skilled artisans with which they are apparently grouped.

In contrast, Table 6 reveals the preponderance of clerical and skilled employees amongst the national officials of Kenyan unions. No less than 43 per cent of the 431 national leaders whose occupations at the time when they first became officials could be discovered were clerical employees, and a further 21 per cent were skilled workers. Of national officials 8 per cent (mainly general secretaries) originated from outside the industry; many of these had held clerical positions in other industries before entering trade unionism as a full-time occupation. Only 8 per cent of officials were drawn from such unskilled occupations as watchmen, office messengers, sweepers, cleaners, and labourers. In fact, more national positions were held by supervisory staff (11 per cent) and professional and technical people (10 per cent) than by unskilled or semi-skilled workers who constituted the bulk of most unions. In six of the fifteen unions, no unskilled worker had ever held a national post. In two unions – the Quarry and Mine Workers and the Building and Construction Workers – tradesmen and skilled workers of all kinds have composed over half of all the national officials whose occupation could be determined. In six other unions, clerical employees have predominated. Other unions have national leaderships drawn largely from professional and technical employees. The Tea Plantation Workers' Union was formed and led during the four years of its existence by medical attendants, dressers (in hospitals) and welfare assistants. Since they constitute the best educated employees in the large estates, their predominance is understandable. The East African Community Union has drawn half of its officials from professional and technical officers, which is not surprising since these employees constitute about 40 per cent of this union's membership. Subordinate employees form only about 20 per cent of the total.[8] Finally, the professional and executive employees of local authorities have traditionally occupied the top positions in the well-organized Local Government Workers' Union, though they form only a small minority in the union's membership.

Although no survey of the occupational background of branch officials was attempted, fragmentary evidence suggests that a higher proportion of these lower-level leaders were manual or subordinate workers.[9] But, in the branches of all unions, clerical, professional, technical and skilled employees were still over-represented in proportion to their numbers in the wage-earning force. Furthermore, the most prestigious and powerful posts – branch secretary, chairman, and treasurer – were almost invariably occupied by the better-educated members. The ability to speak English, the language of communication with employers and head office, is a decided asset even at the branch level.

A concomitant of the occupational gap between union officials and the bulk of the rank-and-file is the gap in average cash monthly earnings. In 1967 the average monthly earnings of male clerical employees was KSh806 while that of male skilled wage or salary earners was KSh521 and of male unskilled labourers was KSh162. The male professional, technical, administrative and managerial grades made an average monthly salary of KSh2,386.[10] According to these figures, therefore, the disproportionately clerical union leaderships would have earned approximately five times as much as the unskilled rank-and-file. Moreover, the union officials drawn from technical and administrative occupations might well have been making fifteen times as much as their manual members. Actually, the figures understate the average monthly earnings of urban unskilled labourers since these are grouped together with agricultural labourers. Labourers employed in urban undertakings made between KSh175 and KSh275 per month in 1967, which was still only about one-third of the monthly salaries of clerical employees.

Given this preponderance of upwardly-mobile clerical, skilled and professional employees in the leadership of predominantly labourers' trade unions, one might have expected that occupational status would constitute a primary basis of cleavage. After all, there is no constitutional or legal requirement

Table 6. *Distribution by occupational groups of the national leaders of 15 Kenyan Trade Unions, 1952–69*[*]

Union	(a) Super-visory (%)	(b) Professional & technical (%)	(c) Clerical (%)	(d) Skilled (%)	(e) Unskilled (%)	Outside industry (%)	Total† (%)	Occupation unknown (no.)
CPWU (n = 14)	21	0	29	14	29	7	100	1
SCPWU (n = 11)	9	0	55	9	9	18	100	5
TPWU (n = 13)	0	46	31	23	0	0	100	7
GAWU (n = 10)	20	0	40	10	10	20	100	2
KPAWU (n = 30)	20	0	50	13	0	17	100	0
KUSPW (n = 9)	11	0	33	22	11	22	99	20
KDCWU–								
KUCFAW (n = 60)	2	0	76	3	12	7	100	6
KQMWU (n = 38)	5	0	10	58	8	18	99	2
KCWU (n = 30)	3	0	33	57	7	0	100	2
KPOWU (n = 42)	2	0	50	31	17	0	100	4
KLGWU (n = 43)	19	47	25	9	0	0	100	2
EAFBCWU (n = 17)	6	0	17	59	0	17	99	13
EACU (n = 20)	10	50	25	0	0	15	100	10
DWU (n = 52)	19	0	54	10	13	4	100	4
RAU(K) (n = 44)	18	14	50	14	0	5	101	2
Total %	11	10	43	21	8	8	101	
No.	46	42	185	92	33	33	431	82

* 'National Leaders' include trustees, as well as the president, general secretary and treasurer, together with their various assistants and deputies. A leader's occupation is taken as the job he held at the time when he first became a union official.
† Percentages do not always equal 100 because of rounding.
(a) Includes supervisors, executive officers, foremen, stationmasters, headmen, farm managers and serangs (work-gang leaders on the docks).
(b) Includes inspectors (e.g. sanitary inspectors), accountants, teachers, welfare officers, medical attendants, etc.
(c) Includes clerks, typists, telephonists, office boys, storesmen, etc.
(d) Includes tradesmen, production process workers, plant and vehicle operators, drivers, mechanics and skilled workers of all kinds.
(e) Includes such unskilled workers as watchmen, office messengers, sweepers and cleaners, etc., as well as general labourers.

SOURCE: Author's survey.

that anyone other than the general secretary and treasurer be literate in English. Yet opposition factions have generally been as predominantly led by clerical, skilled and technical personnel as the incumbent teams, and they have seldom appealed to the distinctive interests of manual workers. This surprising absence of occupational cleavage in most unions can perhaps better be understood in the light of the conditions in the Railway African Union which have provoked just such a cleavage. To this unique case I now turn.

RAU – the deviant case

The East African Railways and Harbours Corporation (EARH), which split into separate East African Railways and East African Harbours Corporations in mid-1969, was an inter-territorial body within the East African Community (formerly the East African Common Services Organization). The railways corporation, which operates extensive rail and lake traffic in Kenya, Uganda and Tanzania, has always had its headquarters in Nairobi. It is organized into departments and districts. Within the district, the basic organizational unit is the depot, at which workers of one or more departments are stationed. There are six departments composed of sections and sub-sections, each having its own sphere of competence. The Mechanical Engineering Department, for example, is composed of Sections devoted to Locomotive Shed, Carriage and Waggon Examiners and Office; but not all of these sections would be present at every district depot, and in some depots, none of the sections might be present.

The EARH's Grading System comprises four main groups: Super-scale, Group 'A', Group 'B', and Group 'C'. Each of these is divided into a number of grades, which in turn are subdivided into salary points. Group 'C' consists of employees in unskilled or semi-skilled jobs, such as general labourers, porters, pointsmen, gangers, firemen, engine cleaners, watchmen, office messengers and workers who assist artisans. Group 'B' embraces both clerical and skilled workers. Clerical grades range from junior clerks (with seven years general education and three to four months occupational training) to chief or executive clerks in charge of large offices or goods depots. Similarly, artisan grades range from a trainee tradesman (ungraded) right up to a foreman in charge of a large electrical or machine shop and qualified technicians of all sorts. Group 'A' staff, largely in middle-management positions, are recruited from either university graduates or experienced Group 'B' employees with a secondary school education. Finally, the small 'Superscale' group comprises higher and top management. A person in this category is generally required to make decisions without reference higher up.

Between 20,000 and 30,000 employees – all Africans – have been classified as Group 'C' since 1959. Before 1962, nearly all posts above Group 'B' Grade IX were filled by Europeans and Asians. Yet Africans have outnumbered Europeans and Asians in Group 'B' positions as a whole since December 1957, though Africans were concentrated in the lower grades. Even as early as 1946, the railways employed a larger proportion of skilled African labour than any other enterprise in Kenya.[11] Since 1962, the number of Africans in higher grades has vastly increased and the promotion rate amongst those in the lower and middle ranges of Group 'B' – especially clerks – has been exceedingly high. When a separate Railways Corporation commenced operation in June 1969, 38,749 of the 41,312 employees were African, including 11,251 of the 13,588 Group 'B' employees and 94 of the 171 Group 'A' staff.[12]

Although there is a multiplicity of gradations between the general labourer at the bottom of the hierarchy and the general manager at the top, a consciousness of status has been fostered by grouping employees into the four categories discussed above. Moreover, the administration has always sharply differentiated amongst employees on the basis of occupational status in such matters as social amenities. For example, a railwayman's grade determines both his basic wage or salary and the location and type of house he occupies. The Railways Corporation has always provided free housing for most of its employees, usually situated on railway estates (there were two in Nairobi). Linked to status are seven house classifications; on the estates, houses in the different classes tend to be situated in different locations. Facilities such as toilets and canteens are also segregated on the basis of rank. Signs on doors reading 'Group "A" Staff and Above Only' may originally have represented a thinly disguised form of racial discrimination when nearly all those in Group 'A' or above were Europeans. But these practices persist today, clearly delineating the so-called *samaki wakubwa* (big fish) from the *samaki wadogo* (small fry).

A final significant point about railwaymen is that they are not, and for a long time have not been, short-term migrant workers. In a sample survey carried out amongst railway employees in Kampala, Grillo discovered that the mean length of service was about thirteen years, with nearly 20 per cent having served twenty years or more. Two-thirds of the respondents had held no job other than with the EARH; of the remainder, most had worked for some time in only one other occupation, before settling down with the railways. Most intended to work with the EARH until reaching the retirement age of fifty-five, when they could return to their rural areas of origin.[13] Since 41 per cent of railwaymen in Kampala were Kenyans, it is likely that these figures would apply equally to railwaymen working in Kenya. All railway union members and officials and railway administrative officials interviewed maintained that employment on the railway had long been considered a secure career.[14] Wastage rates of employees were low in the 1960s. Many of those who left the Corporation were clerical employees who assumed more highly paid positions in private industry during the heyday of Africanization.

The Railway African Union (Kenya), an industrial union, has always drawn its membership from among African railwaymen in Kenya, irrespective of occupational group or grade. Since 1964, the union has listed its membership as 'open' to Europeans or Asians; however, few have apparently taken advantage of the opportunity. The voting membership of the union on 31 June 1958 stood at 3,990, about one-sixth of the potential membership. No membership figures were reported during the period of intense factionalism between 1959 and 1961. On 31 December 1967, the voting membership was 13,549, having declined from a high of 16,090 in 1964, and representing slightly less than half of the eligible workers. Although no records of the occupational status of union members are kept, both union officials and the Corporation's officers who dealt with industrial relations agreed that, in 1969, at least 80 per cent of the union's members were Group 'C' employees, with about 15 per cent drawn from Group 'B' and less than 1 per cent from Group 'A' and Superscale employees. Since, in 1959, there were proportionately fewer African workers in Group 'B' compared to those in Group 'C' than in 1969, the support of Group 'C' workers in any intra-union conflict would clearly have constituted a significant resource.

As of early 1970, Group 'C' workers had never occupied any of the top seven national posts in RAU. These have been occupied mainly by Group 'B' employees – especially clerical workers. Initially, there was an attempt to ensure that each occupation was represented in the union's committees. The union's 1953 Constitution provided for a General Purposes Committee composed of the executive committee and eight members elected by the Nairobi branch to represent the EARH's six departments. In May 1959, the number of members on this committee was increased from eight to forty so that 'every trade and/or vocation in the Railways must be represented to give advice in case of discussion on that particular trade'. The forty positions were distributed among the six departments. However, this stipulation was changed in 1964 when the General Purposes Committee was replaced by a reconstituted National Executive Committee and a new Central Council. Central Council members were to be elected by the Annual Conference on the basis of a maximum of two representatives from each branch. The ten members of the National Executive Committee were to be elected by the Central Council or Annual Conference from amongst their members. Thus, the functional basis of representation was replaced by a geographical one.

Until a popular sixteen-day strike in November 1959 the railway union failed to capture the imagination and support of the mass of railwaymen. Since all union officials were part-time and inexperienced in trade unionism, the failure of the union to make an impact is understandable. The leaders were too moderate and concentrated on issues that affected mainly the clerical, supervisory and skilled staff. Relations with management were harmonious: the General Manager was invited to open the union's conferences and demands were presented in a conciliatory manner. Apart from wage demands, the two most commonly voiced grievances were relevant only to Group 'B' employees. Prior to 1956, the union frequently called for the ending of racial salary scales. When these were terminated, the most frequent grievance became the administration's alleged practice of reserving certain posts in the Corporation for Europeans and Asians.

This then was the context in which factionalism based on occupational lines convulsed the railway union in 1959–61, and recurred briefly in 1966 and 1972. That occupational status was the primary basis of cleavage in the earlier episode is indicated by the composition of the opposing teams. While the cores of both factions were similar in respect to tribal affiliation, most of the activists being Luo and Luhya,[15] they differed markedly in occupational background. All of the incumbent officials were Group 'B' employees whereas the more popular opposition group, led by B. A. Ohanga, was mainly drawn from Group 'C'. Indeed, Ohanga's opponents pointed to the presence of illiterate contenders for key union posts as evidence that Ohanga intended to dominate the union by surrounding himself with officials who would necessarily be dependent upon him. Ohanga also attracted some radical clerks to his faction on the basis of his militancy vis-à-vis management.

More indicative of the basis of cleavage than the occupational composition of the two teams was the kind of appeals made and the response to them. Ohanga always directed his attention to the grievances of the subordinate grades. Since the minimum monthly wage of Group 'C' workers in 1960 was only KSh90 their grievances were substantial.[16] He also exploited the widespread resentment toward the better-paid employees who monopolized union leadership. The basis of this antagonism is most comprehensively and eloquently stated in the following list of grievances submitted to the union's general secretary by a group of Group 'C' workers in August 1957:

It was not long ago that I discovered that the Union was only for a very small number of the Africans on the Railways. But this was not brought about by the fact that many of us were non-members, because those of us who never even attempted to join saw from the very beginning that the Union was really of very little help, particularly the 'SUBORDINATE STAFF'. This Union cannot deny the fact that these people have been entirely left out and forgotten.

I wonder why up to so far no effort has been made to standardize the working hours for every employee on this Administration. I believe that the major reason is that the office bearers are all Office Clerks and therefore do not mind what hell other employees go through. Theirs is a regular system of work, while others have a very irregular system of work. As you are aware Office Clerks and others only work 37 hours a week while many, specially those in the Operating Department, have to work 84 hours a week of which 12 hours are 'compulsory overtime'. Others in the same Department have to work 56 hours a week of which eight hours are compulsory overtime. In both these cases no time is permitted for meals in the course of duty. Imagine a pointsman running up and down the Yard marshalling trains for 12 hours without any meals and that for weeks on end, or a signalman working for eight hours...without meals, or a Station Master attending to the public and passing trains from 8.00 hours to 20.00 hours without any meals. I challenge anyone of you to try that and then perhaps you will be able to taste what hell we are going through.[17]

Given these sentiments, Ohanga mobilized support by claiming that clerical and supervisory employees were already well paid and enjoyed superior facilities, yet they used the union to boost their own salaries at the expense of the lower-paid workers. Furthermore, he claimed that, because they were already satisfied, the present officials were too moderate; how, then, could they represent the interests of downtrodden workers against the exploiting imperialists? He summarized his argument in the phrase: '*samaki wakubwa wameza samaki wadogo*' (the big fish always swallow the small fish).

The long-time officials of the union fully realised the effectiveness of such appeals. As President Muinde remarked to a Special Conference of 3 November 1960:

The General Secretary [Ohanga] has been arranging meetings of Nairobi Branch without the co-operation, consent and consultation with the officials of the Branch presumably with an endeavour to create hate and dislike between those officials and the members more especially those in Group C. This move of course has been de-signed to enhance his fame among the mass of workers. Position in this direction has deteriorated quite considerably at this stage, that it will take ages to restore confidence of the staff of the Group C in any Group B leader.[18]

So successful was Ohanga in winning the allegiance of the mass of railwaymen that the union had been reduced to an empty shell by the time the Registrar refused to register Ohanga's breakaway union in 1961. It took a long time for the registered officials to restore the workers' confidence in them after 1961 – a task that subsequent factional encounters proved was never wholly successful. When Ibrahim Mango, the new President, attempted to speak to the workers at the branches in 1961, he was frequently jeered and threatened with beatings.[19] Since the union had few members in 1961–3, the incumbent officials were forced to use their private salaries to cover some of the operating costs. When, in December 1961, Walter Ottenyo became the full-time General Secretary, he found that the head office did not even have letter paper.[20] As there were fewer than 1,000 paid-up members at the end of 1961, Ottenyo devoted much of his time in 1962 and 1963 to organizational activities, especially convincing railwaymen to sign 'check-off' agreements. He visited the housing estates and ate with labourers along the line in an attempt to show that the union belonged to the subordinate staff too. Indeed, Ottenyo's organizational activities were so successful that when the National Executive Committee dismissed him in February 1966 cleavage based on occupational status reappeared. Ottenyo had somewhat the same mass appeal as Ohanga. However, since Ottenyo was a Luhya while Mango was a Luo, a tribal element was also present in the short encounter in 1966. Because Ottenyo felt that it was too risky, politically, for him to fight to regain his position, a distinct cleavage never had an opportunity to materialize. That, however, is another story.

Why has occupational cleavage emerged as a significant source of cleavage in the railway union but not to any extent in the other unions of the sample? It appears that three related conditions must apply before occupational status can become salient. These conditions have occurred together in the RAU, though not in any other union studied in the period 1960–70. These are:

(i) A high proportion of the prestigious union posts must be held by members of a minority occupational group (e.g. the higher grades of clerical and supervisory employees of the EAR) who are already considered by certain subordinate grades (e.g. the unskilled and semi-skilled) to be a privileged group, and who can be perceived as pursuing the interests of their own occupational group at the expense of subordinate workers.

(ii) The existence of clear-cut status boundaries derived not so much from occupation *per se* as from the differential distribution of privileges (e.g. the segregation and classification of housing and other facilities according to occupational category). Grouping diverse trades and occupations into a common graded hierarchy may also tend to foster consciousness of status based more directly on differential rewards than a particular craft or trade.

(iii) The occurrence of a high level of interaction among workers of particular occupational strata over some considerable length of time. For occupational status to submerge tribal divisions in a polyethnic union, there must be something of an 'occupational community' in which workers with diverse origins meet with one another, both on and off the job (e.g., railway housing estates where sections are based on occupational status; railway clubs).[21] Communications are obviously also aided if a union caters for only a single industry, or if all members are employed in one place (e.g., the existence of a railway line linking all workers; work gangs whose job it is to move up and down the lines; a high transfer rate of employees). Finally, workers must feel a long-term commitment to employment, if they are to develop a consciousness of status or the realization of their vested interest in ensuring that the union works for their economic advantage (e.g., the existence of a low wastage rate among railwaymen for some considerable time). Generally migrant workers develop neither status consciousness nor a desire to participate in union politics.

The absence of these conditions in nearly all the other unions under study may account for the failure of status identity to become salient in their internal politics. Most significant is the low level of interaction among employees in the same categories (discussed in Chapter 3) and, for the agricultural unions, the existence of migrant labour. Without any degree of interaction either on or off the job, employees in comparable positions in the occupational structures of diverse enterprises are prevented from developing a sense of common interest. Such consciousness might develop if oppositionists could gain access to union members and emphasize their common interests. But the stratagems of union oligarchies and the laws of the country prevent such 'agitation'.

The conditions enumerated above have been most closely approximated in the Dockworkers' Union, which has never experienced factionalism based primarily on an occupational cleavage. Although economic grievances have certainly played a key part in power struggles within this union, these have generally been articulated in terms of tribal favouritism or of the alleged incompetence of certain leaders in negotiations, rather than in terms of the divergent interests of occupational strata. The main difference between the two unions has been in the quality and goals of the leaderships. Since 1958, dock leaders have vitiated status identity by never allowing themselves to get 'out of touch' with manual workers, a situation the railway leaders failed to achieve. Although space does not permit me to go into the details, I will merely assert that the dock union has, since 1958, always militantly pursued the interests of manual workers, in the process making them among the highest paid semi-skilled employees in Kenya. In addition, the union's top leaders, who have mainly been clerical and skilled employees, have included manual workers in all the union's decision-making bodies. Of its national leaders 13 per cent have been unskilled workers, while none of the RAU's national leaders had this occupational background. More significantly, the union has assiduously provided for the representation of the various occupations on its main committees. As well, shore workers and stevedores have always been included on the union's delegation to the Joint Industrial Council as a matter of course. In this union, manual workers are far from passive in their attitude toward authority; if representation on the union's various organs was denied them, they would be unlikely to support and vote for the established leaders.

Ethnicity as a frame of reference

While occupational status has constituted a basis of cleavage only in the railway union, ethnicity has represented a far more common line of division. To advance their own ambitions, both established union leaders and challengers have sometimes appealed to the tribal identity of the rank-and-file and branch officials. These appeals are not of course automatically effective; they are most likely to succeed in unions where a differential distribution of power and material benefits exists amongst the various constituent tribes. The distribution of jobs and promotions within enterprises with which a union deals may also become an issue in its internal politics if certain members believe that the established union leader has used his influence to benefit his own tribesmen.

The tribal background

Consider first the ethnic composition of wage-earners and union officials in Kenya. As previously mentioned, the most significant sources of migrants were the four largest self-identified 'tribes': the Kikuyu, Luo, Luhya and

Kamba, with the coastal Mijikenda comprising the largest part of the work force in Mombasa, the second largest city. Besides these tribes, the 1962 Population Census lists thirty-five others; but most of these relatively small Hamitic, Nilo-Hamitic and coastal Bantu have played little part in the money economy. Several of them comprise a significant proportion of the wage-earning force in particular industries, though their overall numbers among wage earners are small. The Nilo-Hamitic Kipsigis and Nandi and the Bantu Kisii, for example, form a large part of the work force on tea plantations in Kericho and Nandi Hills Districts.

The State of Emergency imposed on Kenya between October 1952 and January 1960 significantly affected the tribal composition of both the membership and the leadership of trade unions. Under the Emergency (Movement of Kikuyu, Meru and Embu) Regulations, 1953, the government was empowered to repatriate or to detain members of these three tribes for any period of time. Large-scale security operations during 1953 and 1954 resulted in the removal of many Kikuyu and Meru workers from Nairobi and the Rift Valley Province. 'Operation Anvil', for example, deprived Nairobi of more than a quarter of its working population in the space of a few days in 1954. As the Labour Department's *Annual Report, 1954*, commented:

The removal of so many Kikuyu, Embu and Meru from employment had radically altered the balance between these and other African tribes, particularly in the urban centres. Whereas the Kikuyu had previously dominated the employment scene in many towns (either by weight of numbers or their greater sophistication) and had provided the majority of skilled personnel and of spokesmen for the African, the leadership has now been taken over mainly by the Nyanza tribes [i.e. Luo and Luhya].

Owing to the decline in 'Mau Mau' activities, restrictions on Kikuyu, Embu and Meru were relaxed in 1957, and conditions for most of the wage-earning population returned to normal. Many members of these tribes were permitted to work during the day in the rural areas adjoining their land units, while others, in increasing numbers, were authorized to enter the urban areas daily. Moreover, Kikuyu began to move back onto European farms in the 'White Highlands' area of the Rift Valley. The termination of the Emergency regulations in January 1960 resulted in an influx of Kikuyu into Nairobi and the farming areas of the Rift Valley.

As Table 7 shows, the Kikuyu, Embu and Meru comprised almost one-third of the colony's wage-earning force by the middle of 1960. Most of the workers in this category were, in fact, Kikuyu, as the migration rates of the other two tribes were low. Statistics provided in earlier Annual Reports of the Labour Department reveal that the Kikuyu increased proportionately in the wage-earning force at the expense of the Luhya, Luo and Kamba, who had originally replaced Kikuyu workers during the early days of the Emergency.

Although 1960 was the last year in which statistics on the tribal composition of African wage-earners were gathered, these proportions probably

Table 7. *Tribal distribution of adult male workers within provinces, 30 June 1960**

	Coast Province (%)	Rift Valley Province (%)	Nairobi E.P.D. (%)	Central Province (%)	Nyanza Province (%)	Total for colony (%)	Total for colony (No. thousands)
Kikuyu/Embu/Meru	6.2	31.6	34.7	79.0	2.9	32.3	146.2
Baluhya/Kisii	7.2	25.1	17.7	4.3	35.4	18.1	82.0
Luo	14.5	10.4	15.4	4.2	39.1	15.1	68.7
Kamba	16.1	1.9	23.4	8.5	0.8	11.7	52.8
Kipsigis/Nandi	0.5	16.5	1.3	1.4	18.2	8.4	37.9
Coast tribes	45.4	0.2	1.7	0.4	0.1	6.3	28.7
Others	10.1	14.3	5.8	2.2	3.5	8.1	36.8
Total (%)	100.0	100.0	100.0	100.0	100.0	100.0	
(No., thousands)	58.5	126.4	79.0	89.9	76.6		453.3

SOURCE: Labour Department, *Annual Report, 1960.*

* Note that the figures for employment in Southern Province and Northern Frontier District have been excluded, as these are fairly insignificant. In 1960, only 22,915 out of a total of 453,308 Africans were employed in these areas.

have not changed drastically during the last decade. The Labour Department's *Annual Report, 1960*, claimed that, at the time their data were collected, an equilibrium in wage employment had been reached: by June 1960 there was 'a steady movement back to the tribal areas' of those Kikuyu who had not succeeded in finding employment. Thus, the tribal composition of the African wage-earning force during the 1960s was roughly the following:[22]

Kikuyu, Embu and Meru (mainly Kikuyu)	33%
Luhya	15%
Luo	15%
Kamba	11%
Coast Tribes	8%
Kalenjin (Kipsigis/Nandi mainly)	8%
Others	10%
Total	100%

Consider next the ethnic composition of trade union leadership. Before the collapse of the East African Trades Union Congress in 1950, the leadership and membership of its constituent African trade unions were, according to all participants, predominantly Kikuyu. In those early days, unions were primarily political in aim, using economic grievances to stir up political discontent. Such prominent radical Kikuyu political leaders as Bildad Kaggia and Fred Kubai were also union leaders. Politically conscious Kikuyu in Nairobi were thus apparently drawn toward trade unionism by its political involvement, as well as its capacity to ameliorate terms and conditions of service.

During the Emergency period, nearly all Kikuyu union leaders were picked up for screening, and many were detained or repatriated. For a Kikuyu in 1953–4, union leadership – or even membership – was grounds for suspicion by the authorities. Since Kikuyu union members who were not detained or repatriated were generally unwilling to stand for union office, the Luhya and Luo moved into nearly all union offices.

Once trade unions started to revive after the termination of the Emergency, Kikuyu again competed for union leadership. Many intra-union disputes in the early 1960s were at least partially the result of attempts by Kikuyu to win positions in trade unions proportionate to their weight within the wage-earning force. In many cases, however, the Luhya and Luo incumbents had quite successfully consolidated their positions.

By 1970 the Luo and Luhya were still over-represented among union officials relative to their proportions of wage-earners as a whole, while the Kikuyu remain relatively under-represented. According to Table 8, 27 per cent of the 121 national officials of a representative sample of eleven existent unions in December 1968 were Kikuyu, Embu and Meru, whereas 28 per cent were Luo and 21 per cent Luhya and Teso. The Kikuyu are even less represented among the top echelon of leaders: only 22 of the 101 members of COTU's Governing Council were Kikuyu in 1970, while 28 were Luo, 23

Table 8. *Tribal composition of the national officials* of 11 Kenyan trade unions, December 1968*

	No.	%
Kikuyu/Embu/Meru	33	27
Luhya and Teso	25	21
Luo	34	28
Kamba	13	11
Coast Tribes	12	10
Kalenjin	2	2
Others	2	2
Total	121	101†

SOURCE: the author's survey and name analysis (see Appendix 3).

* 'National officials' include from one to three trustees and a national organizing secretary if elected, as well as president, general secretary and treasurer and their various assistants and deputies.
† Percentages do not equal 100 because of rounding.

Table 9. *Tribal composition of branch officials of 10 Kenyan trade unions, December 1968**

	No.	%
Kikuyu/Embu/Meru	236	28
Luhya and Teso	166	20
Luo	176	21
Kamba	64	8
Coast Tribes	74	9
Kalenjin	28	3
Kisii	25	3
Others	38	5
Don't know	25	3
Total	832	100

SOURCE: name analysis (see Appendix 3).

* 'Trade unions' in this table is ten rather than eleven because the Dockworkers' Union does not have any branches.

Luhya, 14 Kamba and 10 were from coastal tribes.[23] However, Table 9 indicates that the Kikuyu have gained a strong position at the branch level, where Kikuyu, Embu and Meru constitute the largest single membership group. This trend augurs ill for the Luo and Luhya national officials in the long run.

Leadership strategies

A union leader is vulnerable to a challenger's appeal to tribal solidarity if his union has a polyethnic membership or a membership drawn predominantly from a tribe other than his own. Consequently, union leaders usually seek to come to terms with ethnicity by attempting either to exploit tribal loyalties to their own advantage or to neutralize them by establishing a 'non-tribalist' reputation. One aspect of creating such a reputation is the basis on which a union's various offices are allocated. To demonstrate his lack of 'tribal feelings', a leader may either allow the tribes within the union's membership to find their own balance by remaining neutral in contests for office at the branch or national level, or he may run as the leader of a team of officials whom he conscientiously selects with the aim of representing all significant tribal groups. On the other hand, a leader may decide to base his power on a core of loyal tribesmen, who occupy many of the strategic posts at the centre and in key branches. The final possibility is that a leader may not be powerful enough in his union to adopt any consistent strategy. This is frequently the case in the initial phase of a union's existence or after an amalgamation. Each of these strategies or the lack of a strategy will affect the ability of a potential opposition to exploit tribal identity to gain support.

The first strategy, which was earlier called 'individual competition', has been adopted, to a greater or lesser extent, in three of the unions in my sample. Although the delegates' first consideration in choosing office-holders is the capacity of various candidates to work co-operatively and effectively with other officials to advance the workers' interests, they also seem to have a clear idea of what constitutes an equitable tribal distribution of posts.[24]

Individual competition is likely to vitiate tribalism as an exploitable resource, provided the general secretary refrains from using his influence to gain unfair advantages for his tribesmen within the industry for which the union caters. Even if the national leadership is drawn predominantly from a minority tribe within the union, an opposition faction will be unable to win a tribal following as long as the branch officials have confidence in the national officials they have elected. The disadvantage of this strategy of *laissez-faire* is that candidates may be elected who do not owe allegiance to the general secretary and who may, in fact, covet his position.

A second strategy aimed at neutralizing tribal tensions may be termed 'ethnic arithmetic'. In this case, the general secretary does not remain impartial in contests for other national offices and strategic branch posts, but instead builds up a personal machine on the basis of representing the main tribes within the leadership group. The object is always to distribute equitably the available prestige and perquisites amongst all significant groups.[25] This strategy has been employed by various factions who have vied for control of the national trade union federation. For example, Denis Akumu and his allies, before COTU's Triennial Conference in 1969, successfully 'balanced the ticket' by distributing the eleven principal elective posts in the following manner: three each for the Kikuyu, Luo and Luhya, and one each for the Kamba, and Mijikenda. Moreover, the three most prestigious and powerful positions were held by members of the three largest tribes, the president being Kikuyu, the secretary-general Luo and the treasurer Luhya. The same principle of balance was employed in selecting the five appointed COTU directors, seven appointed COTU Area Secretaries and other lesser appointees. In a similar fashion, the leaders of many tribally-heterogeneous trade unions apportion their far less prestigious posts on the basis of tribal affiliation (as well as ability, personal loyalty, etc.).

This strategy is not always successful in obviating tribal tensions. To establish a reputation of being 'above' tribalism, a leader must also be careful not to appear to use his influence to advance his tribesmen within the enterprise or industry with which the union is concerned. Ethnic arithmetic, applied only to union offices, does not guarantee that an opposition group will be prevented from exploiting tribal loyalties.

The alternative strategy – 'ethnic oligarchy' – seeks to base a leader's power on trusted lieutenants at the national and branch level who are tied to him by tribal and even kinship linkages. Reliance on such moral ties provides a leader with some security in a fluid situation. However, the central leadership is required to intervene in branch elections on a large scale in order to ensure that its protégés obtain or maintain office. It must also be quite ruthless in its treatment of opposition elements, especially if the tribe on which the leadership bases itself is not the largest one within the union's membership.

Ethnic oligarchy is not a common strategy in polyethnic trade unions. Leaders in only two of the ten unions in the present sample relied on ethnic ties to any extent: the Commercial, Food and Allied Workers between 1954 and 1969 and the Plantation and Agricultural Workers' Union after 1964.

The costs and benefits of this strategy are fairly clear. In the short-run, reliance on tribal ties may provide some cohesion for the ruling group. In the long run, however, it is bound to provoke conflict based on tribal cleavages. The incumbent group may well be able to defeat any such separatist or majority-bent factions, but the individual members always have recourse to their final sanction: revocation of their 'check-off' agreements. Unions in which one particular tribe seems to dominate at the expense of others are often faced with high rates of membership revocation.[26]

The effectiveness of each strategy will be further assessed in the following section.

Tribalism and intra-union factionalism

From the viewpoint of participants in union politics (which usually means the national and branch officials and a few members of branch committees), an opposition faction appeals to tribal identity either when it denounces the

Table 10. *The incidence of tribal appeals and tribal cleavages in factional encounters until January 1970*

Union	Length of existence	Total no. of encounters	No. of encounters in which tribal appeals were made	No. of tribally based encounters
KUSPW	Since Nov. 1960	6	0	0
CPWU	Nov. 1959–Dec. 1961	2	0	0
SCPWU	Dec. 1961–Aug. 1963	3	3	3
KQMWU	Since Sept. 1961	5	0	0
KDCWU–KUCFAW	Since June 1952	8	6	5
EAFBCWU	Since June 1952	7	5	3
KCWU	Since Aug. 1958	1	0	0
KPOWU	Since Dec. 1957	4	0	0
KPAWU	Since Aug. 1963	6	3	3
RAU(K)	Since Mar. 1953	5	2	2
TPWU	Sept. 1959–Aug. 1963	1	0	0
DWU	Since May 1954	7	4	2
KLGWU	Since Sept. 1953	0	0	0

SOURCE: see note 28.

established leader or leaders as 'tribalists' or when it fields a team composed disproportionately of individuals drawn from one or related tribes.[27] Such appeals are often not successful, as tribal affiliation does not morally bind a person in conflict situations. In fact, blatant public attempts to manipulate tribal loyalty are likely to prove counter-productive, owing to the opprobrium attached to 'tribalism'.

One further point bears emphasizing. To assert that a factional encounter was 'tribally based' is *not* to say that tribal loyalties were the only dimension of the conflict or the only reason for one side's victory or defeat. In some cases, the cynical manipulation of tribal identity for personal advantage appeared to be the sole content of intra-union disputes. Usually, however, the tribal opposition was masked or legitimated by a clash of ideological positions or policies. Until September 1965, the most frequent ideological dimension involved the question of whether a particular union should be affiliated to the allegedly 'imperialist-dominated' Kenya Federation of Labour. In addition or alternatively, issues such as alleged dishonesty or alleged collusion with employers nearly always were raised.

Table 10 shows that the incidence of tribal appeals and tribally-based factionalism vary widely from union to union.[28] Seven of the unions had never experienced an encounter in which ethnic appeals were made. The six remaining unions, on the other hand, had experienced a medium to high incidence of encounters in which such appeals were voiced, and a variable incidence of actual tribal cleavages.

How is this variation to be explained? It will be argued that most of the complexity is explicable in terms of two hypotheses:

(i) Wherever the principal leader of a trade union belongs to one of the smaller tribes within his union's potential membership, the probability arises that a challenger from a more numerous tribe will appeal to tribal identity for support.[29] Whether this probability is actually realized depends on the inclinations of the challenger and his assessment of the possible effects of such appeals.

(ii) Wherever a differential distribution of power, prestige or material benefits exists amongst the various tribes within a trade union, the probability arises that a challenger will successfully activate tribal identity for 'remedial' action, thus initiating a struggle for power in which factions form primarily along self-identified tribal lines.[30] Whether this probability is actually realized depends not only on the inclinations of potential challengers, but also on the tribal composition of a union's potential membership. It is unlikely, for example, that a challenger from a small tribe would try to mobilize ethnic support against an incumbent from a tribe with a majority or strong plurality amongst a union's branch officials and members.

While the first hypothesis is fairly straightforward the second one is not. If it is valid, one would expect to find a differential distribution of power, prestige or material benefits in the cases where tribally-based factionalism has actually emerged, but not in the cases where it has not. But what constitutes a differential distribution of something as amorphous as 'power', 'prestige' and 'material benefits'? From the point of view of participants in union politics, a differential distribution of such values means that a particular tribe is acquiring more than its fair share of elective and appointed union posts, of other union resources such as scholarships and travel grants, and/or of promotions and jobs within the industry or enterprise with which the union deals. A particular tribe is thought to have got more than its fair share of the available benefits if its supposed members within an enterprise's labour force seem out of proportion to the union positions it occupies. If one tribe constitutes a majority or a strong plurality of a union's potential membership, for example, a leader from this group may claim that the general secretaryship should rightfully belong to it. An opposition leader may also successfully mobilize the support of tribesmen among the branch officials by charging that the incumbent general secretary shows 'tribal feelings', as evidenced by his appointing his own tribesmen to key positions in the union. Furthermore, if members of the same tribe as the main union leader win a disproportionate number of jobs and promotions within an enterprise, this fact may be exploited by a challenger to his own advantage. The general secretary may not have used his influence to advance his tribesmen, but in union politics as in all other kinds, it is the appearance that counts.

The two hypotheses were tested by examining the relationship between the tribal composition of each union's potential membership, the proportion of union posts and promotions in industry (where relevant)

Table 11. *Tribal composition of potential union membership and the incidence of tribally based factionalism*

Union	Tribal composition of potential membership	Incidence of tribally based factionalism
KUSPW	Luo majority	Non-existent
CPWU	Kikuyu majority	Non-existent
S&CPWU	Kikuyu majority	High
KQMWU	Luo majority, until 1966; then Luo preponderance.	Non-existent
KDCWU–KUCFAW	Kikuyu largest single group (since 1960), but not a majority. The next largest tribes are the Luhya, Luo and Kamba.	High
EAFBCWU	Varies from year to year depending on the location of building projects. But Kikuyu are the largest single tribe.	High
KCWU	Kikuyu and Kamba, two-fifths; Luo and Luhya, two-fifths; Coastal and others, one-fifth.	Non-existent
KPOWU	Luo are the largest single group, but are closely followed by Kikuyu, Luhya and Coastal tribes, in that order.	Non-existent
KPAWU	Kikuyu, Embu and Meru together constitute at least one-third of the total; next in order of importance are the Luo, Luhya, Kalenjin, Kisii, Coastal and Kamba.	Medium
RAU(K)	Luo constitute about one-third, followed by Kikuyu, Luhya, Kamba and Coastal.	Medium
TPWU	In 1968 Luo constituted about one-quarter, Kalenjin one-quarter, Kikuyu one-sixth, and Luhya, Kisii and others nearly two-fifths.	Non-existent
DWU	In 1968 Giriama, Kamba and Digo constituted about one-fifth each, Taita one-sixth, Luo one-tenth and others one-sixth.	Medium
KLGWU	Kikuyu, Embu and Meru constitute about one-quarter of the total; the rest of the membership is drawn from every tribe in Kenya.	Non-existent

SOURCES: Estimates of ethnic composition were obtained by comparing management's estimates with labour leaders' estimates. In some cases, management kept figures on the ethnic composition of their employees.

gained by the various tribes, and the occurrence of tribal appeals and tribal cleavages within the relevant audience (i.e., either branch officials or rank-and-file). The approximate tribal composition of thirteen unions on which such information could be gathered is indicated in Table 11.

Unions in which One Tribe Constituted a Majority. Four of the thirteen unions had potential memberships in which one tribe had a majority: the Union of Sugar Plantation Workers, the Coffee Plantation Workers' Union, the Sisal and Coffee Plantation Workers' Union and the Quarry and Mineworkers' Union. Only in the sisal union were ethnic appeals made and ethnically-based encounters evident. In each of the other three unions, the most numerous tribe within the potential membership also occupied most of the prestigious and powerful posts within the union, at both the branch and national level. However, the Coffee Workers' Union, drawing about nine-tenths of its membership from Kikuyu and Meru workers, suffered a factional fight in 1961 in which sub-tribal divisions within the Kikuyu were politicized. This conflict eventually led to the demise of the union in December 1961.

During its three years of existence, the Sisal and Coffee Plantation Union experienced three instances of tribally-based factionalism. The main tribal opposition was between the Kikuyu, based largely on coffee estates, and the Luo and Luhya, based solely on sisal estates. Comprising slightly over half the total labour force engaged on sisal and coffee estates, the Kikuyu and the culturally similar Meru held a distinct advantage over their opponents. It is clear that the basis of the disputes was the fact that a Luo, Apolo Owiti, had become the amalgamated union's first general secretary, at a time when few Kikuyu appeared to be interested or qualified to hold the post. Although most of the national officials under Owiti were Kikuyu, the general secretary made the mistake of appointing four full-time Luo organizers. In this situation, Kikuyu challengers soon emerged, charging that Owiti was treating the union as his 'tribal company with monopoly'. The first encounter involved an attempt to split the coffee section of the union off from the rest of the union; it failed. The Kikuyu faction then switched to a majority-bent strategy which was ultimately successful. During this period of factionalism, there was a clear polarization between the Kikuyu branch officials, on the one side, and the Luo and Luhya branch officials (in sisal-growing areas), on the other. Owiti's core group in mid-1963 comprised three Luo, two Luhya and two Kikuyu, whereas the opposing group was led by five Kikuyu and one Meru. This polarization was reflected in the separatist factionalism which followed the ousting of Owiti: a largely Luo faction sought unsuccessfully to win registration for a separate sisal plantation workers' union. Thus, in this case, an ambitious Kikuyu challenger was able to phrase the struggle for power in tribal terms, claiming that Owiti was a 'tribalist'. Given the stereotypes which Kikuyu and Luo held of each other, together with Owiti's alleged indiscretions, the opposition faction's claims were accepted.

Unions in which no tribe constituted a majority. No single tribe constituted a majority of the potential membership of the remaining nine trade unions, though tribal composition varied. The hypotheses relating the incidence of ethnic cleavages to the distribution of power, prestige and material benefits were confirmed in a most dramatic way. In the five unions which clearly experienced these cleavages, a differential distribution of union posts, scholarships and, in some cases, opportunities for advancement within the relevant enterprise or governmental agency was evident. In the four unions which did not experience such cleavages, a differential distribution of benefits did not exist. In other words, there was, in the latter four unions, a rough correspondence between the proportion of the unions' potential membership drawn from the various tribes, and the proportion of the available posts and perquisites allocated to them. There was no such rough correspondence in those unions which suffered distinct tribal cleavages.

It would prove extremely tedious to present an historical summary of factional encounters in each of the nine unions in order to show the basis of the generalizations made in the last paragraph. Instead, I propose to present only two brief examples, one illustrating the cases which have experienced ethnic cleavages, the other those which have not.

In the Dockworkers' Union, registered in 1954, contenders appealed to tribal loyalties in four of its seven factional encounters between 1960 and 1970, though on only two of these occasions did such appeals lead to a significant tribal cleavage. In mid-1961, S. T. Omari, the Rabai (a Mijikenda 'sub-tribe') Secretary-General of the Coast African Peoples' Union, launched a campaign to displace Denis Akumu, the union's Luo General Secretary, by appealing to coastal dockers to liberate themselves from domination by upcountry tribes. However, the appeal had little discernible impact; Akumu heavily defeated Omari at the union's annual elections, even though the coastal tribes (Mijikenda, Taita and Swahili) constituted over half of the Port's labour force at that time. Akumu had successfully established a reputation as an effective defender of the interests of all workers. For example, the union's successful campaign to end the practice of casual port labour in 1960 had mainly benefited the coastal workers, who had formed the bulk of casuals. Moreover, Akumu had carefully pursued a strategy of ethnic arithmetic, drawing Mijikenda into prestigious positions as their proportion of the work force increased. In mid-1961, three of the six principal union officials were coastal and three Luo. In October 1962, when the second encounter involving ethnic appeals began, there were four coastal officials and only two Luo. Although the 1962 struggle for control between Akumu and his former Assistant General Secretary, Juma Boy, a Digo (another Mijikenda 'sub-tribe'), was phrased in ideological terms, there was a clear tribal dimension as nearly all of Boy's supporters in the union were coastal.[31] The factional dispute led to one riot and several fights, but Akumu managed to retain the loyalty of the bulk of union members, including many of the coastal members.

The third factional encounter, occurring in August and September 1965, resulted in an ethnic cleavage among the members which brought about Akumu's downfall. The composition of the union's principal officials at this time was still four coastal to two Luo, with nearly half of the seventeen Executive Committee members also drawn from the coastal tribes. But, on this occasion, the opposition had some concrete evidence to use against Akumu. In the rapid Africanization carried out since 1960–1 by the Landing and Shipping Company of East Africa and its successor, the East African Cargo Handling Services, a disproportionate number who were promoted to senior posts or gained junior posts were Luo. This was largely because the Luo were, on the whole, better qualified than others, but the opposition claimed that Akumu had used his influence with the General Manager to gain this result. This charge obviously was accepted, for Akumu's support fell off drastically, and he was defeated by a coastal team led by a Mtaita. The Luo at this time comprised only about one-fifth of the union's membership.

The final tribally based encounter took place between February and May 1966 in entirely new circumstances. The coast tribes were now manifestly in control, possessing four of the main posts, including president, general secretary and treasurer, and a majority in the Executive Committee. Moreover, the coast tribes represented about 65 per cent of the total labour force on the docks. Consequently, competition for control took place *between* the coast tribes and sub-tribes. In the first instance, there was an alliance between the Taita and Giriama, two of the largest groups at the Port, against the Digo and various 'upcountry' tribes, especially the Luo.[32] Juma Boy, the Digo leader, managed to oust the Taita–Giriama team at a May 1966 Special Conference, partly because the Taita General Secretary had not proven effective in protecting the interests of workers. Since then, Taita have been reinstated in leadership positions, but the Giriama, until 1970, had consistently constituted the core of the opposition, claiming that Boy was using his influence to gain employment for Digo workers. The basis of the dispute was primarily political, however, as the Giriama political leader, Ronald Ngala, had wished to eliminate Boy's trade union base in Mombasa.[33]

In sum, it is clear that the Mijikenda only represented a 'tribe' in opposition to the 'upcountry' tribes. Once this opposition was removed 'sub-tribal' loyalties became salient.

An example of a union that has never experienced a tribal cleavage amongst either its branch officials or rank-and-file is the Local Government Workers' Union (KLGWU), registered in 1953. This union, composed of forty branches (since 1968) located in all parts of the country, has been probably the most tribally heterogeneous in Kenya. Each branch represented the employees of a particular local authority. As local authorities naturally favour members of the local tribe as employees, all branches other than those in Nairobi, Mombasa and Nakuru tended to be tribally homogenous in their membership and leadership. Thus, the largest single group of potential members – the Kikuyu – constituted at the most one-quarter of the total.

Tribal cleavages could clearly tear this union apart, given the combination of tribally homogeneous branches in a tribally-heterogeneous union. There seem to be two main reasons for the absence of tribally based factionalism. Most important is the quality of the union's leadership. Tom Mboya, the Secretary until 1958, together with a group of educated national officials drawn from the major tribes, laid the foundation of a strong, united union. Since 1964, this effective leadership has continued under James Karebe, who was a member of the union's executive when the union was formed in 1953. Second, no tribe has ever controlled the union or sought to use it for its own interests. The general secretary has maintained a neutral attitude in most branch elections; indeed, interference in them would invite a coalescence of the local tribe against the general secretary. Individual competition has also characterized most national elections, at which branch delegates are drawn proportionately from all groups (see Table 12). For example, the author was able to establish that, at the September 1967 Annual Conference, there were only fifteen Kikuyu, Embu and Meru delegates of a total of fifty-five present, even though the general secretary was Kikuyu. In December 1958, there were three Kikuyu, three Luo, one Luhya and one coastal official in the national leadership, the president being Kikuyu, the general secretary Luo and the treasurer coastal. Ten years later the holders of the national posts were just as ethnically mixed, though now both the president and general secretary were Kikuyu. In addition, the KLGWU has sought to represent tribal–regional interests within the union's National Executive Committee. The union's constitution provides that this body shall be composed of the national officials, auditor, three trustees, and nine other members representing the branches. Each province and the Nairobi Extra-Provincial District was to have one representative, with the exception of the tribally heterogeneous Rift Valley Province which was to have two representatives. Hence one-half of this important committee was set aside for regional representation.

The importance of leadership

No union leader holds power simply because he is from the 'right' tribe – i.e., the most numerous tribe within the potential membership. From the members' point of view, the most crucial consideration is not an office-holder's ethnic affiliation but his ability to protect their interests.[34]

The heterogeneity of a union's membership does not, by itself, determine whether a union will experience tribal cleavages in its internal politics. Leaders bear a large part of the responsibility in stimulating tribal identity. According to a leader's inclination and his assessment of the various short- and long-term costs, he may decide either to base his power on an ethnic oligarchy or to make a universalistic appeal by practising ethnic arithmetic

Table 12. *Tribal composition of branch officials
of the KLGWU in December 1968*

	%	No.
Kikuyu, Embu and Meru	27	67
Luhya and Teso	14	35
Coast Tribes	12	30
Luo	11	28
Kalenjin	7	17
Kamba	6	14
Kisii	3	7
Others	14	36
Don't Know	6	14
Total	100	100

SOURCE: Name analysis of branch officials registered with the Registrar of Trade Unions and author's survey.

or individual competition. Ensuring that one's tribesmen assume most of the key positions in the union is a means of building up a reliable clique based on ethnic or even kinship ties. Such a strategy will probably provoke the formation of separatist or majority-bent factions along tribal lines, but such challenges can often be defeated, especially since the government's policy is to discourage these opposition activities. More often, leaders will adopt ethnic arithmetic or individual competition strategies. While these are the most effective ways to neutralize ethnic tensions, office-holders may not feel the same commitment to the general secretary and may be more easily subversible by his opponents. Furthermore, neither strategy is a guarantee against tribal cleavages.

The evidence suggests that tribal identity has been successfully politicized in the situation where the office-holders have apparently used their positions to gain unfair advantages for 'their' tribe. Needless to say, charges of tribal favouritism need not be valid to be believed. In many cases such accusations are indeed warranted as union leaders have succumbed to the exigency of constructing a reliable personal following or to the traditional obligation to favour their kin in appointed union jobs or union-recommended promotions and jobs within industry. The usual audience for such charges is the branch officials, though occasionally the rank-and-file have been aroused to such anomic actions as street fights with an opponent's tribal supporters. Finally, tribalism is seldom the only aspect of a factional encounter; challengers often articulate other legitimate and illegitimate grievances against office-holders.

Tribe is thus not a primeval loyalty necessarily leading to conflict within trade unions. Rather, tribalism is a calculable and hence preventable factor which the astute union leader weighs when making decisions. But, owing to the complexity of the situation, the prevalent tribal suspicions and the traditional pressures to favour one's kin, miscalculations are ever a danger for leaders who must retain trans-tribal support. While this remains the case, union leadership will continue to be a precarious and insecure occupation.

The continuing upheavals within unions are also a result of politically inspired factionalism. It is now time to turn to a consideration of this external political dimension.

PART III

Working-class action

6. Unions and clientelist politics

Government policy, as mentioned in Chapter 2, has been to restrict the scope of permissible political action on the part of trade unions. Legitimate union behaviour in this sphere was to be limited to moderate pressure-group activities regarding policies or laws affecting the immediate economic interests of workers. Beyond this, the ruling elite, concerned with safeguarding its domination, has introduced a strict, informal rule governing the political role of union leaders: they are not to engage in activities deemed detrimental to political stability or to KANU's continuance in power.

Union leaders have largely reconciled themselves to these demands. Meetings of COTU bodies, national union bodies and even branch committees often conclude with a resolution pledging support to the President and to KANU, and with a hearty chorus of 'KANU *Yajenga Nchi*' (KANU Builds the Nation). And, as we shall soon see, COTU's pressure-group activities have been nothing if not moderate and responsible. Union officials have been enabled to adapt to the wishes of the ruling elite in these respects owing to the apparent expectations of union members about their leaders' behaviour. As previously mentioned, Kenyan workers have developed only a 'trade-union consciousness'; they expect unions to concern themselves merely with the members' short-run economic interests. There is no evidence to suggest that workers expect their unions to constitute part of a social movement dedicated to realizing a transformation of the dependent capitalist political economy. The unformed nature of the workers' political consciousness is hardly surprising in the absence of a socialist vanguard. Only a handful of labour leaders have ever consistently challenged the government's capitalist development strategy, and most of these have ended up in preventive detention. Plainly, then, union leaders are presently under no pressure from below to concern themselves with broad political aims that would diverge from those of the political class.

Such hostility as exists between the full-time union officials and the political class is on an individual rather than a group basis, as prominent trade unionists strive to enter the political class. The inchoate nature of the workers' political consciousness provides the workers' leaders with an opportunity to use their official positions to advance personal political ambitions. While trade unionists have been enjoined to undertake no activities detrimental to KANU's domination, this injunction is not incompatible with their participation in *intra*-KANU factional struggles. All of the party's factions vie with one another in professing loyalty to Kenyatta and to the party to which they all formally belong. Hence, top union leaders have long employed the resources to which they have access in advancing the positions of particular KANU leaders who act as their patrons.

There is, moreover, a close interconnection between these broader political struggles and the aspects of internal union politics discussed in the last three chapters. First, the centralization of power within unions permits top trade unionists to employ resources for personal ends, provided these are not in conflict with the union's formal economic goals. Second, the persistence of internal union conflict and of the saliency of ethnicity encourages the intervention of politicians bent on eliminating the trade union base of political opponents. A vicious circle is thus created: internal instability encourages external interference into union affairs, and this external intervention exacerbates internal union conflict. Indeed, this interpenetration of internal union struggles and the broader political struggles makes it difficult to draw clear boundaries between the two.

This chapter seeks to support and expand upon this conception of the unions' political role in the context of clientelism. I first discuss the operation of trade unionism as a *unit*, seeking to influence the content of the government's policies and legislation. Then the focus shifts to union leaders acting as *individuals* to promote certain political personages or factions. It will soon be evident that the reality of union life at the top levels is as much factional struggles for union and political power as it is industrial struggles with employers for enhanced terms and conditions of service.

COTU as a pressure group

Several studies of trade unionism in developing countries have claimed that the locus of the unions' pressure-group activities must be the highest councils of the governing party, for it is here that all important decisions are made.[1] This is not the locus of such activities in Kenya, however, for the excellent reason that KANU, the governing party, hardly exists – its councils, high or low, seldom meet. Instead, COTU has sought to influence legislation and policy by lobbying among members of the National Assembly, both backbenchers and frontbenchers, and by publicizing resolutions of COTU's Executive Board on current topics of concern to labour.

COTU has sought to bring its influence to bear mainly on four policy areas.[2] First, the organization showered political leaders with resolutions, correspondence and threats regarding the return to employees of their private provident fund contributions after a compulsory national social security scheme commenced in January 1965. By 1969 this struggle had largely been abandoned without extracting many substantive concessions respecting refunds. Second, COTU and its predecessors have continually pressed the government to accelerate the pace of Africanization, particularly in the private sector, and to prevent Asian and European employers from circumventing governmental policy on this matter. In 1967, the government created a Kenyanization of Personnel Bureau, an initiative perhaps partly prompted by pressure from organized labour. Third, the trade union federation has long argued that labour legislation needed certain amendments. Labour leaders would certainly have liked to secure a retraction of the Labour Minister's power, granted in the Trade Disputes Act, 1965, to declare strikes illegal. Such a demand, however, was unrealistic. Alternatively, COTU requested that the Labour Minister be empowered to refer trade disputes to the Industrial Court after a deadlock in negotiations had been reached, regardless of whether the employer concerned refused his consent to such referral. Other requested amendments have aimed at curbing management's unilateral right to terminate employment and at providing a voice for labour on any prospective board authorized to establish criteria governing wage increases on a national basis. While the government did make dismissals subject to Industrial Court adjudication in the Trade Disputes (Amendment) Act, 1971, this was in the nature of a sop intended to blunt the unions' criticisms of the other amendments. The final area of COTU's pressure activities relates to the institutional interests of trade unions. Since its creation, COTU has unsuccessfully tried to coax the government into legislating a 'closed shop' or 'union shop' system, whereby all employees in an enterprise would have union subscriptions withheld from their wages once one-half of them had voluntarily joined the appropriate union.

COTU, to judge by the results it has achieved, has been an ineffectual pressure group. In the period 1969–72, the government did not even bother to convene a single meeting of the Labour Advisory Board, the statutory body composed of representatives of labour and employers whose function is to advise the Labour Minister. Moreover, neither the government's announcement in 1969 of a wages policy, nor the Trade Disputes (Amendment) Act of 1971 were referred to COTU for its comments. COTU's ineffectiveness is partly a result of the continual splits within the body which prevent it from speaking with a united voice. In addition, COTU leaders, far from influencing political leaders, are often under the latter's influence as clients in patron–client relationships. Prominent politicials are thus unlikely to take COTU's public fulminations very seriously.

Patrons, clients and union

Consider next the involvement of trade unionists in factional politics, an involvement which apparently has consumed a major part of their energies. Recall my suggestion that this personal participation in KANU's factional struggles is not considered illegitimate, given that such behaviour conflicts neither with the government's injunction to honour KANU above all parties, nor with the economic interests of union members. It is now time to elaborate upon these assertions.

Kenya is not unique in the propensity of its union leaders and political leaders to become entangled in each other's affairs in order to further their own ambitions. Studies of trade unionism in some developed as well as underdeveloped countries have revealed how struggles for power within or between political parties are often mirrored by power struggles within the union movement. In Australia, for instance, one writer has contended that 'struggles within the union movement are always closely related to struggles for control of the [Australian] Labour Party and the neat division between "industrial" and "political" which union officials try to maintain is rarely clear-cut'.[3] In Nkrumah's Ghana, the interpenetration of the governing party (the Convention Peoples' Party, CPP) and trade unions was especially pervasive and complex. One study of this period observed that 'the struggles within each [the 'labour movement' and the CPP] tended to spill over into or involve the other'.[4] Government leaders sponsored labour legislation in 1958 and thereafter to assist their allies in gaining control of the Ghana Trades Union Congress and, through that body, the union movement as a whole. CPP activists were encouraged to enter union politics 'both for the element of CPP control it thus guaranteed and for its removing a politically turbulent group from *direct* involvement in the Party'.[5]

Why do union leaders enter into political alliances? Patron–client relationships are constructed on the reciprocal exchange of material benefits and/or services of different types between two persons of unequal status and power.[6] We must thus examine the participants and terms of their exchange in the Kenyan case.

The situation in Kenya is complex because of the various levels at which informal alliances between politicians and trade unionists occur. Politicians of both national and solely local prominence have entered into patron–client relationships with union leaders, while full-time union leaders at federation, head office and branch levels have served variously as either patron or client or both. The tendency for one person to fill both patron and client roles simultaneously (though, of course, in relation to different persons) means that separate dyadic exchange relationships interlock to form hierarchical networks of power.

Consider first the relationship between nationally prominent political leaders and leaders at the national union federation level. Actually, the distinction between 'politicians' and 'leaders of union federation' is somewhat artificial; the latter have usually been palpably politically ambitious and, indeed, have often held political office themselves. Of the officials of COTU in 1971, for instance, its secretary-general, deputy secretary-general and treasurer-general were Members of Parliament, and its President was defeated for such a post at the last general elections. Conversely, several earlier trade union federations co-opted M.P.s and Senators onto their executives, even though, in some instances, these politicians had had no previous trade union experience. Splits in the unions movement have always had political implications: either the split emerged primarily out of a political division in the first instance, or the contending national union federations sought support from factions within KANU after their rivalry had begun.

Splits at the top – both in politics and trade unionism – inevitably ramify at lower levels in societies where few norms exist to insulate institutions from external interference. Aspirants for power in the trade union federation must necessarily create linkages with the leaders of individual unions; only with the support of affiliated unions can they gain or maintain positions at the top. Hence, struggles for power at the union federation level have often created or exacerbated factionalism within the individual trade unions, as contenders at the top sought to undermine each other's clients within the affiliates. Furthermore, this resultant conflict within individual trade unions – and even within branches of trade unions – has had political implications. Since contenders for power in the trade union federation have involved themselves in political struggles, their interventions on behalf of followers within trade unions must be interpreted as designed not only to advance their positions in the top union body, but also to maintain or eliminate the trade union base of a particular party or intra-party faction.

Just as leaders of the union federation depend on continued support from affiliated unions for their retention of control at the top, so political leaders can operate as national political figures only by virtue of local bases of support.[7] We can roughly classify the levels at which politicians compete for power and prestige as 'central' and 'local' political arenas. The National Assembly in Nairobi is a central political arena, as is the headquarters of a national political party. Local political arenas are found at the district and municipal levels; some examples are the district party branch and county and municipal councils. Politicians within both central and local political arenas seek alliances with union leaders in certain circumstances. As previously hinted, political factions in central arenas generally limit themselves to cementing alliances with clients within the national trade union federation, though occasionally they may enter into factional fights within individual unions. Normally, however, national political figures rely on their trade union federation followers to ensure that supporters of political opponents are excluded from control of any trade union. At the local level, contenders for political power are frequently drawn into struggles for control of a local union where that union constitutes a political base for a political opponent or encompasses a significant proportion of the electorate within a constituency.

How then do the various participants stand to benefit from the alliances into which they enter? Let us begin with the more obvious exchanges among union leaders at different levels. Clearly, the prime service that the heads of individual unions can offer contenders for power in the trade union federation are their unions' votes at the federation's elections. In exchange, the patron at the top provides his clients at the next level primarily with the funds required to capture or maintain control of 'their' unions. Secondly, a patron at the federation level undertakes to protect his union followers against any unfavourable government actions or decisions. To this end, top federation leaders frequently communicate with the Registrar of Trade

Unions and the Ministry of Labour. Federation officials sometimes try to utilize their political contacts to influence the Registrar's decisions about registration of office-holders, though apparently without much success.

Political leaders stand to gain substantially from alliances with union federation leaders and, through them, with leaders of trade unions and union branches. There is much talk in Kenya about politicians who have allegedly used the union movement as a channel for the receipt of clandestine funds from abroad, mainly from foreign labour organizations.[8] Whatever the truth of these charges, the *samaki wakubwa* (big fish) who control a significant part of the union movement certainly gain enhanced prestige from their supposed capacity to instigate industrial unrest. They also obtain institutional backing for certain of their political proposals or criticism of colleagues. While it is considered improper for a cabinet minister to criticize publicly other cabinet members it is (or, rather, was) legitimate for a union federation official to do so. Most importantly, the trade union movement provides a ready-made, polyethnic, territory-wide, organizational network for any politician who wishes to establish his own political machine. The various levels of the union movement provide a multitude of jobs at various levels of remuneration. Moreover many, if not most, full-time officials at the individual trade union and union branch levels harbour political ambitions and are politically active within their own localities. Hence, he who controls the union movement has power over a significant proportion of the politically active stratum in Kenya. The support of such a wide range of ambitious men, who sometimes also hold office in KANU branches or sub-branches, county or municipal councils, is invaluable in any election campaign or intra-party contest.

Paid union officials also benefit from entering into a clientage relationship with a prominent politician. Union office – particularly in a large union – is highly prized in a less developed country where few opportunities exist for attaining status, power and comparatively high salaries or allowances. In addition, many union leaders hope to use their unions as a 'ladder' to obtain political office, to which accrue the highest rewards. To achieve these ambitions, union leaders, or contenders for union office, frequently seek to attach themselves to a nationally prominent politician or his subleader within the trade union federation. Such patrons can provide their trade unionist clients with financial and occasionally personal campaign assistance to advance their positions.

As for union members, they are only marginally involved in these factional manoeuvres. National union officials appeal to the rank-and-file for support on the basis of their members' putative economic interests (in wage increases and fringe benefits) and tribal loyalties rather than on the basis of political loyalties. Since members apparently regard their unions as institutions providing a specific economic service in exchange for their subscriptions, they are unlikely to respond to political appeals in this situation. What is important to part-time branch officials as well as ordinary members is not a leader's political affiliation but his ability to protect and advance the economic status of the membership.[9]

In short, I contend that such supposedly apolitical voluntary associations as trade unions and trade union federations tend to be drawn into political strife owing to the impressive political resources which they control, the prevalence of politically ambitious individuals in leadership positions and the absence of alert memberships who regard unions as more than organizations providing a limited economic service. Politics in underdeveloped countries is the main avenue of upward mobility; yet few if any of these countries contain enough political positions (cabinet ministers, M.P.s, county and municipal councillors, chiefs, etc.) to absorb the large number of aspirants who emerge with the broadening of political participation. Hence, such voluntary associations as exist become arenas within which individuals vie for both leadership positions and the opportunity to translate organizational resources into political influence and political position. Politicians are thus easily drawn into, or initiate, leadership rivalries in the union movement as they seek to extend their own organizational support by recruiting new clients and eliminating union leaders allied to their political opponents.

This model is abstracted from a detailed historical analysis of the political involvement of trade unionists during the period 1960–72. Owing to the limitations of both space and readers' patience, I do not intend to present a complete description of the ceaseless factionalism of this period.[10] What follows is thus only illustrative of the nature and consequences of the participation of union leaders in factional politics at the centre and in the localities.

Unions and central factional politics

Intra-KANU struggles for pre-eminence at the centre have led to or reinforced splits in the union movement on four occasions: 1959–60, 1962, 1964–5 and 1970–2. I intend to refer only to the last two post-colonial episodes.

First, however, it is necessary to sketch the contours of clientelist politics in Kenya in somewhat more detail that that provided earlier. The first election of Africans to the centre took place in March 1957, when eight Africans were elected to the Legislative Council on the basis of a qualitative franchise. Of these, four soon emerged as prominent political figures: Oginga Odinga, then President (*Ker*) of the Luo Union and Member for Central Nyanza; Daniel arap Moi, the Kalenjin Member for the Rift Valley; Ronald Ngala, the Giriama Member for the Coast; and Tom Mboya, the Luo Member for the Nairobi constituency. These men became powerful not only because of their reputations as nationalists striving for independence, but also because their positions in the power structure enabled them to build up personal followings. Before the late 1950s, ambitious Africans sought Europeans and sometimes Asians as patrons. This was inevitable since Europeans controlled all the top positions in colonial Kenya. Whenever an African wanted a particular advantage, such as a trading licence, a job or promotion, school places for his kin, a scholarship or protection before the law, he had to deal with a European or perhaps an Asian, and it was advantageous for him to have a European to intercede with the authorities on his behalf.[11] But, increasingly after 1957, Africans could afford to dispense with European patrons, and to rely instead on foremost African politicians to exercise influence on the power structure on their behalf. This new system of patronage obviously benefited those African politicians who gained their positions at the centre first.

Except for Mboya, prominent national political figures built up their clientage networks and grass-roots support mainly within their own ethnic categories. Mboya presented a trans-tribal image from the outset, since his Nairobi constituency was tribally heterogeneous.

The two most consistently antagonistic prominent politicians in the period 1958–69 were Tom Mboya and Oginga Odinga, whose rivalry continued after 1960 even though both men held office in the same political party, KANU. The bases of their antagonism were conflicting ambitions, personality conflict and, increasingly after 1960, ideological differences. Which motivation was foremost is difficult to assess and not particularly significant. What is important to explain is why their rivalry overshadowed and to some extent subsumed other cleavages. The most important factors seem to be their dominating personalities and their access to considerable political resources with which to construct clientage networks. Since 1957 Odinga has been a wealthy man in his own right, owing initially to his success as head of the Luo Thrift and Trading Corporation. Mboya also launched some successful enterprises after independence in 1963. But both men apparently also gained financial assistance from foreign patrons. Colin Legum has observed how internal party splits in African countries often gain an external dimension, involving foreign powers, as opponents 'shop around' for funds, scholarships and prestigious foreign tours, either for themselves or their followers.[12] Whether opponents go 'shopping' in Western countries, other African countries, or communist ones depends partly on ideological proclivities. In Kenya, since Mboya went West for practical assistance in the late 1950s, Odinga, his rival, went East.[13] Both did well.

Both Mboya and Odinga distributed a large, though unspecifiable, number of foreign scholarships in the early 1960s – Mboya returned from his trips to the United States in the late 1950s with offers of scholarships for both trade union leaders and college students. In 1959, he organized the so-called 'Operation Airlift' which sent several hundred young Kenyans to U.S. universities. Odinga sent comparable numbers East, some of them for military training in China and Bulgaria. Needless to say, the young Kenyans who were sent abroad owed much to their patrons, for a university education was a passport to a prestigious career.

Another important type of patronage which nationally prominent politicians such as Mboya and Odinga controlled were jobs and offices. First, they and their respective allies in the cabinet (after KANU formed the government in May 1963) were responsible for appointing individuals to a wide variety of governmental and quasi-governmental boards, tribunals, advisory committees and commissions falling within their ministries' jurisdictions. In 1968, there were 403 such bodies, ranging from state corporations to small committees.[14] Although the rates of remuneration are not public knowledge, the indications are that sitting and other allowances or salaries are high enough to make many of the appointments highly prized.[15] Second, before new legislation regulating local government elections was passed in 1970, national political leaders and their allies could informally select those who would become county and municipal councillors in districts where they controlled the nomination procedures of the KANU branch. KANU branch nominees were assured of election in the local government elections of August 1968, for example, because no independent candidates were legally permitted to run, and opposition Kenya Peoples' Union nominees were disqualified *en masse*. Finally, some political leaders have successfully evaded the universalistic and achievement norms of civil service recruitment to place their own followers in positions. As one observer has commented, 'patronage is...so closely interwoven with the formal apparatus of the state that it is often more intellectually rewarding to consider both in the same stride of political analysis.'[16]

The crucial role of Jomo Kenyatta has not yet been alluded to. Information on his alignments and leadership strategies is difficult to obtain, mainly because Kenyans fear contradicting the prevailing myth of Kenyatta as a person somehow 'above' politics. But a few points can be made with a high degree of certainty.[17] Kenyatta emerged from nine years of imprisonment and detention in August 1961 as the living symbol of independence to whom all other political leaders paid homage. But homage is one thing and power another: though Kenyatta was undoubtedly popular among the masses in certain areas of the country, his lieutenants in KANU, especially Mboya and Odinga, had already developed their own independent power bases and clientage networks. In this situation, Kenyatta publicly adopted a stance of neutrality in his lieutenants' rivalries while at the same time he sought to centralize power to himself and lessen the influence of his lieutenants.

Until the end of 1964, Kenyatta mistrusted Mboya more than anyone else within KANU and tended to side with Odinga, especially in attempts to undermine Mboya's trade union base. Kenyatta's dislike of his Secretary-General apparently arose from a belief that Mboya had colluded with the British over Kenyatta's detention in order to emerge as the foremost nationalist leader. Mid-1962 marked the nadir in relations between Kenyatta and Mboya, symbolized by several clashes in Nairobi between youth-wingers loyal to the two leaders. But Kenyatta clearly grew increasingly suspicious of Odinga's intentions throughout 1964, finally throwing his weight behind the anti-Odinga coalition in early 1965.[18]

The political situation in 1964–5, therefore, was that divisions within KANU, the sole party between November 1964 and May 1966, polarized around Mboya (the 'Conservatives') and Odinga (the 'Radicals').[19] 'In seeking to strengthen their respective positions within the Cabinet both Odinga and Mboya actively campaigned for the support not only of fellow Cabinet Ministers but also of their fellow parliamentarians. Each privately sought to establish a parliamentary following which would strengthen his position in the Cabinet and also in the party.'[20] Why were M.P.s sought as followers? One reason was that the only functioning groups in KANU were the Parliamentary Group and the district branches, the latter often under the control of M.P.s. Since the constitutional provisions for the election of the President, before amendments in June 1968, gave the M.P.s, not the electorate, responsibility for selecting a new one, it was assumed that the man with majority support in the Parliamentary Group would succeed to the post when Kenyatta either died or retired. Moreover, since M.P.s dominated a majority of the KANU branches and, hence, the choice of party delegates, it was further assumed that majority support among M.P.s would assure leadership of KANU as well. Factionalism at the centre thus spilled over into local political arenas as the main contenders sought to extend their clientage networks through the country.[21]

Factionalism at the centre also created or worsened factionalism at the various levels of the union movement as the 'radicals' sought to deprive Mboya of his trade union base. The union movement at the beginning of 1964 consisted of one registered national trade union federation, the Kenya Federation of Labour (KFL), twenty-seven affiliated trade unions with a total reported voting membership of 223,796, and well over 200 branches of trade unions throughout the country. Why Mboya's political enemies should expend resources to capture control of the union structure can only be understood in the light of the earlier discussion about the resources controlled by union leaders and the use Mboya made of them for political advantage.

One advantage Mboya gained from his alliances with union leaders was prestigious followers who could be relied upon to deliver public denunciations of his rivals within the cabinet. When Mboya relinquished day-to-day leadership of the KFL in April 1962 in order to become Labour Minister, he left his own nominee in command as Acting General Secretary. In fact, Mboya's hold on the national union federation was not broken by his political enemies until February 1969. During the period 1962–9, KFL and COTU officials often launched attacks, directly or by implication, on prominent political leaders. In August 1962, union leaders even publicly denounced Kenyatta for 'undemocratic actions' and 'irresponsible statements'.[22]

More significant was Mboya's use of the union movement's organizational network as a polyethnic 'political base' from which he could extend his influence throughout the country. He successfully used the threat of this union base against his political opponents within KANU in August 1962, for instance. When Kenyatta called a special meeting of KANU's Governing Council to resolve the party's internal conflicts, especially the one involving Odinga and Kenyatta, on the one hand, and Mboya, on the other, Mboya prevailed upon the KFL to convene a 'Trade Union Leaders' Conference' to overlap with the KANU meeting. The KFL conference was called to discuss the political situation and, its organizers hinted, the formation of a new political party.[23] With this trade union conference proceeding only about a mile from the KANU gathering, Mboya could afford to warn his KANU rivals that he would resign from the party unless unwarranted attacks against him ceased. 'If you want me to resign, I shall resign. I can help the country in other ways than by being a member of KANU.'[24] The significance of this remark could hardly be lost on his listeners, given the rumours connecting Mboya with the formation of a Kenya Labour Party. Kenyatta, apparently realizing that Mboya would leave the party if pushed too far, made some conciliatory remarks and later adjourned the meeting without seeking to censure Mboya. A labour party thus never emerged; the Trade Union Leaders' Conference contented itself with a few resolutions establishing a 'KFL political committee' and condemning politicians 'who may be working for the downfall of the Federation'.[25]

Given the way in which Mboya exploited the union movement for political advantage, his political opponents predictably sought to replace his union followers with their own. Union factionalism in 1964–5 was thus related to intra-KANU conflict as described above, though it was not, of course, a mere function of political strife. The two main leaders of the anti-KFL body, first named the Kenya Federation of Progressive Trade Unions (KFPTU) and later the Kenya African Workers' Congress, were Denis Akumu and Ochola Mak'Anyengo, both of whom were Luo, and both of whom had originally been brought into the trade union movement by Tom Mboya. They had, however, begun to quarrel with their mentor in late 1962 and thereafter associated themselves with Odinga's 'radicals' within KANU. At the ideological level, both men disagreed with Mboya on the question of the KFL's continued affiliation to the then American-dominated International Confederation of Free Trade Unions, and (after 1964) on the nature of African socialism. Indeed, foreign affiliation was the key issue in the labour split right from the start. Not only did the KFPTU affiliate with the radical All-African Trade Union Federation, but Mak'Anyengo was elected Assistant Secretary-General of this pan-African body. The two union leaders also condemned Mboya's brand of socialism as a mask for capitalism under which a few well-placed individuals grew steadily wealthier at the expense of the masses.[26]

At the personal level, the antagonism may best be summed up by a Luo proverb: 'You can't cook two cocks in the same pot.' It was difficult for Mboya to maintain a co-operative relationship with either of the two Luo, as they were both as energetic and ambitious as he was. Mboya, realizing that he could never hope to control or manipulate either Akumu or Mak'An-yengo, passed them over for the top KFL posts when he finally withdrew as formal head of the Federation in August 1963. Instead, the then Minister of Justice and Constitutional Affairs exerted his considerable influence on behalf of Clement Lubembe, a Luhya lieutenant who had just been elected Senator for Nairobi. Lubembe's defeat of Akumu for the Secretary-Generalship infuriated the latter, partly because he felt he was better equipped to handle the post. There were, therefore, personal as well as policy reasons for the split of March-April 1964.

The so-called 'rebel' union leaders aimed, from the outset, to end Mboya's influence in the trade union movement. Both sides within the union movement and within KANU clearly recognized this. Akumu and Mak'An-yengo were at pains to emphasize that they were not disloyal to Kenyatta's Government (as Mboya and Lubembe alleged), but only opposed Mboya's position. In a letter to Prime Minister Kenyatta in April 1964, the two sought to make it clear 'that any implications by an individual or a minister (such as the speech made by Mr. Mboya last weekend at Nakuru) that we are quarrelling with the government is false and unfounded'. Instead, they were against 'individual politicians using the Trade Union movement as a lever in their fight for power with others'. They thus concluded that 'if any leader who is attempting to use the Trade Union movement for political reasons or one making a vague statement on possible neutrality and finds himself in conflict with us, we submit, sir, that in any case it is not the government that we are in conflict with but the individual.'[27] KFL leaders also clearly realized the political implications of the split. A KFL 'Reorganization Plan' of May 1964 asserted that 'the divisionist activities within labour movement...aim at breaking down the strength of the KFL for the benefit of some politicians....It is well known that...if the rival group would win the battle then it is obvious that our beloved former General Secretary of KFL will have lost a great deal in public life and also his successor the present General Secretary.'[28]

The anti-KFL federation was closely linked to Odinga. He supplied it with funds, as did the AATUF, though the Congress was never as wealthy as the KFL. Some of the 'rebel' federation's officials were office-holding politicians linked to Odinga's faction. For example, a Senator, Tom Gichohi, was its President, two M.P.s, G. F. Oduya and Gideon Mutiso, were its Vice-President and Financial Secretary, respectively, and a Member of a Regional Assembly was its Assistant Financial Secretary. Denis Akumu, the Director of Organization, became Chairman of the Odinga-dominated Central Nyanza branch of KANU in early 1966. Furthermore, the KFPTU–Congress interests were defended within the House of Representatives by members of Odinga's faction,[29] and M.P.s linked to Odinga also addressed several Congress rallies in various parts of the country.

As usual, the split at the national trade union federation level produced struggles for control of the individual unions. Officials of the opposing federations almost daily issued conflicting claims of union support. Factional fights between KFL and Congress-supported groups often pervaded the branches of trade unions as well as their head offices. Indeed, few, if any, parts of Kenya where unionized employees worked escaped organizational (or disorganizational) visits from the principal contenders or their agents.

Trade union conflict in Mombasa was probably more intense than elsewhere, owing to the central position in labour affairs held there by Denis Akumu and his well-organized Dockworkers' Union. Before his expulsion in March 1964, Akumu had been the KFL's Coast Branch Secretary, and most of his supporters in unions and union branches at the Coast left the KFL when he did. During 1964–5, conflict occurred not only within the Mombasa branches of unions affiliated with the KFL, but also between unions with different affiliations, as Congress leaders sought to recruit workers outside their jurisdiction. Akumu, for example, handled trade disputes on behalf of the sugar workers at the large Ramisi plantation in Kwale District and the sisal workers at Vipingo Estates, Kilifi District, when these workers refused to obey the upcountry leaders of the KFL affiliates, the Union of Sugar Plantation Workers and the Plantation and Agricultural Workers' Union, respectively. Furthermore, in June 1964, the Dockworkers' Union revived its claim to represent workers in the high level area of the Port, then represented by the Distributive and Commercial Workers' Union and Printing and Kindred Trade Workers' Union; it also started to enroll members from amongst those employed by a transport company, the Tally Clerks' Organization and a fumigation company which operated on the dock. All four of the unions which the Dockworkers' Union raided happened to be staunch affiliates of the KFL. Following a number of 'wild-cat' strikes involving these concerns, designed to persuade employers to recognize the Dockworkers' Union, the Labour Minister appointed a Board of Inquiry to inquire into the dockworkers' claims and labour strife in Mombasa. This Board recorded the following conclusion regarding the causes of labour unrest:

As was inevitable the split in the trade union movement figured prominently in the proceedings before the Board...Mombasa being Akumu's headquarters, was the natural centre of the trade union war. Whereas in the past Mr. Akumu had made half-hearted attempts to encroach on other unions, after his expulsion, he went all out in his pursuit of enlisting as many members into the Dockworkers' Union as possible. He has certainly shaken the whole structure in Mombasa. This split is assuming bigger proportions as time goes by. The dissident group is busy forming rival unions to the ones that are affiliated to the KFL.[30]

It is thus understandable why Mboya, his political allies at the Coast, especially Ronald Ngala, and Lubembe expended so much effort in trying to oust Akumu as General Secretary of the dockers. They finally succeeded at this union's election of September 1965.

If the struggle had been permitted to continue, the Congress might quite conceivably have defeated the KFL, even though the latter still had thirteen affiliates in June 1965, while the former had only five. But President Kenyatta halted the competition in June, and appointed a Ministerial Committee to examine ways of forging unity in the union movement. Since the radical wing in trade unionism had sought to remove Mboya's independent power base, Kenyatta had initially sympathized with it. But when, in early 1965, Kenyatta switched to support for Mboya's broad 'conservative' coalition, the President was unwilling to see Odinga's union allies capture control of the union structure. To avoid this eventuality, the President accepted his Ministerial Committee's recommendation that unity be imposed from above, in the form of a new federation, the Central Organization of Trade Unions (Kenya), created from an amalgamation of the KFL and the KAWC. As long as union leaders balanced one another off within a single organization, they could not threaten anyone.

This brief case study illustrates how political conflict tended to spill over into trade-union arenas, thus creating or exacerbating factionalism at all levels of the union movement. This was also the pattern that characterized the factional episodes of 1959–60 and 1962. While some of the characters had changed by 1970–2, the plot remained substantially the same.

By 1970, one of the major characters, Tom Mboya, had been removed, cut down by an assassin's bullets the year before. But powerful politicians continued to encourage splits in the union movement when such served their personal ambitions. In the post-Mboya era, Denis Akumu's position as Secretary-General of COTU grew less secure. A group of Kikuyu cabinet ministers (commonly referred to in 1968–9 as the 'Kikuyu Group') had originally backed him when he had seemed to be the man most capable of defeating Clement Lubembe, Mboya's ally in the top COTU post. Before COTU's triennial elections in February 1969, Akumu's stature among trade unionists and his long-standing opposition to Mboya had weighed more heavily than suspicions that he retained a secret loyalty to Oginga Odinga (then the KPU leader) and nurtured political ambitions of his own. But the death of Mboya in July had ended Akumu's usefulness. When Akumu was elected an M.P. in December 1969 and continued to use his COTU position to forge contacts all over Kenya, some prominent Kikuyu ministers favoured replacing their erstwhile protégé with a more pliant individual. In May 1970, two Kikuyu COTU officials created a group to gain control of COTU from Akumu; this became known as the 'Kenya United Group'. Akumu countered with the formation of his own group the 'All Workers' Group'.

The struggle between these two groups has persisted from July 1970 to December 1972, the time of writing. Three COTU elections were held in 1972, but none of these resolved the crisis. The second election was supervised, according to the author's own count, by not less than nineteen officials of the Ministry of Labour, backed up by fifty or sixty uniformed policemen responsible for maintaining order. Yet the Registrar of Trade Unions, who personally dealt with the objections of both factions prior to this election, felt unable to register the victors, Akumu's 'All Workers' Group', without a direction from the Trade Union Tribunal. No such direction was forthcoming in this instance.

This most recent instance of intra-union factionalism gives one a distinct feeling of *déjà vu*. As before, the split was linked to intra-KANU factionalism, as prominent political leaders struggled for the succession to Jomo Kenyatta. The 'Kenya United Group' is apparently fully behind the Defence Minister, Dr Njoroge Mungai, the current favourite in the succession struggle. Labour Minister Ngala Mwendwa publicly admitted as much when he stated, in an address to COTU's Governing Council in September 1970, that 'some of the politicians think that the President is retiring tomorrow and that they could take over by capturing COTU leadership.... They think that by enlisting the assistance of trade unionists and applying tribalism they would eventually manage to achieve their goals.'[31] Again, in a National Assembly debate on the estimates of the Office of the President, introduced by the Minister of State, Mbiyu Koinange, Mwendwa commented that 'people say COTU has problems. COTU has no problems.... But some big fish somewhere are messing around with it. I even get calls saying "I don't want him" for a candidate in an election.'[32] Akumu's 'All Workers' Group' has also had covert support from cabinet ministers, mainly coastal, Kamba, Luo and Luhya ones who fear Kikuyu domination.

As before, the disputants at the top instigated factionalism within individual unions as they sought to replace their opponents' followers with their own. Bribery and intimidation of union officials reached new heights, and hardly a union escaped involvement in the internecine warfare. The two factions competed at the branch elections of individual unions held in early 1971, at the subsequent elections of national officials and at the COTU elections in 1972. At no time have issues relating to the welfare of workers been seriously debated by the two factions.

Unions and local factional politics

Have local factional struggles had the same tendency to permeate the internal politics of locally prominent unions or union branches? To answer this question, I originally selected three localities for study on the grounds that each had experienced long-standing political disputes and that each contained a trade union or union branch which catered for a significant proportion of local wage-earners. One of these case studies – that of the sugar workers in Nyanza Province – I had to abandon owing to the declaration of a state of emergency in Nyanza in 1969 just as I was about to undertake field research there. The two remaining cases included Mombasa Town and Murang'a District in Central Province. In Mombasa, the involvement of the Dockworkers' Union in local politics dates back to 1958. In

Murang'a, intra-KANU factionalism has emerged sporadically since 1962, though the Plantation and Agricultural Workers' Union was uninvolved until 1967–8.

I found that it was not unusual for a union leader to use the prestige, ready publicity and other resources attached to his official position to advance either himself or a particular party or intra-party faction within a local political arena – such as a county or municipal council or the district branch of a political party. And, predictably, when leaders of such organizations took sides in local politics, they were likely to encounter politically inspired opposition within their own ranks. Hence, political involvement, at the local as well as the national level, was detrimental to the stability of union leadership.

In Mombasa, the dockers' leaders have participated in local politics ever since the dock union's emergence as a powerful organization in 1958 under Denis Akumu. The union was entangled in the struggle for control of the Mombasa African Democratic Union in 1958–9, the fight for supremacy between KADU and KANU in 1960–4 and the intra-KANU factionalism after the governing party absorbed KADU in 1964.[33] Politicians of local or national stature took a direct part in the union's internal politics in 1960, 1961, 1962, 1965, 1966 and 1967–8, either by the provision of financial assistance and tactical advice or by participation in union election campaigns. Sometimes politicians would devote several weeks to such activities; for example, S. T. Omari, then a coastal M.P., spent three weeks before the September 1965 union election campaigning amongst dockers against Akumu, assisted on occasion by cabinet ministers and other M.P.s who belonged to Mboya's broad coalition of 'conservatives' at the time. This time the politicians' efforts succeeded, as Akumu was voted out of union office in a fair election. But – and this is a crucial point – both Akumu and the politicians involved emphasize that political alignments *per se* did not interest the hard-headed stevedores and longshoremen; the issues used against Akumu were his alleged tribalist tendencies in influencing promotions in the docks and a recent unfavourable settlement with the employer.

As the reader will have recognized by now, one cannot describe the complex series of alliances characterizing factionalism within the political class without getting immersed in historical detail. Perhaps the consideration of one discrete episode of factionalism involving the Plantation and Agricultural Workers' Union (KPAWU) in 1968 will best illustrate the pervasiveness of conflict in the shortest space. The main actors (participating either directly or indirectly) in the struggle for control of this union included Jesse Gachago, then a KANU M.P. for Makuyu in Murang'a District, Dr J. G. Kiano, then Minister of Health and KANU Branch Chairman in Murang'a, Denis Akumu, an aspirant to COTU leadership, Shadrack Njoka, the Meru President of the union and Philip Mwangi, the Kikuyu General Secretary.

To understand this union's involvement in politics, one must know something of the background of political conflict in Murang'a. In the

post-Emergency period, factionalism erupted in late 1962, spurred by competition for official KANU nominations in the 1963 General Election. The
leading antagonists were Dr J. G. Kiano, Member of the Legislative Council
for all the Kikuyu districts between 1958 and 1961, and M.P. for various
Murang'a District constituencies since 1961; and Bildad Kaggia, a militant
and prestigious Kikuyu ex-detainee who was released with Kenyatta in 1961.
Involvement in the Mau Mau rebellion was the split's main ideological
dimension. Whereas Kaggia presented himself as the defender of the former
'freedom fighters' and all dispossessed Kikuyu, Kiano portrayed himself
as the unifier of Mau Mau fighters and the Home Guard.[34] Among Kiano's
supporters were the other Murang'a M.P.s including Jesse Gachago. Kaggia's threat to the established politicians diminished in 1966 when he
resigned from KANU to join the newly-formed, radical opposition party,
the Kenya Peoples' Union. He was defeated in the 'Little General Election'
which was held in June 1966 to test the popular mandate of those M.P.s who
had resigned from the governing party.

With Kaggia's defeat, competition for power among the various anti-
Kaggia Murang'a political leaders soon surfaced. This conflict centred
around efforts by challengers to undermine Kiano's position of pre-
eminence in the District. At an encounter in September 1966, Kiano managed to assert his dominance, largely because he was able to bring the
influence of KANU's national leadership to bear in his favour.[35] But the
main instigator of the plot to oust Kiano, Jesse Gachago, then Assistant
Minister for Lands, survived the defeat without losing his position as
Vice-Chairman of KANU's Murang'a Branch.

Manoeuvring for position continued in 1968 and 1969. Legislation passed
in 1968, stipulating that only official party candidates could contest public
office, stirred up dormant factional conflicts in many parts of the country,
including Murang'a. Obviously, the elimination of independent candidates
meant that control of the local party machinery was crucial for political
survival. The subsequent struggles for control of KANU sub-branches in
Murang'a led to a further encounter early in 1969 between Dr Kiano, on the
one hand, and the four other Murang'a M.P.s led by Gachago, on the other.
The four KANU M.P.s announced on 28 February that the Branch's
executive had dismissed Kiano from his post as Branch Chairman; but
Kiano once again managed to use his influence among KANU leaders at the
centre to reverse the decision.[36]

When a system of 'preliminary' elections for the selection of all party
candidates for the National Assembly was legislated in mid-1969, factional
struggles for the control of KANU branches diminished in intensity. Control
of party branches diminished in importance, since no limits were placed on
the number of party candidates who could run in the preliminary elections,
no tests of party service were required of candidates, and all registered
voters could cast a ballot to select the KANU candidate for a constituency,
provided each declared that he was a KANU supporter. Popular selection of

party candidates thus prompted political opponents to switch their energies from seeking control of the KANU branch to seeking influential allies in enemies' constituencies to run in the preliminary elections. Such was the pattern in Murang'a.

Gachago's involvement in the triennial election of the Plantation and Agricultural Workers' Union in October 1968 can be explained in terms of his anxiety about maintaining support within the Makuyu KANU sub-branch and within his constituency. Most of his constituency consisted of large sisal, coffee and mixed farms, many of them still owned by Europeans, and employing several thousand Kikuyu workers in all; in December 1967, 2,570 of these employees belonged to the Makuyu branch of the KPAWU. If each farm labourer had a couple of dependents of voting age, the wage-earners' vote clearly was crucial for success in a constituency where the total vote in the December 1969 preliminary election for the National Assembly was only 15,813. Gachago had initially been a favourite among the workers because, as KFL National Organizing Secretary, he had played an important part in organizing sisal and coffee unions in Thika, the district within which his constituency was formerly located. Following his dismissal from the KFL in 1961, he had tried to form his own 'Coffee Plantation and Agricultural Workers' Union' as a means of re-entering trade unionism. Gachago's attempt failed, however, as prominent KFL leaders were determined to abort the registration of an anti-KFL union. But his image as a man committed to bettering the lot of farm labourers undoubtedly helped him to win the Makuyu seat in the 1963 General Election. By the time of the preliminary election in November 1969, his image had definitely changed. The wealthy owner of a large farm within Makuyu Division, Gachago had apparently lost his popular appeal.[37]

Many of the national, provincial and branch officials of the Plantation and Agricultural Workers' Union were active in KANU politics within Murang'a District – often at the originally crucial sub-branch level. In a situation of endemic political factionalism, few of these trade unionist-politicians escaped identification with a particular faction. It is hardly surprising, therefore, that political conflict spilled over into trade union matters. Indeed, several recorded cases show where political conflict intruded into employee–employer relations in Makuyu; for instance, one Kikuyu official of the KPAWU pressured a European estate owner to fire an employee – a sub-branch official who belonged to an opposing political faction.[38] Employers, in such cases, generally retreated behind the normative rule that political squabbles must not impinge upon industrial relations matters.

By 1968, Shadrack Njoka, President of both the plantation union and COTU, was, in addition, an Estate Manager and a Director of the largest sisal estate within Makuyu Division. (Of course, co-opting a union president into management is one means of guaranteeing the enterprise's industrial peace!) If the ambitious Njoka had not tried to use his economic position to advance the political interests of Dr Kiano, he probably would have survived in this anomalous situation for some time. But Njoka found his ability to build up a personal following through his responsibility for hiring and firing on the large estate and through his union's resources too tempting to play cautiously. In the following letter of August 1968, Njoka issued Gachago a serious political challenge:

Mr. Gachago has surveyed his political future of which he had reached to a point of no survival at the forthcoming General Elections, if the undersigned still exist at Makuyu with such an overwhelming majority support of workers.... To prove Mr. Gachago a failure I would ask him to come forward democratically and share a platform with me on both political and economic fields instead of beating around the bush. This I mean he should antagonise me within KANU which is our political body, KPAWU or COTU, whichever he prefers....

If Mr. Gachago claims to [have] any moral support of the workers or other inhabitants of Makuyu Constituency, he would have stopped them from electing me to the office of Vice-Chairman of Makuyu KANU sub-branch at the election which took place on the 22nd of June, 1968.... If he cannot compete with me in KANU of which he is an officer then any attempt to point his finger at me in the labour movement tantamounts to his political death. He should have known by now that the workers in the countryside are 'bega kwa bega' with me, and that Plantation Workers' Union has made me a life member eligible to hold any office in the union.[39]

Accepting Njoka's challenge, Gachago set about undermining Njoka's trade-union base, preparatory to destroying him politically. One tactic was to complain to the Minister of Labour about the anomaly of Njoka being both a union leader and a member of management. Thus, in a letter of August 1968 to E. N. Mwendwa the Assistant Minister complained that:

The Kenyan trade union movement is headed by a person who is, by the virtue of his appointment, an employer.... The workers, especially in this District, view this anomaly with serious concern and have repeatedly asked me to find out from you whether it is a part of Government policy to allow employers to maintain this manager, under the guise of previous trade union officials, to look after their [employers'] interests...

It is recognized that any person in the trade union's offices could be appointed to a management position, but when this happens, the management taking up such a person requires him to relinquish his position in the Trade Union.... In the case of this individual under reference, it is said that pressure was brought by your predecessor [Dr Kiano] on political grounds to return him [as Estate Manager and Director] and as such the anomaly was created purposely to satisfy an individual to the detriment of the workers of Kenya.

Gachago also formed an alliance with Philip Mwangi, the union's General Secretary, who had his own reasons for wishing to see Njoka eliminated from union leadership.

Before discussing Mwangi's role, however, we must consider how COTU's politics also played a part in the union's internal affairs. Through Shadrack Njoka, COTU's President, Clement Lubembe's regime controlled the three votes of the KPAWU in COTU's Governing Council. Hence, Akumu's COTU faction, dedicated to the ouster of Lubembe, was keen on assisting any faction within the KPAWU which sought to overthrow Njoka.

Thus, in September 1968, Akumu offered Mwangi the nomination for the post of Deputy Secretary-General of COTU in his team at the forthcoming COTU elections. Mwangi, however, afraid of creating further powerful enemies within the trade union movement, declined the offer.

Philip Mwangi could never be secure as General Secretary as long as Njoka was President of KPAWU. Njoka was the single most powerful man within the union: since 1964, he had participated in the dismissal of three general secretaries and had virtually appointed Mwangi to that position in December 1966. Moreover, under Njoka's influence, the union's constitution had been amended to give the President, rather than the General Secretary, 'overall powers over the Union's affairs'. Nor was Njoka reluctant to use his extensive powers; during 1965 and 1966 the President ruled the KPAWU virtually by decree, bothering neither to call Central Council meetings nor to consult the General Secretary. Thus, when Mwangi saw the opportunity of allying himself with powerful forces against Njoka, he took it.

This alliance spelt disaster for Njoka and his allies within the plantation union, including the Treasurer and the Provincial Secretary for Central Province. Five days prior to the union's Triennial Conference on 27 October 1968, Mwangi informed the President that he had been requested by 'the paid-up members' to dismiss Njoka from his union post, because he was an employer, not an employee. At the Conference held in Nyeri – far removed from the area of Njoka's influence – the President, Treasurer and Provincial Secretary were replaced by men loyal to Mwangi. The new President, for example, a Kikuyu supervisor on a coffee estate, spoke little English and, therefore, constituted no threat to Mwangi's position. When Njoka resigned as President of COTU and lost his job with the sisal estate (owing to political and trade union pressure on his employer), he was through politically, especially since he was a Meru in a Kikuyu area. Defeated, he returned to his place of origin on the other side of Mount Kenya. Njoka had been strong enough to defeat his opponents within each separate arena, but when these diverse enemies coalesced against him within a single arena, his days were numbered. He ended up by losing everything.[40]

After the election, Mwangi and his team attempted to root out all of Njoka's supporters within the union's branches, especially the Makuyu branch. In a short-lived resistance campaign, Njoka and his followers fought back by prevailing upon union members to revoke their 'check-off' agreements. Although this tactic proved to be a fairly successful one, the campaign ended when Njoka lost his influential position in the Makuyu sisal estate.

Conclusion

This chapter has uncovered a clear contradiction in union–government relations, a contradiction between the private and public aims of prominent politicians. The government as an entity has a policy towards trade unions as an institutional sphere: this is, in brief, to encourage unions to enhance political stability and to adopt a productionist orientation. Yet the personal ambitions of government leaders and politicians in general push them toward actions which help to undermine this policy to which they are collectively committed. By acting as patrons to factions within the national union federation and individual unions, political leaders create or exacerbate intra-union conflict, thus augmenting the insecurity of union leadership at all levels. Such conflict can degenerate into violence, as in Mombasa in 1965, which threatens political stability. In addition, as I have already hypo-thesized, the more intense the personal insecurity of trade unionists, the greater the incentive for them to adopt militant and uncompromising stands in industrial relations. In short, the factional manoeuvres of cabinet ministers have been detrimental to their government's formal goal of instilling a productionist orientation.

7. Militant economism (1)

A trade union, according to the famous definition of Sidney and Beatrice Webb, is 'a continuous association of wage-earners for the purpose of maintaining or improving the conditions of their employment'.[1] This definition is certainly congruent with the expectations of union branch officials and the rank-and-file in Kenya who, placing their immediate economic interests before other considerations, regard unions as organizations providing a specific service for them. In this respect their expectations have not been markedly different from those of workers in other parts of the world.

The Kenyan government, on the other hand, increasingly views the union movement as a junior partner in the enterprise of promoting economic growth. Prominent political leaders either oppose the 'traditional' consumptionist goals of trade unionism or wish to supplement this with an overriding productionist orientation which would, in effect, negate the traditional aim.[2] In the succinct phraseology of Mwai Kibaki, Kenyan Minister for Finance and Economic Planning, 'the unions have a role, a very positive role, and in fact a duty, to promote productivity in each industry so that the national income may grow rapidly and so that with greater productivity we may get further opportunities for those who are now not taken care of.'[3]

Union leaders, responsible for guiding their unions' activities, are thus caught between conflicting expectations of their behaviour. Since the specific dilemmas confronting trade unionists in the definition of their economic role were treated in Chapter 2, I will merely summarize these here. One relates to the unions' whole tactical approach to industrial relations: should they utilize militant tactics to gain their ends or advocate the peaceful and orderly settlement of all disputes? Another is their attitude towards improvements in terms and conditions of employment: should union leaders push for as much as they can get or advocate sacrifice and wage restraint? A third dilemma relates to the choice between grievance handling and workers' discipline: should unions concern themselves primarily with articulating and channeling workers' individual and collective grievances or with propagandizing among workers on the necessity for hard work and obedience to rules and supervisors? While not a dilemma, a final question union leaders must decide is whether they should adopt the new social welfare and 'nation-building' functions advocated by the ruling elite.

This chapter and the one following seek both to describe the choices made by trade unionists in defining their economic role and to explain these by reference to the conflicting pressures operating on them, as outlined in previous chapters. On the one hand, the state disposes of many penalties and rewards which can be used to discourage intransigent union behaviour. On the other, a union's members, including the branch officials, are unlikely to support their leaders' or retain their membership unless they produce concrete results. Workers cannot be persuaded that unions fulfil a worthwhile function for them if such patently is not the case.

Militancy or peaceful settlement?

On the question of the proper approach of unions toward industrial relations, the government has consistently demanded moderation. The Labour Minister, in a speech to a union audience in 1971, touched on a recurring theme when he observed that 'the relationship between workers and employers should not be one of conflicting interests. It is the atmosphere of peace and logical negotiations that achieve the required results.'[4] Employers' representatives also disseminate this viewpoint on the many occasions on which they address national or branch officials or shop stewards at various trade union seminars. It is a notion, moreover, that is implicit in the trade disputes legislation of 1964, 1965 and 1971.

There are, on the other hand, strong internal pressures on union leaders to articulate their demands in an aggressive manner, perhaps reinforcing them with dire threats of industrial war. The aim of such behaviour, I hope to demonstrate, is not only to coerce employers into granting concessions, but also to establish the impression among members and branch officials that their leaders are uncompromising in the defence of the workers' interests against a powerful and unregenerative management. Suspicions among workers of management's motives and intentions are largely a consequence of the initial exploitation of African workers, the racial structure of employment and management's early attempts to weaken and 'guide' trade unionism. Hence, moderate and 'co-operative' trade unionists are vulnerable to challenge from more militant opponents. The usual charge is that a particular leader has been 'pocketed' by management; this implies either that he has been bought off with promotions or bribes, or that he is afraid to stand up to management. The potency of such allegations can only be fully appreciated in the context of the development of union–management relations in Kenya.

Union–management relations

Kenyan employers, like those in other parts of the world, generally reacted antagonistically to the emergence of trade unions representing their employees. Employers were not, of course, unanimous in their response; foreign-controlled firms which began to operate in Kenya after the Second World War tended to display a more positive attitude toward trade unionism than the longer-established, locally-owned companies. On the whole, however, managements before 1956 were prone to regard industrial disturbances as the work of political agitators. Instead of trade unions, companies often favoured the formation of consultative works councils for their employees through which petitions on individual grievances could be channelled to management.[5] Even when the colonial government formally encouraged trade unionism after 1947, many firms were reluctant to recognize the appropriate unions, and often tried to make union organization as difficult as possible.

By 1961 most unions had won recognition from the larger employers or the relevant employers' association. But the signing of a recognition agreement did not necessarily signal an end of the power struggle between union and management. At the worst, the agreement merely resembled an armistice treaty imposed by a victorious army upon its defeated opponents: this type of union–management relationship may be termed an 'unstable truce'.[6] In this type, management either makes no effort to safeguard the prestige of union leaders or attempts to weaken the union by assisting 'co-operative' challengers or by victimizing or buying off the more militant leaders with promotions, better pay or special privileges. Union leaders, for their part, do all they can to stir up resentment toward management and to capitalize on workers' discontents. They also favour strike action to bring employers to terms. This relationship is thus frequently accompanied by mass firings, strikes and, occasionally, acts of physical violence and sabotage.[7]

An unstable truce characterized the initial period of union–management relations in many cases. Relations have always been hostile in the sugar plantations and were hostile in such other agricultural enterprises as tea until 1963 and coffee until 1965. An indication of the state of industrial relations in the coffee industry in 1964 is the following remark by the European chairman of the Kenya Coffee Growers' Association:

I doubt any Industry, anywhere in the world, could produce a worse Trade Union history than ours. It is indeed remarkable that we have survived at all... The saddest part about it all is that the very organization which is designed for the employees has caused them more harm than anyone else. All the foolish pointless strikes have gained the workers nothing, unless it be loss of wages. I viewed the introduction of Trade Unionism at the time as crass idiocy, subsequent events have proved the opinion to be typical British understatement.[8]

An unstable truce characterized the union–management relations of at least four other non-agricultural unions in the present sample, usually in the earliest period of such relations.

A second type of relationship is a 'tutelary relationship' in which the union becomes a kind of junior partner of management, reflecting its view. Recognizing the utility of a mechanism to permit employees to 'blow off steam', management judges that this may best be achieved by a union led by 'responsible' and 'loyal' employees. The policy is thus to recognize the relevant union and to contain or guide its development. The company provides assistance to the union in the form of training schemes and time off with pay for leaders. Management also understands that union leaders must not be put in a position where they might alienate their members; it is thus prepared to discuss major grievances and make a few concessions. Finally, management may easily be drawn into the union's internal struggles for power if its protégés are threatened or replaced by so-called 'irresponsible elements'.

The tutelary relationship was favoured by many of the larger and more progressive enterprises in the 1950s. Convinced that trade unionism was inevitable, these employers created the Association of Commercial and Industrial Employers in April 1956.[9] This Association's policy toward the development of trade unionism followed that recommended by the Overseas Employers' Federation in January 1956, namely that 'the climate of world opinion is such today that the question is not whether employers are to encourage or discourage workers' trade unions, but what sort of trade union is going to develop.... Workers' trade unions will only develop responsibly if they are nurtured by employers.'[10] Thus, one of the aims of the Kenyan employers' federation was 'to attempt to guide the corresponding develop- ment of employee trade unions along the right lines'. The original idea was that only those trade unions led by 'responsible' leaders were to be recognized.[11]

A tutelary relationship is obviously easiest to establish where a union represents the employees of a single large enterprise or department. Among the unions in the present sample the three clearest cases of a tutelary relationship involved house unions. This type of relationship occurred in these unions during periods in which their foremost office-holders occupied responsible positions within the relevant corporations; in all cases, the general secretary retained his position in the enterprise and either worked part-time for the union or was seconded to the union to work full-time, without loss of seniority privileges. Instances of tutelary or collusive rela- tionships existed within the agricultural sector too, but these generally involved branches of unions rather than a union as a whole.

While a tutelary relationship may provide employers with tranquil indus- trial relations in the short-run, it is unlikely to be a viable long-term solution to the tensions inherent in the employer–employee relationship. One writ- er's observations regarding the Uganda Textile Workers' Union applies equally well to many Kenyan cases:

The idea of basing a union upon management trainees will secure a responsible leadership for the moment, but it will pose as many problems as it will solve. There is a danger that the leaders will cease to represent the rank-and-file in their desire to impress management and confirm their promotion chances. What management regards as responsibility may be regarded by the workers as subservience. Radical leaders, perhaps more in tune with the masses, will be frustrated by their inability to reach controlling positions in the unions.[12]

The tutelary relationship may either disintegrate into an 'unstable truce' as union and management struggle for the loyalty of employees, or it may evolve peacefully into a more equal 'stable truce'. As well, an 'unstable truce' may move towards a 'stable truce' relationship as the employer abandons the struggle to control the union and the union leader decides to accept the *modus vivendi*.

At the very least, the stable truce requires a mutual recognition by both management and union that their interests are best served by accepting a more equal relationship in which each side stays out of the other's internal affairs entirely. More positively, management may decide that a strong, independent union is beneficial, in that it would be able to ensure that employees honour their obligations under collective agreements and refrain from making unreasonable demands on the company. Realizing that the absence of intra-union factionalism is a prerequisite for establishing a harmonious relationship, management must be willing, as a minimum condition, never to force the established leader to 'lose face' before his members. At the other extreme, an employer may be willing actually to enhance the established leader's reputation by granting significant concessions. Employers are not always the unrelenting 'profit-maximizers' of economics textbooks; they may sometimes decide to grant high wages and accept lower profits, provided they can thus establish a reputation as progressive employers and avoid industrial disturbances. Of course, it takes two to make a relationship. To establish a stable truce, a union's leaders must be willing to adopt a more compromising position in private, if not in public. Ultimately, this relationship involves an understanding between 'professionals' in both the union and the enterprise whereby they drop all rhetoric in private in order to work out an agreement that is acceptable to both sides. This agreement is then formally adopted at a larger meeting.

Few enterprises have advanced beyond the minimal condition of the stable truce relationship. With the establishment of the 'check-off' system and strict legislation regulating the right to strike, and with experience in negotiations, employers have discovered that their initial fear of trade unions was largely unfounded.[13] Moreover, initial attempts to establish a tutelary relationship often failed, as moderate leaders were replaced by militant challengers. There has thus been an overall trend toward the stable truce situation, whereby management has adopted a non-condescending and neutral attitude towards union leaders and union politics. Occasionally, a relationship has advanced beyond this state as both sides accept the other's sincerity and regard the other's interests as legitimate.

Dangers for union leaders are inherent in the stable truce situation. Under pressure from both management and the government to act 'responsibly', union officials must increasingly conceive of their role as the gaining of substantive concessions from management in exchange for obtaining their members' compliance with all contractual obligations, rules of the enterprise and labour legislation. Union leaders must often counsel moderation, advice which may be interpreted as reflecting the will of the company or the government rather than the interests of the workers. Challengers can thus portray office-holders as paid-off lackeys of management, particularly since the incumbents generally occupy better-paid positions than the average manual worker. At this early stage of industrial relations, the 'strong-man' leader rather than the 'moderate' negotiator still evidently has the greater appeal to workers.

Perhaps the best way to demonstrate the relationship between internal union power considerations and a union's tactics in industrial relations is by means of a couple of brief case studies. The two that follow have been selected because the structures of the unions involved are so dissimilar: the first is the most highly organized union in Kenya while the other is the least organized. The Dockworkers' Union, on the one hand, is a union with an urban membership concentrated in one small area – Kilindini Docks. The work force has been fairly stable over time: many of the founders of the union in 1954–5 were still employed on the docks in 1969. Because the national officials are directly elected by their members, factional struggles tend to involve many rank-and-file members. In the Kenya Plantation and Agricultural Workers' Union, on the other hand, the rural membership is widely dispersed, transient and largely uninvolved in intra-union struggles for power. Yet in both cases moderate leaders have lost out to more militant ones, and radical leaders have successfully mobilized support for their union and themselves by their daring behaviour.

Case 1: Union–management relations at the port, 1958–9

The Dockworkers' Union constitutes an interesting though somewhat atypical case of a union in which membership commitment was forged in a struggle for power between management and union.[14]

On many occasions during the colonial period Mombasa Port was the focus of labour disturbances throughout Mombasa Island. Low wages and depressed living and working conditions led to strikes and violence on the docks in 1939, 1944, 1947, 1955 and 1957. Although the dock union was registered in October 1954, it remained ineffectual until 1958–9, playing no part in the strikes of 1955 and 1957. These strikes were only ended by the intervention of Tom Mboya, General Secretary of the KFL.

Unlike the situation in most other industries, the registration of the dock union had the full approval of the most important member of management, the General Manager of the Landing and Shipping Company of East Africa, Captain G. R. Williams.[15] Williams, a progressive individual for his time, recognized the inevitability of trade unions and believed employers would be wisest not to fight trade unions, but to 'guide' their growth along 'responsible' lines.[16] To this end he managed, as Chairman of the Port Employers' Association (PEA), to persuade his colleagues to enter into a proper recognition agreement and always to adhere to its provisions. He also ensured that the union's inexperienced leaders were given time off with pay to attend six-week courses in industrial relations arranged by the Labour Department. Francis Thiongo Gathuna, the Kikuyu General Secretary until

April 1958, was granted an indefinite leave of absence in order to work full-time for the union. As well, all union officials could easily gain access to Williams at any time. Finally, Williams began in 1958 to argue with the directors in favour of a 'check-off' system for the union. Among other things, he felt that this provision could be used to keep the union responsible: 'The threat of withdrawal is a considerable deterrent against the union executive adopting an unreasonable attitude at any time.'[17]

In the union's election of March 1958, all the 'responsible' (i.e., moderate) leaders favoured by management were defeated by militant opponents led by Denis Akumu, then Secretary-General of the Nairobi Peoples' Convention Party. A measure of the union's weakness at that time was the small turn-out for the election: only 510 voted out of a potential membership of approximately 6,000. Participants with differing allegiances agree that the most important reason for the defeat of the office-holders was their close identification with management. According to one of the defeated officials, dockers knew that Gathuna was only on leave of absence from his job. Doubting the company's sincerity in granting such leave, many felt that the former General Secretary should have left his job entirely if he wished to become a full-time union leader. Akumu, on the other hand, was an outsider with no ties to employers. Akumu, ebulliently militant, also gained from his association with Tom Mboya. Mboya, then a widely-known member of the Legislative Council, had won a 30 per cent wage increase for dockers at the arbitration tribunal following the strike of 1955.

Relations between the PEA and the union's new leader soon deteriorated. This was inevitable once Akumu refused to continue the former tutelary relationship, with the union in the position of junior partner to a wise and benevolent management. More than this, the young Luo was determined to forge a strong, independent union on the basis of a common hostility to the employer. This certainly was not Captain Williams' expectation. In welcoming Akumu to the Port's Joint Industrial Council (JIC) he stated that:

...he was sure [Akumu] would receive the same co-operation from employers as the previous Union Secretary, *as long as the same relationship was maintained.* The strength of the union had so far lain in the fact that officer's primary interest had been in the welfare of the Port employees and the betterment of the industry as a whole. As long as these objectives pertain exclusively, the employers would continue to assist the union in its desire to grow into a well-organized body.[18]

The first phase of the union–management struggle originated in the dismissal of the union's new President from his job as clerk, in late April 1958, on the grounds of incompetence. While such action may have been justifiable, its timing was bound to appear provocative to the union. Claiming 'victimization', Akumu's reaction was to issue a Swahili leaflet to dockers which, for the first time in the union's history, attacked management. Since this leaflet had such an impact on union–management relations, it deserves to be quoted at some length:

You obviously know that our President is sacked. After considering this, we found out that he was sacked because of his support for you.... This is because of the employers' liking for people who only say 'Yes, sir!' [' *Watu wa "Ndio, Bwana"* '].

If we allow the employers to sack our leaders who work for the Union, this Union will perish at once. If we let them sack our President, the next man to be sacked will be the leader of your Section.

And finally, you yourself, will get the sack.

After getting rid of all your leaders, the employers' aim is to play tricks on you – he will sack you today, and engage someone else tomorrow....

Are you prepared to be tricked in this way?

Brothers, I call upon you to join me to decide our future action. Let us stand firm, and this will assure this man [i.e., Williams] that truly we have a strong union, for it is he who disturbed the hornet's nest.

Apparently enraged by this leaflet, the PEA responded by posting six notices in Swahili around the Port, attacking Akumu and defending the records of the previous union leaders. The first notice accused the new General Secretary of lying about the employers' intentions and argued that the former union representatives had served their members well. Subsequent notices enumerated all the gains that dockworkers had received since 1955. The final one (in May 1958) summed up the Association's case against Akumu:

This new Secretary from Nairobi who says himself that he does not know anything of Port working – HOW WAS HE ELECTED? HE WAS ELECTED BY 277 VOTES OUT OF 6,000 WORKERS. He has never worked in the Port and knows nothing of its ways. WHO THEN IS THIS MAN TO SPEAK OF TRICKS AND YESMEN? WHAT HE DOES IS TO DISTURB GOOD RELATIONSHIPS BY HIS WORDS.

All your previous union representatives have gone out from the union, but these were people who got the good results you have read about in these pamphlets. How then could they be men who only said 'Ndio, Bwana' and how can the employers, who have agreed to grant these good things be called Tricksters and Victimizers?

Akumu's retort, in this struggle for the loyalty of the workers, was to restate his arguments for a strong union independent of employers. In a leaflet, he asked the dockers why, if the former union leaders had been so good to the workers, it was the employers who praised them.

The union, as far as I know, is yours and you have the right of disposing of any representative at any time when you think he is worthless and should not have allowed the Employers to interfere in your Union in such matters, in the same way you don't interfere in the Port Employers' Association. WHO IS YOUR PRESENT LEADER? IS IT THE EMPLOYERS OR MYSELF? The conclusion is that, run the Union as you wish or run it as the Employers wish.

Akumu thus offered members the alternative of either following the employer or following him to build up the union. The workers' decision was never in doubt. At a general meeting on 11 May, the audience refused to listen to Francis Gathuna when Akumu gave him the floor; later, they gave the new General Secretary a vote of confidence by a show of hands.[19]

The immediate issue of victimization was resolved before the end of May, owing to several conciliatory gestures made by Akumu. He withdrew his notice of a trade dispute with the Labour Department so that the JIC could be used to settle the matter. Moreover, the union issued two leaflets in late May stating that Williams was, above all, a 'trustworthy man', who had aided the union's establishment. As a result, Williams agreed to resume his Chairmanship of the JIC.

An 'unstable truce' situation existed for the next four months. The dismissal of a clerk led to one four-day 'wild-cat' strike in June, but the union agreed to undertake the unpopular task of persuading the dockers to return to the job. While Akumu was abroad in July and August 1958, the PEA frequently complained to the union about the activities of its Vice-President, Msanifu Kombo, who allegedly used his privileged position to agitate and create unrest, rather than alleviate it. A retrogressive step was the management's cancellation of the practice whereby union representatives were permitted to collect union dues while members were still in the Port area.

After Akumu's return, he soon moved toward another confrontation with the employers. One of his first leaflets concerned wage demands that the union intended to press on the PEA. These ranged from a 64 per cent increase for *askaris* (watchmen) to a 13 per cent rise for workshop boys, with the median demand being a 47 per cent increase. As the Senior Labour Office, Coast commented, 'it would appear that "vote-catching" has not been overlooked in this claim, because it is noticeable that generally the highest increases are made up for those categories from which Mr. Akumu has the least support, i.e., *askaris* and casual workers'.[20] Another demand made in leaflets and speeches was the removal of the 'clocking-in' system for shore-handlers, a very unpopular innovation. Akumu also denounced management for revoking the union's privilege of collecting subscriptions in the Port area and for permitting 'abusive' supervisors to get away with such activities.

It was this last emotional issue that eventually destroyed the unstable truce between the union and management. On 25 September 1958, the union's newsletter asserted that 'those supervisors and Foremen who abuse human beings as grass, ape or donkey, give their names, and we will show them. Though we are after peace, if we are stirred even grass can make an elephant fall.' Five days later, work at the Port was brought to a halt by a 'wild-cat' strike, arising from the management's refusal to consider the complaints about abusive behaviour on the part of an Asian supervisor. At a JIC meeting of 2 October, called to discuss this strike, Akumu disclaimed any responsibility for it, charging that management had provoked the stoppage. 'The Union would take no part in persuading the men to return to work. The employers were attempting to make the Union a scapegoat and [he] would repeat that...the Union would not persuade the workers to resume work in the case of a strike not called by the Union.'[21] Msanifu

Kombo, the Vice-President, added that the union would undertake the unpopular task of persuading the dockers to abandon the illegal strike only if an Asian supervisor and his European superintendent were suspended for two days while charges against them were investigated. Williams and his colleagues refused. The following day, the PEA decided that it could no longer recognize the Dockworkers' Union 'as it is presently represented'.[22] Employers then set about breaking the strike themselves: a para-military force, the General Service Unit, was called to Mombasa to deal with any trouble, and a number of shop stewards were arrested for encouraging an illegal work stoppage.

The employers' decision amounted to a revocation of its recognition agreement with the union. Only if Akumu and Kombo were 'completely excluded' from all industrial negotiating machinery would the Port employers agree to re-establish recognition of the union. But it was obvious, from various general meetings and executive committee meetings, that the union stood behind Akumu. Thus, in desperation, management began to establish its own machinery for settling individual grievances in December 1958. This move was thwarted when the union managed to have its own shop stewards elected as representatives for each Section under the new scheme. Yet another response of the union was to threaten that a strike would be called in January 1959 unless the union was recognized and several wage and related demands were met. This strike notice was withdrawn in mid-January in order to give the Labour Department an opportunity to conciliate.

The basis of a sound relationship between employers and the union was established in June 1959 with the signing of a new recognition agreement. Supervised by Labour Department officials, the union's annual elections in late February 1959 had demonstrated massive support for Akumu and his colleagues. When all of the office-holders except the Treasurer were returned unopposed by approximately 4,000 union members it was abundantly clear that continued refusal to deal with Akumu was unrealistic.[23] Moreover, the Parkin Board of Inquiry into conditions at the Port had made recommendations in 1959 which, when accepted by all parties, laid the basis for relatively harmonious labour relations.[24] Prompted by this Board of Inquiry, radical changes were introduced at the Port in 1959–60, including improved working conditions, new rates of payment for overtime and shift work and the termination of casual labour employed on a daily basis. Improved conditions of employment allowed the union to temper its demands and accusations without losing its members' respect.

Hence, in the space of thirteen months, Akumu and his officials were able to forge a strong and independent union, largely on the basis of hostility to employers and wide-ranging demands. One measure of its enhanced strength was the discrepancy in the number of members attending the two consecutive Annual General Meetings. Whereas 510 attended in April 1958, approximately 4,000 voted in the elections held only ten months later.

Case 2: Union–management relations in the agricultural sector, 1964

Although the circumstances differ markedly from those obtaining in the Kilindini Docks, this case also illustrates how a moderate leader can be outflanked by a more radical challenger. The evidence suggests that the agricultural employers favoured Herman Oduor, the first General Secretary of the Kenya Plantation and Agricultural Workers' Union, because he was a reasonable and temperate man, not because he colluded with them at the expense of the workers. In fact, the sisal and tea workers won quite sizeable wage increases in 1963–4. That Oduor was an exceptional administrator can be gauged from the following commendation, contained in a letter from Mboya to Oduor in March 1961 when the latter had been General Secretary of the General Agricultural Workers' Union (GAWU): 'If all our unions could work with the same efficiency and conscientiousness, I am sure the KFL and the Labour Movement generally would advance considerably by now.'[25]

Oduor's relations with employers had nearly always been excellent. This was not surprising, given that he himself had been the assistant manager of a large European mixed farm until 1958. Indeed, Oduor would never have devoted his energies to organizing the GAWU between 1958 and 1960 if he had not felt so personally frustrated in this job.[26] An African managing a European farm in the 1950s was subject to various petty humiliations: he was paid less money than a European with comparable responsibilities; he was provided with inferior housing (Oduor was given a stable to convert into a cottage!); and he was not permitted to attend farmers' conferences (these were entirely European affairs at this time). Denied the status that was rightfully his as a manager, Oduor had turned to trade unionism as an outlet for his talents and leadership abilities. But his stint as a manager had enabled him to appreciate the farmers' point of view. GAWU was the epitome of moderation. Oduor had selected as the other national office-holders men like himself who spoke English and held responsible positions on European farms. The recognition agreement, which came into effect in February 1961, had committed the union to pursue the peaceful settlement of all disputes and to resort to strikes only after a lengthy period of negotiation and conciliation. In practice, the union had only called one strike – and this had been terminated after two days for 'humanistic reasons' (the cows' udders would soon have burst!).[27] While there were many other 'wild-cat' strikes, the union had never supported these. Furthermore, the General Secretary had been willing to transfer any of his branch secretaries who offended European farmers by their 'irresponsible' actions. His view had been that more concessions could be extracted from employers through co-operative rather than antagonistic relations. Judging by the negligible gains won for farm labourers (in contrast to the substantial gains won for the higher categories of employees) in 1960–3, the validity of this view is doubtful.

European farmers had reacted predictably. They had initially been extremely hostile to the formation of a union liable to undermine their paternal-istic relationship with their labourers. But Oduor's organizational efforts had soon received the support of two very influential Europeans, Lord Delamere and the Senior Labour Officer, Nakuru, who persuaded most farmers that, since trade unionism was inevitable, their interests lay in backing a moderate like Oduor before he was replaced by a firebrand. Hence, the new General Secretary had quickly established cordial relations with the farmers' association, the Kenya National Farmers' Union. Com-menting on this relationship, the Labour Department's *Annual Report, 1961* was unusually lavish in its praise, noting the 'high sense of responsibility shown by the leaders of both organizations...'. The monthly reports of the District Commissioner, Nakuru, also reveal the employers' sympathy for the union. In late 1961, for example, this officer had reported that 'the GAWU is being kept afloat mainly by the efforts of some farmers who do not wish to see it sink without a trace. With extraordinary incompetence, they [the Union] even seem unable to take advantage of the offer of many farmers to collect union fees for them.'[28]

The Plantation and Agricultural Workers' Union was formed in August 1963 by the amalgamation of three unions, GAWU, the Tea Plantation Workers' Union and the Sisal and Coffee Plantation Workers' Union. As the omnibus union had only been created because of the determination of Herman Oduor, it is not surprising he was selected the first General Secretary. That the agricultural employers welcomed Oduor's appointment is clear. A resolution passed by the Federation of Kenya Employers' Standing Committee of the Rural Employers in November 1963 asserted that 'the Federation and members concerned should give what support they could to the leadership of the present General Secretary.' This was felt to be necessary because the union was facing 'many divisive influences and centrifugal forces'.[29]

By June 1964 a campaign emerged within the Plantation Union to oust Oduor, organized mainly by Kikuyu (Oduor was Luo), and linked to the current struggle for pre-eminence between the Kenya Federation of Labour and the Kenya Federation of Progressive Trade Unions (KFPTU). While the incumbent General Secretary was a firm supporter of the KFL, his main opponent, the militant former General Secretary of the Sisal and Coffee Plantation Workers' Union, had accepted aid from the KFPTU. Several of Oduor's other prominent Kikuyu opponents were careful to keep a foot in both camps, so as not to create enemies unnecessarily.

Fearing the deleterious effect that the emergence of Oduor's opponent as General Secretary would have on industrial relations in the coffee industry, the Kenya Coffee Growers' Association became 'very uneasy' regarding 'undesirable, undercover activities within the union'. They remembered only too well how the challenger had exploited the grievances of their Kikuyu coffee workers, both political and economic, to build himself up in 1962. Thus, in early July 1964 the Association presented a memorandum to

Oduor and 'the Government' explaining 'what was going on, by whom, and where. We stated that in our opinion the weight and nature of the well-financed opposition being constructed against Mr. Oduor would defeat him unless he received considerable help urgently.'[30]

The European employers' obvious solicitude for Oduor's predicament was extremely embarrassing for him. It merely lent weight to his opponent's charge that the General Secretary was 'in the pockets of the employers'.[31] Consequently, Oduor felt compelled to assert his independence by issuing the following inflammatory statement in late July:

> The union gave notice that all Europeans of British nationality who owned farms were to 'pack up and go'. Their farms would be taken over by the workers. Non-co-operation, go-slows and strikes would be carried out from the 20th of August onwards, and farming for the British people would be made impossible. The unemployment consequent upon the mass-deportation would be welcomed by the union.[32]

When questioned by the Chairman of the Coffee Growers' Association about his motives for issuing such a statement, Oduor apparently replied that he 'had to do it'.[33]

None the less, Oduor was ousted in a 'palace coup' on 27 August, while he was out of the country. Since his principal opponent was visiting the USA at the time, another Kikuyu, Christopher Wachira, became General Secretary after a factional encounter lasting about two months.

It is difficult to assess how significant the charge of collusion with employers was in Oduor's defeat. There was an obvious tribal dimension to the struggle for power in that Oduor's supporters were mainly Luo and Luhya, whereas the opposition was largely Kikuyu and Meru. Moreover, it must be remembered that factional struggles in this union involve national and branch officials almost exclusively, with little involvement by the rank-and-file membership. From all accounts, the branch officials – especially the full-time branch secretary/treasurers – are much more concerned with being on the winning side than with questions of principle. Yet, suspicion of European employers is pervasive in certain rural areas of the country, particularly in Central Province.[34] One can only conclude, therefore, that the employers' clear sympathy for the moderate Oduor was an added liability for him.

The strike weapon

In the light of these internal pressures toward union militancy, how have union leaders employed the strike weapon? Strikes can be very effective in mobilizing the workers' support for both a union and its leadership, in addition to intimidating recalcitrant employers. Union officials, particularly before the establishment of the 'check-off' system, frequently provoked strikes as a means of arousing workers to the point where they would join the union or pay their subscriptions. Strikes also gave these leaders the opportunity to present themselves as the fearless champions of the down-trodden. As well, opponents during factional encounters sometimes engineered work stoppages in order to mobilize and demonstrate their power and force employers to recognize them as the official leaders. Of course, a challenger could only successfully employ this tactic when the loyalty of the workers to the incumbent leaders was weak, and when machinery for the resolution of disputes either did not exist or was not understood. Factionally inspired industrial disturbances thus generally occurred in the more poorly organized unions before any single leader had managed to consolidate his authority. In the present sample the most obvious cases in which these circumstances initially existed were the unions catering for agricultural workers and those in the widely scattered quarries and building sites.[35]

As legal restrictions on the right to strike were made increasingly stringent after 1964 (see Chapter 2), trade unionists had to take greater personal risks in advocating work stoppages. Such restriction has now reached the point where an Assistant Minister can publicly assert that 'if I had my own way I would curb the question of strikes for ten years. Any trade union calling a strike when there are so many people hungry in the countryside – I would lock them up.'[36]

Given this conflict between internal union pressure toward militancy and external governmental pressure toward peaceful settlement, what has been the outcome in terms of work stoppages? Table 13, indicating a quite remarkable lowering of the incidence of strikes since 1965, suggests that the government's firmness on this matter has met with success. There are now few strikes, and those that do occur rarely last more than two days. Of course, the ruling elite's determination to eliminate strikes is likely only partly inspired by calculations of the economic losses they occasion. Strikes not only 'cost the nation output, the workers wages, the companies profits and the government taxes': they may also threaten the position of the ruling elite. While the formal sector of the economy employs a relatively small number of people, it contributes a substantial proportion of the national income. A government that has assumed responsibility for economic growth looks ineffective if it allows the most strategic section of the economy to be paralysed by strikes. Strikes, furthermore, introduce an element of uncertainty. It is never entirely clear how far industrial unrest will spread in dependent capitalist countries, or whether direct action will be limited solely to peaceful picketing against employers. Restricting the right to strike thus neutralizes one of the union leader's most important *political* resources.

The injunction against strikes has required adjustment in the behaviour of union leaders. One aspect of their adaptation to new circumstances is their skilful use of the strike threat. While dutifully following the various stages and procedures for the peaceful settlement of disputes through negotiation, conciliation by the Labour Ministry and arbitration by the Industrial Court, union leaders frequently resort to dramatic announcements about impending

Table 13. *Work stoppages, Kenya, 1962–70*

Year	No. of stoppages	No. of workers involved	No. of lost man-days
1962	285	132,433	745,799
1963	230	54,428	235,349
1964	267	56,011	167,767
1965	200	105,602	345,855
1966	155	42,967	127,632
1967	138	29,985	109,128
1968	93	20,426	47,979
1969	124	37,641	87,516
1970	84	18,941	49,517

SOURCE: Kenya, *Statistical Abstract, 1971.*

strikes. Their hope is both to placate members and branch officials who demand action, and to prod a lethargic Ministry of Labour into processing a trade dispute which may have remained unresolved for months. While no statistics on the frequency of strike threats exist, one has the distinct impression, bolstered by a perusal of the local newspapers, that dire threats reach a peak just before the unions' national elections. Of course, nearly all such strike notices are revoked at the last minute 'in order to give the Ministry of Labour a final chance to resolve the dispute'. But a union leader can only revoke so many strike threats before he loses his credibility with his members. This is another aspect of the dilemmas trade unionists face.

Another facet of the union leaders' adjustment to the government's firm stand is tacit support for and even organization of 'wild-cat' strikes. Although 'wild-cat' tendencies were not more pronounced in 1972 than earlier, such a trend is likely if restrictions on union activities increase further. Trade unionists, management representatives and Ministry of Labour officials were unanimous in pointing to dismissals of popular workers and alleged abusive behaviour on the part of expatriate supervisors as the two most frequent causes of unofficial work stoppages. Since such stoppages are often led by shop stewards and result from a deep seated sense of grievance, a union's leaders really have no choice but to support the strike unofficially. To denounce the strike as 'illegal' and order the workers to return to the job would brand the leader involved as a flunkey of an unpopular employer or of the government.[37] But, in the view of many employers and officials of the Labour Ministry, the refusal of union leaders to prevent or condemn illegal work stoppages is evidence of irresponsibility.

Wage restraint?

Although the government announced an incomes policy in late 1969 and translated it into legislative form in the Trade Disputes (Amendment) Act, 1971, the sections of this Act relating to wage control had not yet been brought into effect by the middle of 1973. The ruling elite thus had to rely on exhortation of trade unionists and on the good sense of the Industrial Court to limit wage increases in the late 1960s and early 1970s. Unions, in the absence of appropriate legislation, were assigned the unenviable task of restraining their members' demands.

The key to the incomes policy is the government's justifiable concern over the worsening problem of urban unemployment. Although no official statistics on the extent of the problem have been available since 1960, unemployment is manifestly endemic in Kenya. The Labour Department, which first alluded to the problem of 'idlers and unemployed' in its *Annual Report, 1941*, has periodically remarked on its magnitude. The hostility generated by widespread unemployment is reflected in newspaper reports, such as the following one in 1970: 'In Mombasa fighting broke out among a crowd of more than 4,000 and six people were taken to the Coast General Hospital with injuries received after police had charged a section of the crowd which smashed its way into the Labour Office in Nkrumah Road where the unskilled were being registered.' Kenya's predicament is further illustrated by an issue of *African Development*, devoted in part to a survey of Kenya's economy in 1970, which began with an article entitled '1970 – A Golden Year' and ended with one called 'Unemployment: The National Obsession'.[38] The government's concern over the problem is indicated by its appointment in 1970 of a Parliamentary Select Committee on Unemployment to gather views on possible solutions, and its request to the International Labour Organization for a team of experts to study the question in 1972.

A final indicator of unemployment is the number of people who registered under the two 'Tripartite Agreements for the Immediate Relief of Unemployment', which were in force from February 1964 to April 1965, and from July 1970 to June 1971. These agreements, 'voluntarily' signed on behalf of the government, the Federation of Kenya Employers and the appropriate trade union federation, provided, as previously mentioned, for all employers to take on an extra ten per cent of employees in exchange for a one-year standstill in wage increases and a strike ban. During March-April 1964, no less than 205,051 men and women reportedly registered for employment under the first agreement at the five major urban centres.[39] Approximately 291,000 people registered as unemployed in June-July 1970 as the prelude to the second agreement. Of course, these figures represent only a very rough estimate of unemployment because, on the one hand, considerable numbers of unemployed, particularly women, did not register in the four or five days available and, on the other, some of those who registered already had jobs but hoped to find better-paid positions under the agreement.[40] Still, it is worth noting that 291,000 unemployed would represent about 46 per cent of all the people currently employed in the 'modern' sector of the economy, where trade unions concentrate their attention. One survey of eight urban areas in Kenya concluded that the unemployment rate in towns was about 17 per cent of the total labour force.[41]

In this difficult situation, the government can advert to convincing economic arguments in support of its policy to restrict urban wages. Economists are broadly in agreement, though not unanimous, about the detrimental economic effects of relatively high wages in a poor country. First, rapid increases in real wages encourage employers to economize on labour, perhaps by substituting capital for labour, thus either reducing total employment or limiting its expansion. Second, rapid increases in real urban wages enlarge the gap between rural and urban incomes, thus stimulating high rates of rural–urban migration and aggravating the unemployment problem. Harris and Todaro have developed a persuasive mathematical model which stresses the interaction of two variables – the rural–urban income differential and the probability of obtaining an urban job – in determining the rate and magnitude of rural–urban migration.[42] Apropos this income gap in Kenya, a commission appointed by the government claimed that the average African wage-earner in 1965 earned twice as much total income and ten times as much money income as the average small farmer.[43] The urban–rural differential is compounded, moreover, by the urban workers' fringe benefits and relatively secure income and his access to a higher quality and greater range of social services than are available in most rural areas. Third, economists often claim that high wages in the 'modern' sector militate against economic growth by diminishing resources available for capital accumulation. A high-wage economy, it is argued, prevents the rate of economic growth from attaining its potential maximum, thereby limiting the expansion of employment in the long run.

Union leaders confronted with these arguments usually react by denying their validity. They are especially scornful of the notion that organized labour constitutes a privileged and selfish segment of the population standing in the way of employment creation and economic development. While their objections generally lack conceptual elegance, they are often not without a foundation in common sense. Anyone believing that urban workers are a privileged group should drive in Nairobi from those areas where most politicians, top businessmen, higher civil servants and economists reside (such as Westlands and Karen) to an area where many semi-skilled and unskilled workers live (such as Pumwani). Urban–rural income comparisons are notoriously difficult to perform.[44] Although some urban workers earn ten times as much as some peasants, they also have vaster responsibilities and expenses. Price levels vary enormously between rural and urban areas. Food supplied at little cost in the countryside fetches high prices in the cities. High rents force urban workers into overcrowded and sometimes unsanitary accommodation. Transportation to the place of work and fuel are further expenses for the urban dweller. Furthermore, workers in Kenya, as in other African countries, have accepted responsibility for providing for unemployed kinsmen in the city and assisting their families in the rural areas. One large-scale survey of 2,148 adult males in medium and high density areas of Nairobi discovered that, in December 1970, 23 per cent of the net income of all respondents had been transferred to the rural areas.[45] Similar findings have been reported for Ghanaian and Senegalese industrial workers.[46] On the basis of obligatory expenditures such as these, one authority has contended that 'the higher income of the urban dweller is...more apparent than real'. Consequently, it is 'increasingly apparent that the nutritional problems of Africans in urban and peri-urban areas are as bad as, if not worse than, those encountered in the rural areas'.[47]

The intent of these remarks is not to refute the overriding importance of the economic motive in rural–urban migration, confirmed in survey after survey. A job provides a money income, no matter how small, and this opens up new opportunities both for the worker and his children. Even in countries where real urban wages have declined – such as Ghana – people continue to crowd into cities seeking work. But the avidity of the job-seekers should not obscure the fact that the urban worker's life is still a hard one. And while the idea of narrowing the rural–urban earnings differential is commendable in principle, the ones who would probably suffer the most from its implementation are the unskilled and semi-skilled urban wage-earners. This is the case because it is much easier to suppress wage increases in the small 'modern' sector than to raise incomes in the large agricultural sector. To create an equilibrium between job-seekers and available jobs, wages would have to be low indeed. In political terms, one must doubt whether a country like Kenya possesses the requisite means of coercion to impose sacrifices on a strategically located working class, as the European countries did in the nineteenth century. In economic terms, a low-wage economy would have the undesirable effect of undermining labour stability and commitment, thereby reducing the quality and efficiency of labour. Since labour is not a homogeneous entity, it cannot be treated like any other factor of production whose supply will be forthcoming in the right amount at a given price.[48] But even if one could argue that economic growth in the early stages can only proceed at the expense of the workers, there is still the question of social justice. Should workers be expected to acquiesce in their own impoverishment, especially when the small political class and bourgeoisie are steadily augmenting their own comfortable standard of living?

Kenyan union leaders clearly believe not. They continue to aim at high wage and related gains for members in spite of both the economic arguments and the government's admonitions. They could hardly do otherwise: their interests in maintaining their own positions and in holding or creating a large membership push them toward embracing the traditional economism of unions. As one authority has succinctly remarked in the context of British trade unionism, 'trade union officials who can regularly announce wage increases need fear nothing from...members'.[49]

Publicly Kenyan trade unionists have not been recalcitrant on the question of wage restraint. Since 1970 they have indicated their willingness to accept wage controls, provided a number of conditions were met. But these provisos have been so wide-ranging as to suggest that their implementation would require a thorough restructuring of both economy and society. Consider, for instance, the recommendations of COTU's seminar on a wages and incomes policy, held in Nairobi in May 1971. The participants, twenty-five leaders of national unions, accepted the government's call for wage restraint, 'provided that such a sacrifice by us is accompanied with the following': a programme of redistributing income in favour of the poorer strata through the use of a reformed tax system, an increase in the price of agricultural products and the introduction of certain free social services; a programme of job creation supported by the excess profits generated by wage restraint and dependent upon official encouragement of labour-intensive productive technologies; an upward revision of minimum wages in response to increases in the cost of living; a system of controlling profits, prices and rents as well as wages; and a provision that workers would be represented on all public bodies authorized to implement the incomes policy, including the body that determines the wage 'guidelines'.[50]

Until the government meets these conditions or employs more coercion against unions, labour leaders will persist in placing their members' short-run interests before the vaguer but officially articulated public interest. Their orientation is evidenced by their persistent pursuit of high wage increases and by their un-co-operative stand on 'voluntary' short-term agreements to create employment through wage freezes.

Consider, first, wage increases. The average earnings of Africans certainly rose precipitously in the decade 1960–70, especially in the earlier years. Table 14 indicates that African average earnings rose from K£68.3 in 1960 to K£182.5 in 1970, an increase of about 167 per cent over ten years.[51] These figures cannot, of course, be taken as a measure of the rise in the wages of the manual workers for whom unions mainly cater. Africanization of top posts in the public and private sectors as well as the upgrading of African employees have contributed considerably to the increase in average earnings. The exact effect of these factors on earnings is difficult to gauge, as no data on the distribution of African earnings amongst the various occupations has been available since 1960. One study of wage increases granted by the Industrial Court between its creation in 1964 and 1967 and by four firms claimed that wages for urban, unskilled workers increased at a rate of approximately 10 per cent per annum between 1960 and 1966.[52] As the wage-earners' cost of living index rose by a total of only 14 per cent in the same period, this author concluded that the real income of urban manual workers rose by the high rate of approximately 8 per cent per annum during

Table 14. *Average earnings per African employee, 1960–70*

Year	Average earnings (K£)	Percentage increase
1960	68.3	9.3
1961	76.0	11.3
1962	80.1	5.4
1963	94.6	18.1
1964	110.8	Non-comparable
1965	126.6	14.3
1966	149.3	17.9
1967	158.4	6.1
1968	168.7	6.5
1969	173.7	3.0
1970	182.5	5.1

SOURCE: Compiled from Kenya's *Statistical Abstract, 1969* and *1971*. (Note that since there was an improved coverage of employers in 1964, the figures before and after this date are not comparable.)

this period. This rate probably declined somewhat after 1967, owing largely to restraint on the part of the Industrial Court.

One way of determining the maximum rate of wage increase for manual workers is the analysis of wage rates in 'pace-setting' firms. These are firms that influence wage levels throughout the economy. Owing to their oligopolistic or monopolistic position, they are able to pass on the cost of wage increases to the consumers. Since they are typically large-scale, highly capital-intensive enterprises requiring considerable entrepreneurial ability, new firms with lower costs can rarely establish themselves and drive the higher-cost firms out of business. One such pace-setter in Kenya is the largely foreign-owned petroleum refining and distribution industry, which has usually led the field in wages and fringe benefits. By May 1967 (when the third collective agreement between the oil companies and the Petroleum Oil Workers' Union was signed), employees worked a 40- or 45-hour week and received 30 days' annual paid leave, paid maternity leave, religious holidays, leave for trade union conferences, 60 days' yearly paid sick leave, free medical treatment, shift differentials, leave allowances, housing subsidies and allowances, redundancy payments and long-service increments.

However, as Table 15 shows, wage increases for manual workers have not been too remarkable. Over the period 1963–75, the money wages of a 'general hand' will have increased 87.3 per cent, at a cumulative annual rate of under 6 per cent. The annual increase in real wages is under 4 per cent, since one has to reckon on an annual rise in the cost of living of at least 2 per cent. It should be noted, moreover, that the wages of 'general hands' were chosen in order deliberately to *overstate* the annual increments. Employees

Table 15. *Wage increments for 'general hands', oil industry,*
Kenya, January 1963–January 1975

Year	Wage (KSh)	Percentage increase
1963	231.28	
1965	249.28	7.8
1967	297.92	19.5
1969	319.48	7.2
1971	339.08	6.1
1973	370.44	9.2
1975	433.16	16.9

SOURCE: Compiled from information supplied by the Joint Industrial Council of the Oil Industry, Nairobi.

in the oil industry are classified into four 'staff' categories and ten grades of 'operatives'; of these, only one 'operative' grade received higher proportional increases than the 'general hands'. This was the lowest grade, in which labourers serve during their initial three-month probationary period. The other categories and grades received closer to an annual rate of increase of 2 or 3 per cent in money terms. In addition to their basic wage, all 'operatives' have received since 1967 a housing allowance and subsidy of KSh70, and possibly a long-service increment.

Manual workers in the oil industry do about as well as or better than comparable grades in the other pace-setting firms and industries. Other pace-setters include the East African Cargo Handling Services (at the Kilindini docks), the brewing and tobacco firms, banks and the foreign-owned chemical companies. The dockers, for example, have won a higher rate of increase in their monthly wages than the workers in the oil industry, but they have not done as well as the latter in terms of fringe benefits. Although dockers achieved a cumulative annual rate of increase of just over 8 per cent between January 1961 and January 1971, the highest proportional increases were won in the early part of the decade.[53] By 1972 a manual worker in the oil industry received a slightly higher wage (inclusive of housing allowance and subsidy) than a docker. In practice, however, dockers normally earn far above their basic monthly wage owing to their unique opportunities for overtime work. All the workers in the pace-setting firms do better – in some cases far better – than other urban workers employed by unionized establishments.

While there are discrepancies in the rates of pay of urban workers, these are overshadowed by the wage differential between organized workers in the urban and agricultural sectors. It is difficult, of course, to compare the merits of urban employment as opposed to work on an estate or farm which pays a low wage but provides free housing and a plot of land for each family.

Conditions are best in the large, foreign-owned plantation enterprises. These tend to be highly organized undertakings, with large numbers of labourers and a small number of specialized and skilled men employed on standardized rates and supervised in somewhat the same way as industrial workers. The larger tea, sisal, coffee and sugar plantations and estates provide housing (of varying standards); some of the best, especially tea estates, also provide primary schools, dispensaries, recreation grounds and clubs or a social hall. The smaller ones generally offer only rudimentary facilities and welfare activities.

Owing to the poor and often oscillating world price for primary products, the plantation unions have not been very successful in boosting the wages of their members. The world market for sisal was so poor in the 1960s that the plantation union had to accept a seven-year moratorium on wage increases just to avoid bankrupting the remaining sisal estates. In 1970 the tea employers led the other agricultural employers in terms of wages and fringe benefits. But even a tea labourer's monthly wage, at KSh111, was less than one-third of that of a general hand in the oil industry.

In short, while 'modern'-sector urban wages have risen much higher than agricultural wages, the annual rate of increase of real urban wages has been far from spectacular. It is unclear, moreover, how much credit – or blame, depending on your viewpoint – should accrue to unions for the general rise in urban wages. One study of the determinants of wage levels in Kenya did conclude that 'unionism is the principal cause of high wages in the modern sector'.[54] This conclusion is apparently based on finding a significant union–non-union wage differential – a wage advantage of 30 per cent in private industry and 11 per cent in government employment. But this evidence poses the famous question of the chicken and the egg: did strong unions force wage rates up in firms they organized, or did strong unions emerge in firms which were best placed economically and most willing to pay higher wages? If the latter proposition is closer to the truth, as I suspect, then one would expect the unionized sector to pay higher wages regardless of union pressure. The brief comparative analysis of wage rates engaged in above suggested that success or failure in obtaining material gains for workers depended much more on the financial position of the firm than on the union's bargaining power. The oil industry and the Cargo Handling Services both offered the best terms and conditions of service because they could most afford to; additionally, in the case of the oil companies, head office policy dictated that the local subsidiaries should act as model employers. Aside from these factors, minimum wage laws have contributed to wage increases in some of the more dispersed industries which unions find difficult to organize.

Whatever the part actually played by unions in wage determination, union leaders have not hesitated to claim credit for all wage advances. This, as I have already mentioned, is one indication of their economism. Another indication is their unco-operative attitude toward short-term policies to relieve unemployment, where such schemes require sacrifices on the part of organized labour.

Union leaders have usually refused to acknowledge any relationships between their demands for higher wages and increasing unemployment. Denis Akumu, the Secretary-General of COTU, articulated the unions' viewpoint on unemployment in a speech to the National Assembly in 1970. After an Assistant Minister suggested that unions accede to another 'Tripartite Agreement' whereby 10 per cent more jobs would be created in exchange for a wage standstill, Akumu introduced a motion noting that such an agreement was unacceptable to the workers, 'employed or unemployed', and urging the government to find a permanent solution to unemployment. He argued convincingly that the National Assembly was hardly in a position to recommend a wage freeze for urban workers, some of whom earned as little as KSh150 per month, when M.P.s had awarded themselves wage increases totalling 300 per cent since independence. Less convincingly, he argued that only private employers would benefit from a wage pause, since they would prefer to use the money saved through wage increases foregone to take higher profits rather than to create new jobs. His own solutions to unemployment were the rapid Africanization of all jobs held by non-citizens and greater control of private enterprise with the aim of encouraging recalcitrant employers to increase job opportunities.[55]

Despite these sentiments, the trade union movement has entered into two pacts with the government and the Federation of Kenya Employers requiring a temporary wage freeze. While the leaders of individual unions expressed distaste for both Tripartite Agreements, the trade union federation, under pressure from the political authorities, signed them. Popular expectations regarding the economic benefits to be derived from *Uhuru* were high immediately following independence in December 1963, while the economy was in a slump, owing mainly to foreign investors' uncertainty about the intentions of the new African government. Government leaders thus proposed to use the Tripartite Agreement in 1964–5 to help bridge the gap between expectations and the economy's capability to fulfil them by providing an extra 40,000 jobs. Clement Lubembe, the Secretary-General of the KFL at the time, was particularly vulnerable to political pressure on this matter owing to his close relations with Tom Mboya, the government's spokesman on the 'Tripartite Committee', and his position as a newly-elected KANU Senator for Nairobi. In addition, sacrifice, in the first few months of independence, could more readily be justified to workers as a patriotic duty than in later years when the new political–bureaucratic elite had entrenched its privileges. Also, the agreement was made more palatable to union leaders by the inclusion of assurances that no union member would be permitted to opt out of his 'check-off' agreement during the life of the pact, and that the authority of existing union leaders would be assisted by the official discouragement of 'splinter unions'.[56]

It is difficult to assess the success of the first agreement. Although the

Ministry of Labour claimed that 38,307 workers were engaged under its terms, one does not know how many of these would have been hired in any case, or how many employees were laid off at the termination of the agreement. What is clear is that many union leaders vociferously rebelled against the pact, denouncing employers and the government for not fulfilling their part of the bargain and threatening and carrying through strike action in support of wage and other demands. Although strikes were forbidden, the total work-stoppages in 1964 numbered 267 and involved 56,011 workers, as compared with 230 strikes involving 54,428 workers during the previous year. However, the work stoppages were of shorter duration in 1964 than a year earlier, so that the total man-days lost was 167,767 as compared with 235,349 in 1963.

Designed to create 50,000 new jobs as a token of the government's concern over unemployment, the second Tripartite Agreement ran for twelve months from July 1970. It was unilaterally announced by President Kenyatta in his *Madaraka* (Internal Self-Government) Day speech on 1 June, and only later did representatives of employers and labour sign the pact. Again, most union leaders outside COTU were openly hostile to the proposal; only after two extended meetings of general secretaries at COTU's Solidarity Building was agreement reached to accept the *fait accompli*. If President Kenyatta had not personally announced the agreement, it would probably not have been signed for, as Denis Akumu later commented, 'it was only respect trade unionists and workers had for President Kenyatta and Mr. Mwendwa [the Labour Minister] that created the climate of industrial relations which made the agreement possible.'[57] A refusal by COTU to sign the agreement would have been perceived as an affront to the President, with possible dire consequences for top COTU leaders and for the union movement as a whole.

Both union leaders and ordinary workers soon showed their dissatisfaction with this agreement. Denunciations of employers and threats of strike action were soon rife. There were many 'wild-cat' strikes, though the union leadership felt constrained from supporting these publicly by the Trade Disputes Act, 1965, which gave the Labour Minister the power to declare strikes illegal and impose penalties on their perpetrators. Trade unionists were especially irritated that, while they were denied wage increases, M.P.s and superscale civil servants received pay rises in January 1971. Union leaders generally chafed under the restraints of the agreement; how could they retain their members and their personal support if they were unable to produce demonstrable results?

8. Militant economism (2)

I have so far explored two of the specific dilemmas that confront union leaders in interpreting their unions' economic role. I now continue this analysis by examining further fundamental decisions trade unionists must make in reconciling the short-term interests of their members with governmental demands. In light of the earlier discussions about the insecurity of union leadership and the vulnerability of unions as institutions, we can well understand why union leaders persistently place a high priority on their members' interests.

Grievance articulation or disciplinary agent?

In numerous addresses to union audiences (especially trade union seminars) the Labour Minister, some of his colleagues and civil servants have requested national and branch officials to assume more responsibility for shaping their members' attitude toward work. Unions should 'educate' workers in the necessity for hard work and obedience to both supervisors and the established procedures in order to increase production. In practice, however, trade unionists have largely ignored this disciplinary role in favour of articulating and pursuing the workers' grievances against management. But they have not acted irresponsibly. Most of them have sought to ensure that shop stewards and branch officials follow the agreed stages in dispute-settlement. They have also occasionally counselled hard work. For instance, when the dockers' general secretary tours the port area, he may unexpectedly join a gang of shore-handlers in moving a cargo, urging them on to greater effort. The rationale he offers for such advice is a very pragmatic one: higher productivity enhances the union's bargaining power in the next round of negotiations with management. The orientation is explicitly consumptionist.

Most grievances never reach the general secretary; they are resolved on the shop floor or in the office or in the fields by the shop stewards. Although these low-level leaders play an important part in the unions' activities, few constitutions make any provision for them. Their duties and responsibilities are usually set forth only in the recognition agreement between a union and an employer. Consequently, there are often no established rules governing either their tenure in office or procedures for their election. Shop stewards may be elected annually, biennially or triennially or at no set period, either by a show of hands or secret ballot. This lack of procedure has usually meant that a shop steward who gets out of touch with the workers is immediately replaced by them. Many national union leaders complain, in fact, about the high turnover of shop stewards which retards the growth of an experienced and reliable lower level leadership. In practice, top union leaders complain that shop stewards tend to assume that the workers are always in the right, thus occasionally embarrassing the head office which is held responsible for the activities of shop stewards. Grass-roots democracy ensures that low-level leaders are close to the rank-and-file both in occupational status and attitudes toward work and the employers. Their militancy necessarily acts as a prod to branch and national officials as long as unions remain dependent on the rank-and-file.

Internal union pressures thus encourage office-holders not only to emphasize the wage-determination function previously discussed, but also to pursue individual and group grievances with alacrity. Indeed, it is doubtful that wage increases are the highest priority for workers in underdeveloped countries with high unemployment and a history of acrid industrial relations. Allen, who helped organize the plantation and mining ùnions in Uganda and Tanganyika, has suggested, for instance, that East African workers 'showed most concern for the failure of managers and employers to treat them as human beings: often they complained about abusive treatment. Next, they wanted improved medical facilities, then better accommodation, and, lastly, higher wages.'[1] Warmington, in his detailed study of the Cameroons Development Corporation Workers' Union, discovered that the workers considered their individual grievances – especially the sacking of an employee without apparent reason – as crucial in their estimation of the union. 'When union officials act promptly and energetically on receipt of a complaint, there is every reason to be grateful to them, and hence to be willing to pay such reasonable dues as are demanded in return.'[2] The evidence suggests that Kenyan workers regard as critical the same kinds of grievances as their brothers in Uganda, Tanzania and Nigeria. Since strikes in Kenya have become so fraught with difficulties and dangers over the past few years, the causes of the short ones that have been undertaken should provide some indication of the most deeply felt issues in industrial relations. As the statistics in Table 16 show, there have been more strikes over dismissals of employees than over wage and salary disputes. In addition, more strikes occurred in some years over alleged victimization and abusive behaviour on the part of expatriate supervisors than over wage questions. Also important in a period of Africanization and upgrading of African skills is the question of the classification and grading of employees. The overriding importance of job security as an issue is further and even more strikingly demonstrated by the statistics on trade disputes. Of the 765 trade disputes declared by unions to the Ministry of Labour between July 1969 and August 1972, 68 per cent related to dismissals while only 11 per cent concerned terms and conditions of service![3]

Impressionistic evidence also leads to the conclusion that the grievances just discussed are the most salient ones from the workers' point of view.

Table 16. *Causes of strikes, Kenya, 1969–72 (percentages)*

	1969 (n = 131)	1970 (n = 82)	1971 (n = 75)	1972, until July 20 (n = 61)
Wages and salaries	25	12	23	12
Dismissals	26	18	11	23
Redundancy	0	1	4	0
Alleged victimization or abuse of workers	11	28	19	23
Task*	12	18	15	12
Classification and grading of employees	5	3	5	15
Refusal to recognize union	6	6	3	3
Allowances (e.g. for housing)	3	0	8	2
Non-payment of wages	3	3	4	2
Rations	1	0	0	0
Miscellaneous (e.g. severance pay; conversion from casual to permanent employment; challenges to managerial prerogatives)	8	11	8	10
Cause unclear	0	0	1	0
Total†	100	100	101	102

* 'Task' refers to disputes involving agricultural workers over the proper task they must complete (e.g. volume of coffee berries; footage of sugar cane) before they get credit for a day's pay.
† Totals do not equal 100 because of rounding.
SOURCE: Compiled from data supplied by the Ministry of Labour, Nairobi.

Why are these the issues which an astute union leader must be careful to monopolize?

Workers' dignity

The existence of antagonism between employers and employees is natural, especially in the early period of trade unionism. But where management and supervisors are largely European or Asian while the relatively lowly paid workers are African, a further ethnic dimension is added to the primary conflict of economic interests.[4] Hostility and suspicion can be expected to be even more intense when the alien employers are (or were) associated with colonial rule and frequently regard themselves as culturally or occasionally racially superior to their employees.

Conducted by European chairmen, several boards of inquiry into trade disputes since 1960 have alluded to discrimination on the basis of race as a cause of industrial disturbances. An investigation into labour unrest at Macalder–Nyanza Mines during 1962–3 revealed, for instance, that the basic cause of unrest was management's failure to pay adequate attention to the 'human factor'.[5] The Board noted that, in the course of a single year, one European manager was dismissed for striking a worker, three senior supervisors were officially reprimanded for using abusive langage and a Labour Ministry investigator had recommended the immediate transfer of a personnel officer. Allegations of similar conduct towards subordinates by two other heads of department were still under investigation. In addition, the Board claimed that the company's policy of awarding salaries on the basis of race rather than occupational status, together with its slow pace of Africanization, were further reasons for discontent. Another Board, investigating a trade dispute in the sugar plantations in 1962, made a similar point in its report. It noted that, in the largest companies, the racial structure was clear-cut, with very few Africans earning over KSh200 and nearly all the senior posts filled by Asians. 'Such a situation is bound to lead to frustration and resentment, and this certainly was the case.'[6] A Board inquiring into industrial relations in the Nairobi City Council also discovered that the attitudes of certain European officers to their subordinates was 'harmful to good industrial relations'.[7]

Maltreatment of African workers by European and Asian supervisors is an extremely emotional grievance, one that union leaders must take care to articulate. It is, in fact, an allegation frequently voiced by many trade unions, both agricultural and urban. In the agricultural industries, charges of racialist attitudes on the part of management and of 'abusing' workers are most frequently raised in the sugar and coffee industries, where labour relations have always been most strained. Many of the 'wild-cat' strikes in these industries have been caused by such allegations.[8]

Amongst most urban-based unions, charges that employers have abused African workers have also been common. These have most frequently been voiced by officials of the Railway Union, Dockworkers' Union and Distributive Workers' Union, though the frequency has diminished with the Africanization of many top management positions. The Railway Union, for example, called its first and longest strike (nineteen days) in November 1959 over the charge that a white building superintendent had beaten his African subordinates.[9] Significantly, almost all African railway employees walked out, though the trains were kept running by European and Asian staff aided by European volunteers. During the period of Walter Ottenyo's tenure as General Secretary of the Railway Union (between December 1961 and March 1966), he occasionally referred ominously to a 'black list' of European and Asian members of the railways administration who had insulted Africans or displayed a 'colonial attitude'. He claimed that the union was seeking to have these officers Africanized 'immediately', and threatened that the union would have to resort to a mysterious 'Master Plan' if the administration proved intransigent.[10]

Africanization and 'Brotherization'

Allegations that some expatriates insult their African subordinates lend force to continual union demands for rapid Africanization and an end to racial salary scales. The latter demand was granted by both public and private undertakings before independence in 1963. Africanization, of course, is a popular issue not only because of the emotional satisfaction of seeing the members of one's 'own' group move into higher positions, but also because African employees in clerical, skilled and semi-skilled grades are in a position to benefit directly from such a policy. As the bulk of part-time branch and national officials are usually drawn from these grades, they are unlikely to endorse leaders who fail to press aggressively for more rapid Africanization.

Almost invariably, as soon as substantial Africanization has been achieved in a particular enterprise or industry, union leaders begin to denounce the Africans who assumed the higher positions. They frequently charge that the new African members of management are 'no better than the colonialists' in their treatment of subordinates and engage in nepotism and favouritism in selecting people for vacant positions and promotions. A typical union point of view is the following:

For many years, the Kenya Meat Commission has been engaged in recruiting luxurious management personnel who care for themselves and not workers or the society, as a result dissatisfaction has overstayed for years before and after independence. What is most deplorable is that even the so-called African management who were expected to show more human understanding than the expatriate employer have shown no grade at all.

The Industrial unrest at K.M.C. is the hangover or the inheritance of colonial heritage. Most of the present African management especially those who champion personnel policy had been associated with colonialism as so-called past intellectuals and this has been very difficult for the Union to clean after independence for few have not changed glory of 'Ivory Tower' enjoyed during the days of white domination.[11]

Charging that 'brotherization' rather than Africanization was the policy in certain enterprises, leaders of many unions have publicly stated that people who did not belong to a 'particular tribe' (usually unstated) could not win promotions, no matter what their qualifications. In addition, leaders of the Railway African Union (Kenya) and the East African Community Union (Kenya) have attempted to exploit feelings of Kenyan parochialism by claiming that the top positions in the East African Railways Administration or the East African Community civil service were going to nationals of Uganda and Tanzania at the expense of Kenyans. When Kenyans working for the East African Railway in Uganda were sacked in September–October 1970 as part of the policy of 'Ugandanization', the Railway African Union went so far as to suggest that all Ugandan employees in Kenya should be forcibly removed from their jobs.[12]

All the evidence suggests that 'brotherization' is rapidly becoming a key issue in trade unions. Where union leaders previously tried to unite all their African members on the basis of opposition to the European or Asian management, they are now tempted to appeal to a particular section of their potential membership on the grounds of tribal solidarity against allegedly unfair advantages being gained by another tribe.

Victimization

This issue has been used by nearly all union leaders at one time or another. To overcome the many divisive forces at work within their unions, they have relentlessly pursued and publicized cases in which union officials or members were apparently discharged or penalized because of their union activities. The Commercial, Food and Allied Workers, for example, has, on many occasions, charged an employer with victimization. One case, involving the sacking of a shop steward at the Kenya Co-operative Creameries, was pressed for four years; the dispute eventually reached the Industrial Court in September 1969. In the intervening period the union had twice threatened countrywide strikes over the issue.

Since the potency of victimization as an issue depends on the extent to which union members believe the charge, a discussion of the validity of such allegations is largely irrelevant. Yet it is clear that enough documented cases of victimization exist to give some plausibility to union leaders' claims. In the case of a trade dispute between the Distributive and Commercial Workers' Union and the Distributive and Allied Trades Association in 1963, for example, a Board of Inquiry commented that 'sufficient evidence was produced to show that, in the case of two firms, there were undoubted cases of victimization of Union members after the strike. The Union also produced evidence, which was not refuted by the Association, of numerous cases of employees having been penalized by employers prior to the strike because of Union activities.'[13] Leaders of the Railway Union have often levelled charges of victimization against the East African Railways Administration. As all employees must sign a contract agreeing to be transferred at any time, it is an easy matter for the Administration to rid itself of a bothersome branch official. That the union's claims are not always imaginary is indicated by the following comments of the Deputy Secretary of the Ministry of Labour regarding the Administration's actions in 1966: 'The principle involved here is victimization and it would be very difficult for any Union officials to resist the temptation of taking the case as direct victimization. ...It would appear that the Railways Authorities is avoiding dealings with strong representative Trade Union officials and would like to take part in helping to build up officials of their choice....'[14]

Job security

More strikes are threatened and called over dismissals of workers than over any other single grievance. While wages, unemployment rates and landlessness simultaneously increase, job security undoubtedly represents the single most crucial union issue. As the General Secretary of the Local Government Workers' Union told delegates to his union's Annual Conference in September 1967, 'the main task in the last four years remained as in the past, that is to ensure the security of the members in their employment. The Union has handled cases of dismissal with great determination and has achieved remarkable results....'[15] The nature of these results was indicated in a document circulated by the General Secretary to union delegates:

Other major disputes were the dismissal of 103 employees of Meru County Council, this was processed up to conciliation level and resulted to continuation of services of all dismissed employees. ...*The result brought the Union back into life at Meru.* Another dispute which was also settled at conciliation level was the dismissal of over 140 employees of South Nyanza County Council. Again this dispute was processed ...with the results of reinstatement of the whole lot. At Mombasa, seven employees of the African Trust Fund were dismissed by the Council. Employees of that department went on strike for a few days, the strike was called off and the case was processed and a settlement was reached at the conciliation level which resulted in reinstatement. *Here again the result meant more membership to the Union.* There were several dismissals during the period under review which were settled at the Branch level. I would like to emphasize that the primary duty of the Union is to make sure that the security in employment is safeguarded, and it is because of this stand that the Union took strong action...[16]

Job security is obviously an especially critical issue in industries which frequently declare redundancies. For instance, such capital-intensive and technologically advanced industries as the oil and chemical ones have reacted to rapidly rising minimum wages for manual workers by increased automation. Oil companies have also tended to rely increasingly on contractors for necessary labour work; they can save money in this way, because the contractors pay their employees much lower minimum wages than the oil companies. The result of these decisions has been a shrinking labour force in these two industries. In the mining industry, the Quarry and Mine Workers' Union lost about 600 of its members between 1965 and 1969 when Macalder–Nyanza Mines curtailed its operations. Finally, the agricultural unions wage a constant battle with owners of large farms, estates and plantations who wish to lay off employees owing to the vagaries of weather and world and domestic markets.

Discussions with union members and branch officials suggest that the determination with which union leaders pursue such individual grievances as the discharging of one or more employees is extremely important for their popularity. It was often said of Ochola Mak'Anyengo, General Secretary of the Petroleum Oil Workers' Union, that, regardless of how unpopular he was with political leaders, he would continue to win re-election as union leader as long as he continued personally to handle individual grievances.[17] His tenacity can be seen in the case of three employees declared redundant by Kenya Shell Company in April 1969. Mak'Anyengo, arguing that the proper procedures had not been followed, took up their case with the company. Failing to get satisfaction, he declared a trade dispute, and forced the case to the Industrial Court. This Court ruled in September 1969 that the three men should be deemed to be still in employment. If the company still wanted to dismiss them, it should give fourteen days' notice to the union.[18] Denis Akumu, as General Secretary of the Sugar Workers, frequently threatened strike action over the laying off of sugar workers. Consider, for example, the strike he called on 20 August 1968, just prior to his union's triennial elections. On the issue of the alleged 'summary dismissal' of seven sugar workers at Miwani, Akumu called out 1,400 employees at Miwani Sugar Mills and 800 workers at nearby Chemelil. The strike, declared illegal by the Labour Minister on 21 August, continued until management agreed to submit the dispute to the Industrial Court.

Illustrations could be multiplied, but the essential point has been established: as wages have increased and the number of people seeking employment has escalated, the union's main task has become the protection of the jobs of the employed. To be popular with his members, a union leader must demonstrate that he is willing to handle individual as well as collective grievances.

Social welfare functions for unions?

At the same time that the government has restricted the unions' bargaining powers and advocated productionism, it has also encouraged unions to undertake new social welfare functions. If trade unions are not to atrophy as their core bargaining functions contract, they must develop new activities to engage the energies of their leaders and the enthusiasm of their members. The government cannot be sanguine about the decay of unionism, for the absence of popular organizations capable of channelling and regulating worker protest may lead to costly industrial unrest and dangerous urban discontent. Hence, unions have been steered toward social service and commercial activities designed to enhance the collective welfare of workers without endangering plans for economic growth. As the government's key policy statement, Sessional Paper No. 10 of 1965 asserted, 'the Government will assist trade unions to become involved in economic activities such as co-operatives, housing schemes, training schemes, workers' discipline and productivity and, in general, to accept their social responsibilities' (p. 56). Later official statements echoed this theme.[19]

Training schemes

What has been accomplished by the national union federation and individual unions in the way of educational programs? A survey of these revealed that their emphasis has been overwhelmingly on training low, middle and high-level union officials in how to fulfil effectively their industrial relations functions. This finding again confirms the prevalent orientation toward traditional union goals in Kenyan unionism.

Union movements elsewhere in Africa have run quite extensive pro-grammes in vocational training, skill-improvement and workers' literacy. The Ghanaian Trades Union Congress, for instance, maintains vocational train-ing centres in two cities, one of which provides day and evening courses in tailoring and domestic sciences, while the other offers day and evening courses in typing, accountancy, elementary economics and English language training. Workers thus have the opportunity to upgrade their skills at night. In addition, this TUC operates a large Workers' College in Accra with programmes to combat illiteracy and to permit workers to earn higher academic qualifications.[20] In Kenya, only two small vocational programmes are even remotely connected with a trade union: a tailoring and cutting institute, and a course at a polytechnic designed to upgrade the skills of those already engaged in the printing trade. In addition, the Kenya Federa-tion of Labour established an 'Education Centre' in Nairobi in 1964, financed by an American foundation, the Fund for International Social and Economic Education. During the eighteen months of its existence, this Centre mounted an evening literacy programme for workers. However, a mere sixty students remained in this programme a year after its initiation.[21] The closure of the Education Centre, occasioned by the government's ban on foreign assistance to Kenyan unions in early 1966, ended the union movement's experiment in literacy schemes.

The training of union officials has therefore constituted the main thrust of the unions' educational efforts in Kenya. In 1964–6, the KFL's Education Centre offered two-week, six-week and weekend courses designed 'to provide a basic understanding and the modern know-how of trade unionism as it applies to the present day needs and realities of Kenya'.[22] After the demise of the Centre, COTU and individual unions continued to run short seminars on an *ad hoc* basis for high- and middle-level officials. COTU's seminars increased in number in 1970 with the arrival of a Workers' Education Consultant from the International Labour Organization. Between early 1970 and mid-1972, COTU had run, with the assistance of the ILO consultant, four seminars for shop stewards, ten for branch officials, one for 'specialists' (national treasurers) and three for 'high-level' union officials. These seminars, financed almost wholly by the International Confederation of Free Trade Unions and the African–American Labour Centre, were usually only five days in duration. Lecturers for these seminars were usually provided by COTU, the Federation of Kenya Employers, the Ministry of

Labour, the University of Nairobi and, where senior trade unionists were participants, the cabinet itself. The topics covered in the seminars for shop stewards, branch officials and specialists provided basic information on the Kenyan industrial relations system, grievance procedures and the relevant labour legislation. In addition, the seminars gave both the representatives of employers and the government a chance to exhort trade unionists to act 'responsibly' and respect the 'public interest'. The three successful seminars for top-level leaders in 1971 were broader in scope, dealing with the following topics: wages and incomes policy in Kenya; trade union participation in planning and development; and workers' participation in management.

National unions have supplemented COTU's training program. Most unions in 1970–2 managed to provide at least one five-day seminar for branch officials and shop stewards; several provided three or four. These seminars, involving twenty-five to thirty participants, also focused on the basic duties and responsibilities of union officials in the present system of industrial relations. In nearly all cases the expenses of the seminars were defrayed in whole or in part by the relevant International Trade Secretariat, the African–American Labour Centre or an American international union. Kenyan unions have taken full advantage of foreign financial assistance since the government lifted its ban on this in late 1969.

Co-operative and commercial schemes

In principle, unions should be in a superior position to justify their existence to members if they sponsor successful co-operative and commercial ventures. The record of Kenyan unionism in this area of activities has been far from distinguished, however, for reasons that will soon be clear.

Tom Mboya, who had early in his career been impressed by the involvement of Israel's *Histadrut* in commercial and welfare activities, envisaged a similar role for the KFL before he left its active leadership in 1962.[23] He specifically wished to establish a KFL-sponsored medical clinic and a consumers' co-operative for union members. While neither of these schemes ultimately succeeded, the Federation did obtain its own printing press in 1962 through the generosity of a New York based organization called Peace with Freedom. But even this venture was a débâcle; the foreign donor prevailed on the KFL in 1963 to accept KSh15,000 in exchange for the machinery after the experiment had collapsed. Politically-inspired factionalism within the union movement after 1962 effectively diverted attention and funds away from the implementation of commercial and welfare projects.

Upon his election as head of COTU in February 1969, Denis Akumu promised to launch a variety of workers' co-operative and commercial schemes.[24] Yet circumstances mainly outside his control prevented him from implementing any of these during the following four years. COTU's Directorate of Co-operatives was almost moribund in this period, its

Director being detained under the Preservation of Public Security Act in 1971. Of the eleven extant unions studied, only three boasted even a single functioning consumers' co-operative in 1972. Other consumers' co-operatives had opened at various times, often with initial technical assistance from Israel or West Germany, but most quickly failed when the foreign sponsor retired. Aside from plain dishonesty, one of the main reasons for failure has been the involvement of a co-operative's officials in intra-union factionalism. A faction controlling a co-operative will be tempted to employ its funds in fighting opponents, whereas the opposing faction will try to destroy the shop's financial viability. For this reason, the head of the sugar union has a policy forbidding incumbent union officials from also serving as officers of consumers' co-operatives. Owing to the discouraging experiences with this sort of co-operative, unions have lately shifted their attention to the establishment of credit and saving societies for members. There are many successful credit unions in Kenya, but these have generally been sponsored by the management of an enterprise for employees without any assistance from or connection with a trade union.

Another project Akumu undertook to promote was workers' co-operative housing. In a country where urban workers are forced into overcrowded and unsanitary accommodation by high rents, low-cost housing deserves to rank high in a union movement's list of priorities. In Ghana, the Trades Union Congress built 136 such houses in Kumasi and Takoradi in 1970–1; these were leased to union members on hire-purchase terms. It planned to have constructed another 500 units in Accra by 1974.[25] In Kenya, COTU has not yet established a workers' housing scheme. Akumu managed to interest labour organizations in the United States, West Germany and the Scandinavian countries in providing initial financial and technical assistance. But intra-COTU conflict in 1970–2 aborted the project; in the face of persistent power struggles the foreign sponsors understandably backed out. A project of this magnitude will not succeed until there is a united and committed leadership in COTU.

A final scheme proposed by Akumu was a workers' investment trust. This trust was to be composed of private provident funds, a donation by the government of KSh5 million and contributions deducted from the wages of union members. In July 1970 the Labour Minister promulgated a rule, under the Trade Disputes Act, 1965, which permitted unions to apply for an order directing employers to deduct special levies from members' wages for nation-building projects. Before such an application would be granted, the union would have to prove that two-thirds of the membership had approved the levy. The workers' investment trust was to be directed by a board on which the representatives of workers would have a majority. As the Finance Minister explained, 'the idea here is that the workers themselves will through a board be able to determine what are the investments which would help to promote the welfare of the workers and then to invest in them.... This is a challenge to bring more responsibility to those who lead the workers and to give them a sense of participation.'[26] One cannot but doubt whether workers' leaders would really have been given the predominant voice in investment decisions, especially in view of the government's large contribution. In any event, the question is hypothetical, as the idea of the trust died in 1971; it is unlikely to be revived until a pliant leadership captures control of COTU.[27]

The unpalatable fact is that neither the national union federation nor the national unions is capable today of mounting comprehensive training, co-operative and business schemes. As I have already hinted, politically inspired factionalism in COTU in 1970–2 has rendered that body quite ineffectual. Both the shabbiness of its headquarters – the so-called Solidarity Building – and the absence of much of its staff during working hours are indicative of COTU's sad decline. To manage complex projects, COTU and its larger affiliates require competent and efficient administrations. However, such administrations are unlikely to emerge as long as most jobs are distributed on the basis of patronage rather than competence. COTU's employees, during factional struggles, spend most of their time out of their offices campaigning for their patrons. This situation will continue until a leadership has the courage to hire neutral and qualified staff – preferably bright young Sixth Form school-leavers or university graduates outside the union movement – at higher salaries.

A second problem concerns finance. While COTU and its affiliates can probably obtain funds to start projects from foreign labour organizations, such reliance might well reintroduce the externally financed rivalries which plagued trade unionism before 1966. If Kenyan workers are to be asked to provide the wherewithal to finance their unions' commercial and welfare projects, they must be informed how these projects will ultimately benefit themselves. Union members may otherwise conclude that levies for a workers' investment trust, for example, are simply a disguised form of taxation. Workers may decide that union membership is a burden rather than a boon if their subscriptions are increased at the same time that their unions' core bargaining function is further limited.

Conclusion

Whatever union leaders decide should be the basic responsibility of unions, they annoy some group. If they adopt a basically productionist orientation, their memberships will likely lose interest in trade unionism. If they stubbornly insist upon militant economism, the government may pass legislation seeking to convert the union structures into an arm of the state. No one has more colourfully described the acute dilemma confronting unions in Kenya (and, by extension, other capitalist countries of the Third World) than Clement Lubembe, who likened a union leader to 'a poor orphan boy surrounded by a great fire in a great desert.... We are called upon to co-operate to the full with the Government and everybody else in the society in the new struggle for economic and social re-construction of our country, and at the same time, assure the ordinary workers...that his hopes and expectations will not deliberately be disappointed in the course of this co-operation.'[28]

In these circumstances top union leaders have tended to favour the traditional consumptionist aims of trade unionism, though not to the extent where their actions might invite retaliation from the political authorities. Of necessity, they have become expert temporizers. Where legislation exists to govern their behaviour, they generally adhere to its provisions. Unions follow the time-consuming and often frustrating procedures for peacefully resolving disputes; but, at the same time, they threaten numerous strikes and accord tacit approval to 'wild-cat' strikes. In the absence of legislation requiring unions to practice wage restraint and act as promoters of production, union leaders have largely ignored the government's appeals for co-operation. They have quietly proceeded to press high wage demands and give precedence to workers' grievances rather than management's requirements. In addition, unions have shown neither great enthusiasm in the social welfare and commercial activities urged upon them, nor a capacity to implement them successfully. In sum, top union leaders have conformed more closely to the expectations of their lower-level officials and the workers than to those of the political class.

9. State control and worker protest

In a seminal article Berg and Butler have argued that 'almost everywhere' after independence 'labor organizations were taken over by governing parties. This process differs in degree of control: the levers of control are manipulated more gently and discreetly in the Ivory Coast than Guinea, for example. But the result is the same: the labour movement, if not completely subordinated to the party, is at least pliable and responsive to party pressures.'[1] At a later point, the authors expanded upon these remarks by observing that 'it is only on party suffrance that they [the unions] are given a role to play, and they are constrained to be "reasonable" and "responsible" organs which emphasize productivity and hard work.'[2]

The preceding chapters suggest the need for some revisions in this general formulation. In the first place their conception that a relationship exists between two entities – a 'governing party' and a 'labour movement' – is misleading.[3] While I do not mean to suggest that such perspicacious observers as Berg and Butler were unaware of internal divisions within the two organizational spheres, their model, in over-simplifying a very complex relationship, does retard a full understanding of trade unionism. By conceptualizing 'governing party' and 'labour movement' as entities, almost as individuals, their framework diverts attention from the internal dynamics so crucial in determining what role unions actually play. In Kenya, the governing party hardly exists as an organization; it is more in the nature of a congeries of clientage networks competing for pre-eminence at various levels. This was true even when opposition parties existed for various intervals before October 1969. At the national level, KANU has not had a life independent from that of the government, which has itself always been severely split. Neither the governing party nor the government has thus acted monolithicly to control trade unionism; indeed, many top union leaders have themselves been prominent KANU politicians with powerful political allies looking out for their interests. Even less tenable is the concept of the 'labour movement' as an entity.[4] The Kenyan union movement has long been composed of at least one national trade union federation, about thirty national unions, hundreds of union branches and approximately 300,000 paid-up members. While the national union federation has been susceptible to governmental demands, it has been unable to enforce its wishes upon member unions, in whom sovereignty formally resides. In fact, some leaders of national unions have rejected all requests, advice and suggestions emanating from the national union federation, owing to antagonisms generated by the persistent factional splits in the union movement.

Most significantly, one must never forget that the 300,000 union members and lower-level leaders, possessing their own aims and sources of influence, have not passively accepted all decisions made at the top of the union hierarchies.

This brings me to a second point. Kenyan unions have not, on the whole, been 'pliable and responsive to party pressures', though, as I have already mentioned, the trade union federation often has been. Unions have tended to respond more to the pressure from their members than to those from the ruling elite. That this has been the case is not surprising, given the leaders' reliance upon their lower-level leaders and members. This dependency is not, of course, complete: top union leaders have freedom to pursue some goals not shared by their members. In Kenya, for example, full-time union officials have taken advantage of their positions to further their own ambitions in the political sphere, where the greatest personal rewards can be obtained. But until they are ensconced in political life, their immediate interest must be the retention of their union posts.

Perhaps it is worthwhile to recapitulate the bases of the union official's dependency upon his membership, since such dependency has been instrumental in frustrating some of the government's expectations of the unions' economic role. Given the lack of democracy within Kenyan unions, why have their leaders remained responsive to their members' demands and interests? Union democracy requires that members can hold their leaders accountable for their actions, that leaders, in other words, retain their positions at the pleasure of the majority. While the forms of democracy – triennial elections, annual reports, the convening of various committees – persist in Kenyan unions, the reality is central, increasingly oligarchical control. In most unions only about 10 per cent of the rank-and-file actually vote for the branch officials, a small proportion of whom then elect the national officials every three years. Vote-buying and other stratagems appear fairly widespread in some unions. Moreover, almost no office-holders accept the legitimacy of organized opposition groups, which they denigrate as 'splinter groups' or 'anti-union factions' determined to undermine the workers' solidarity for selfish motives. The absence of a continuing opposition allowed to voice criticisms of office-holders limits the opportunity for union members to hold their leaders directly accountable for their actions.

Yet the lack of democracy in Kenyan unions is not raised as a criticism. Since almost every Western trade union studied has been found to exhibit oligarchical leadership,[5] we should not be surprised to find the same feature in Kenyan unions. Furthermore, even the British colonial authorities, who introduced the idea of union democracy into Kenya, did not want real internal democracy, if this meant unions would be used against their interests. What the colonial Labour Department championed was more akin to 'guided democracy', whereby public officials intervened in the internal affairs of unions to prevent so-called 'irresponsible agitators' from pursuing aims of which they disapproved. 'Guided democracy' was extended and refined in the post-colonial era.

In these circumstances, the responsiveness of union officials is dictated by their sense of insecurity. Internal conflict has been rife in most unions. The government passed the Trade Unions (Amendment) Act, 1964, in the hope that enhanced leadership stability would encourage 'responsible' behaviour on the part of union leaders, i.e., behaviour not directly tied to short-term internal union power considerations. However, legislation has not yet reinforced the position of union leaders to the point where they can afford to ignore the aspirations of branch officials. Full-time leaders still manoeuvre in an uncertain milieu. Tribal identity remains strong; established leaders who fail to take it into account invite the formation of a rival faction. Occupational status will likely become a more salient source of cleavage, owing to the increasing stability of the urban wage-earning force, and to the declining opportunities for upward mobility as the process of Africanization is completed. Whether the growth of status consciousness will negate or reinforce tribalism depends on the emerging ethnic structure of employment. If the frequent charges of 'Kikuyuization' in certain sectors of the economy have any basis, status groups may, to some extent, become coterminous with tribal categories, with the Kikuyu in the higher echelons. Tribalism, in this case, would represent an explosive element in both internal union and national politics. In addition, both politicians and contenders for control of the national union federation continue to channel money and organizational resources to challengers within unions led by individuals whom they oppose. In these uncertain circumstances, full-time union leaders must continue to depend upon the support of the voluntary branch officials and, hence, to respond to their wishes.

From the point of view of the rank-and-file, the absence of union democracy is unimportant as long as members have the right to resign from the union without suffering reprisals. If a leadership disregards the interests of workers, present members can withdraw their financial contribution while potential members will not join the union. Since any diminution of the membership and influence of a union diminishes the prestige and power of its leaders, the self-interest of office-holders dictates their attention to the individual and collective economic well-being of workers. In short, as Allen has argued in a much different context, the ultimate dependence of the unions' economic power on the consent of their members is crucial to their operation in the workers' interests.[6]

Bates, in one of the few studies comparable to the present one, came to similar conclusions. He sought to understand why the Zambian Mineworkers' Union 'failed' to fulfil the role ascribed to it by the government in post-independence Zambia. 'Out of a regard for the national interest in rapid economic growth, the government asks the workers to restrain their wage demands, eschew strike action, work hard, and defer to the authority of their supervisors.'[7] Yet the Mineworkers' Union refused to transform itself into an agency dedicated to control and regulate its members' actions, just as Kenyan unions have largely refused. According to Bates, the main reason for the union's 'failure' (or, from the workers' viewpoint, success) was the existence of deep cleavages between the union's national and branch officials. Since national officials received recognition as leaders of national importance, were frequently lectured by politicians about their union's role in the development process and could aspire to mobility into top public-sector jobs, they tended to adhere to the government's formulation of the public interest (at least in public). In contrast, the branch officials were not granted national recognition, seldom were exposed to government propaganda on labour's role in development, sought advancement in the mining companies rather than the government and remained in face-to-face contact with aggrieved and protesting mine employees. Consequently, these lower-level leaders tended to be militant, identifying their interests with those of the mineworkers.[8] Given this conflict in orientations between the national and local union officials, the government's policy could only prevail if the national leaders could enforce their views of the union's proper role. But they could not impose development priorities on the union because of its 'decentralized' power structure.

Hence, Bates also stresses the primacy of intra-union power relations in determining the union's actions, though he does not emphasize the union's dependence upon its members' financial contributions. My findings differ from those of Bates in that, firstly, I did not discover any marked cleavage between the views of national and branch officials on the question of the proper aims of trade unionism. Both levels were oriented towards traditional consumptionist goals, though lower-level leaders were prone to be less cautious in their approach to industrial relations. Owing to the economic importance of copper in Zambia, national leaders of the Mineworkers' Union were apparently offered more inducements to honour the officially enunciated public interest than their counterparts in Kenyan unions. No single union in Kenya dominates the economy to nearly the same extent. Furthermore, I did not feel, in the Kenyan situation, that communication was a difficulty accounting in part for the unions' low commitment to the government's objectives. Government spokesmen often admonished both national and branch officials at various seminars and conferences. But my impression was that no amount of exhortations will persuade trade unionists to forego what they regard as their members' just reward – unless the speakers themselves practice the restraint that they preach.

Given the unions' constant demands, strike threats and factiousness, one might expect an impatient and increasingly authoritarian government to pass legislation forcing unions to act as instruments of its labour policy. Indeed, there were strong voices in the government in 1970–2 advocating an extensive reorganization of the union structure. The suggested changes included the following: a 'streamlining' of the union movement to amalgamate the existing thirty unions into a smaller number, perhaps sixteen; a *de jure* centralized union structure in which all unions must belong to a scheduled federation with legal powers over some of its affiliates' activities; a compulsory 'check-off' system of the union shop variety, in exchange for which the government would set salary scales for all levels of paid union officials and channel a certain proportion of the subscriptions into a workers' investment trust; and a virtual strike ban as a result of compulsory arbitration of all disputes. The effect of these changes would clearly be to establish close governmental control over the union movement, with full-time union officials expected to act as *de facto* public servants dedicated to the ruling elite's definition of the public interest. Accompanying such amendments would be a programme of wage restraint whereby urban workers would forego their customary wage increments in order that the money so saved could be reinvested or used to improve social services in the rural areas. Is this likely to represent a viable solution to the labour problem in economic development and political stability?

I think that such an approach in a country like Kenya is likely to prove untenable. This is because of the political tension and instability which are liable to be fomented by the growing contradiction between workers whose wages and living standards are held down and a small but affluent elite. This contradiction would, of course, recede if the political class volunteered to forego some of its privileges. But is this likely to happen? The dangers of downgrading the economic interests of urban wage-earners without restricting the consumption of the political class and bourgeoisie are illustrated by the case of Ghana, among others. A brief reference to this case may be helpful at this point.

The Ghanaian government, under the Convention Peoples' Party (CPP), sought to bring trade unions under government direction after independence. An Industrial Relations Act, 1958, together with later amendments to it, placed unions under the control of the Ghana Trades Union Congress, which was itself informally dominated by CPP leaders. By 1960, the TUC was empowered to supervise the 'efficient organization, management, working and disciplinary control' of its sixteen affiliates. Only these sixteen unions, formed through legislated amalgamations, could legally exist and negotiate on behalf of their members. Furthermore, these unions could communicate with the Ministry of Labour over trade disputes and matters of certification only through the TUC. Strikes were virtually outlawed, as the Labour Minister could refer an issue in dispute, which had not been resolved through negotiation and conciliation, to arbitration if either of the parties consented to such an action. Legislation also made union membership compulsory for all workers in 1960; employers were obliged to deduct union subscriptions from all their employees' wages each month. As for the full-time union leaders, the TUC officials, headed by the Secretary-General, John Tettegah, were CPP stalwarts, while the leaders of the national unions were, according to the public utterances of cabinet ministers, to be 'CPP militants'. Informal government influence over the TUC was further fortified by the provision of generous loans and other financial aid to the labour body. Hence, between 1958 and 1960, the Ghanaian union movement ceased to constitute a protest movement seeking 'more' for workers and became, in large part, an adjunct of the state, rendering automatic support for government policy and extolling the virtues of hard work and discipline on the part of workers. In 1960, the TUC even lent its support to a policy of wage restraint.[9]

Urban wage-earners did not take lightly this disregard of their economic interests. There were a series of small-scale 'wild-cat' strikes throughout 1959 and 1960, for which, in each case, the appropriate union denied responsibility. These were followed in September 1961 by a much more prolonged and serious strike which began in the railway yards of the twin industrial towns of Sekondi–Takoradi, and then spread to other enterprises and to railway towns upcountry, including Accra. The incident which precipitated this work-stoppage was the deduction, in August 1961, of 5 per cent of each worker's wages in respect of a 'compulsory savings scheme' introduced by the government in its austerity budget of July. Workers were particularly incensed by this scheme since prices had been rapidly rising while wages had been frozen. Much of their hostility was directed at the TUC, which had acquiesced in the government's policies. In fact, top union leaders, including those in the Railway Union, disavowed any responsibility for the illegal Sekondi strike and sought to persuade the workers to return to their jobs. The lower-level union leadership and rank-and-file were, however, defiant, especially in Sekondi, and especially among the railway workers. The latter workers finally returned to work after seventeen days when President Kwame Nkrumah threatened that any person who refused to do so would be considered guilty of sedition.

It should be emphasized that the aims of the strike were initially economic, not political. The striking workers were 'interested...in restoring traditional trade union privileges such as the right to bargain collectively and to withhold their labour if they could not secure what they wanted. ...They were unionists with an "economist" ideology.'[10] Yet widespread strike action inevitably has political implications in an underdeveloped country where a weakly-based government confronts, as principal employer and economic manager, angry and sometimes violent urban workers. The political import of such industrial action is magnified when, as in Ghana, strike-leaders express grass-roots hostility towards the acquisitive activities of the *nouveaux riches*, foremost among whom are the top politicians. In the case of the Sekondi strike, one authoritative writer has claimed that, though it was 'perhaps' not a major threat to Nkrumah's regime, it might well have become so.[11] At the least, the workers' defiance forced Nkrumah to terminate his tour of communist countries in order to return home to handle the crisis. Moreover, during the second week of the strike, leaders of the opposition United Party (UP) came forward to encourage and exploit the industrial unrest for their own political purposes. Government spokesmen later claimed that UP leaders had, in fact, encouraged the insurrectionary features of the strike by providing strike-leaders with advice, finances and moral support.[12] In the aftermath, forty-seven persons were detained, including UP leaders, union officials and a former cabinet minister.

Ten years later, history repeated itself in Ghana. By 1971, the main protagonists were still the government and the Sekondi–Takoradi workers. But in the interim much else had changed. A rejuvenated TUC now championed the cause of the workers, and the Progressive Party (PP) government was led by individuals who, ten years earlier, had formed the opposition UP which had supported the strikers against the CPP. However, the grievances were much the same as in 1961. Throughout 1970 and 1971, the TUC argued that rapid increases in the cost of living justified a considerable increase in the minimum wage. The government resisted the TUC's demands, contending that all would have to sacrifice for the cause of economic development. Yet the political class and business elite were plainly unwilling to surrender any privileges, while the real wages of workers diminished. In the civil service, for instance, a salaries review commission in 1967 recommended increases which provided the highest paid category of public servants with a salary thirty-eight times that of the lowest paid category.[13] This was the context of inequality in which the government introduced an austerity budget in July 1971. The item in this budget which most infuriated urban workers was the imposition of a 'National Development Levy' on all those earning over a certain minimal amount. This levy was more onerous than the compulsory savings scheme introduced ten years earlier, since contributors could never expect to get their contributions back, with interest, at some later date. Relations between the TUC and the government rapidly deteriorated over the issues of the minimum wage and the levy. In September the Labour Minister, accusing the TUC of communist sympathies and of 'exploiting industrial disputes to cause disaffection and confusion in the country', introduced a bill dissolving the TUC.[14]

This move touched off another general strike in the Sekondi–Takoradi area, the initial demands of which included the termination of the National Development Levy and the restoration of the TUC. Lasting four days, the strike closed down the harbour, railway and most offices in the twin cities, and sparked off demonstrations by thousands of workers.[15] In the space of a decade, therefore, the wheel had come full circle; many of the opposition leaders who supported the workers in 1961 now belonged to a government that had introduced an austerity budget far harsher on urban workers than the earlier Nkrumah budget. The resulting disaffection of organized labour was one of the factors forming the background to the army *coup* in January 1972. The urban workers were as jubilant about the overthrow of the PP government in 1972 as they had been about the CPP's fall in February 1966.[16]

Income inequalities within the 'modern' sector also lay behind the 1964 general strike in Nigeria, which lasted thirteen days and paralysed practically the entire economy. The Nigerian federal government also expected wage-earners to sacrifice improvements in their standard of living for the sake of its development goals. Wages had remained almost stationary between 1960 and 1963, while prices had increased 12–15 per cent overall, and by as much as 22 per cent in the Enugu and Port Harcourt areas.[17] Furthermore, a six-year development plan published in 1962 declared that wages would be held down in favour of encouraging further investment. But the unions were unwilling to accept the necessity for wage restraint, especially since the government refused to reduce the vast disparities in income between the highest and lowest categories in the civil service.[18] The obduracy of the government in the face of workers' demands led to the general strike in June.

The aim of the Nigerian general strike, as in the case of the earlier Ghanaian strike, was thus economic in the first instance. But, while the strike began over wages, 'it quickly broadened into an attack on the Establishment as a whole – its corruption, its tactless ostentation and its flagrant inefficiency.'[19] The Joint Action Committee (JAC) of the union movement justified its position on wage increases by comparing workers' wages to the ostentatious wealth of the small political class, rather than to the miserable conditions of the bulk of the labour force who were engaged in agricultural pursuits. As Wahab Goodluck, one of the JAC leaders, commented at the time: 'What is the meaning of independence for a worker? Did he fight for independence so that only the pot-bellied politician will continue to grow fatter and more secure, while he vegetates in insecurity?'[20]

If the Kenyan government enforces its own policy of wage restraint, backed up by more stringent controls of trade unionism, is the outcome likely to be different from that in Ghana and Nigeria? Kenya's latest development plan, published in late 1969, commits the government to equalizing income through a programme of rural development and an incomes policy. Yet the sincerity of this commitment must be questioned in light of the increasing disparities in wealth in Kenyan society.

Consider, for instance, the public services. In July 1971, 160,000 civil servants received pay increases adding some K£4.6 million to the annual wage bill for the public sector[21] and widening the income gap between the highest and lowest paid civil servants. The reasoning of the Commission of Inquiry which recommended these increases is perhaps indicative of the attitude toward nation-building at the higher levels of the civil service and government. Throughout its report, the Commission of Inquiry grappled with the conflicting demands of equity and incentives for senior staff. In the final anlysis, it gave precedence to the need to provide incentives for skilled and administrative personnel, so that they would 'rededicate' themselves to the development effort.[22] The report asks whether 'the country can afford *not* to pay? In our view this question has special application to the middle and higher grades of the service in whose ranks are found the technician, the staff with professional qualifications, and the senior administrators. They are the people upon whom successful Government and development depends...'[23] The Commission consequently concluded that the 'top cadres' deserved a 'considerable increase', which rose to 12 per cent at the highest levels. Hence, one of the most privileged segments of society, the top civil servants who had inherited a salary structure designed to attract British administrators out to the colonies, benefited disproportionately. True, the gap between the highest and lowest salary was reduced in relative terms from 46:1 to 38:1. But, in absolute terms, the top civil servant now received K£4,464 per year more than the lowest-paid civil servant, rather than K£3,522 per year more as previously.[24]

Increasing social inequality has prompted many KANU M.P.s to warn of the possibility of disruption and even revolution unless reforms are undertaken. Representative is the following comment in a debate on the Presidential Address in February 1970:

I am going to let the President know what the *wananchi* [common people] say about *Uhuru*. They say *Uhuru* came only to a handful of people, to a privileged class...Those people are referred to by the *wananchi* as the Ministers, the civil servants who can buy things, who can get loans, who can get forms to fill when applying for loans, those who can buy land. These are the rich people and the poor are left without anything. *Wananchi* say it is they who died [for independence]...It is the very common class of people, they say, who suffer nowadays even though they are the people who fought for *Uhuru*...I warn this House to be careful when blaming the *wananchi* outside because they do say they are hungry. In most cases they are hungry and because of that they are angry too.[25]

On the question of sacrifice for the public interest, another M.P. observed that there was little use in discussing projects for relieving unemployment and promoting economic development 'when we are not even prepared to sacrifice. If the President and leaders of this country are not prepared to sacrifice then how do we expect the office messengers who are earning only about Shs.150 to accept a redirection of salary down to Shs.100?'[26] Many other M.P.s, all belonging to the 'governing party', have made similar comments.

It is probable, therefore, that a policy of wage and salary restraint and state control of unions will lead, in Kenya, to a growing contradiction between the urban workers and the small elite. Top civil servants, army officers, politicians and businessmen are clearly in a superior position politically to protect their interests under the present regime. Moreover, many members of the political class have access to non-salary income through their participation in business. It is considerably easier in a capitalist system to establish machinery to control wages and salaries than to control private profits and other non-salary income. Direct public control of profits appears inconsistent with a free enterprise economy in which relative profitability determines the flow of resources into the various activities. Such control is certainly incompatible with the attempt to attract foreign investment. The state can regulate profits indirectly through price controls, but this requires such complex machinery and expertise that even Western countries have hesitated to impose price controls except during wartime. Hence, an incomes policy is likely to have its greatest impact on the living standards of the urban wage-earners.

It is naïve to believe, moreover, that aggrieved workers will not protest if their unions are controlled by the state. Depending on the extent of such control, worker protest will either be expressed through trade unions or in spite of them. If governments allow unions enough freedom to bargain effectively on behalf of workers and to articulate their grievances, worker protest will probably be limited to non-violent, orderly channels. This does not mean there will be no strikes, but that work-stoppages will probably remain peaceful and non-political. But if self-seeking ruling elites allied to business interests dominate the trade unions, worker protest will probably take the form of passive resistance, with high absentee rates and low productivity, and of spontaneous, potentially violent 'wild-cat' strikes, which may take on political aims. Denied legitimate channels to express their grievances, workers will simply resort to their traditional weapon – the strike. Governments will then compromise or increase repression. But, given the limited coercive power available to governments in African countries, especially where armies are none too reliable, the policy of repression is probably not viable on a long-term basis.

One must doubt, therefore, that a government takeover of the union movement in Kenya is tenable in the context of the prevailing political economy. More restrictions on union bargaining powers may be necessary to buttress a policy of holding down urban wages, a policy crucial to securing external investment capital, a more equitable distribution of benefits between town and country, and a consequent abatement in destabilizing rural–urban migration and rampant urban unemployment. Since economists still do not agree about the independent impact of trade unions on wage rates in underdeveloped countries, even the necessity for further restrictions on unions cannot be firmly established. But even if one accepts that the acquiescence of unions is critical to the successful implementation of wage stability, one can still doubt that simply imposing this policy on a subdued union movement, supported by pious pleas for discipline, frugality and hard work, is a sufficient answer. There is no reason to believe that wage-earners are inherently selfish or immune to appeals for sacrifice for the common good. But they are naturally refractory if there is no equality of sacrifice, if more privileged segments of the population – such as politicians, top civil servants and the small African bourgeoisie – refuse to curb their acquisitive activities. M.P.s who complain about living on K£6 per day should not expect workers earning slightly more than K£6 per month to respond enthusiastically to their appeals for self-denial in the public interest. The example of sacrifice must come from the top if its necessity is to be accepted further down.

Is the Kenyan proletariat likely to move from a trade-union to a revolutionary consciousness if its economic interests are disregarded by the political class? Frantz Fanon's sketch of the role of organized labour in an economically dependent former colony is largely correct in its application to Kenya. Top union leaders, drawn from the more privileged occupations, receiving relatively high rewards, and apprehensive of the sanctions wielded by the ruling elite, have generally seen their role as obtaining a larger piece of the pie for the workers within the capitalist political economy. Workers, on their part, are not committed to a radical critique of the present system. Yet Fanon was incorrect in believing that the proletariat was clearly differentiated from, and out of sympathy with, other social strata, such as the peasantry and the urban unemployed. He also underestimated the disruptive potential of the workers. If one rigorously defines revolution as 'a rapid, fundamental and violent domestic change in the dominant values and myths of a society, in its political institutions, social structure, leadership and government activity and policies',[27] then urban wage-earners are definitely not potentially revolutionary. They have neither the power, nor the cohesion, nor the radical ideology to bring about such far-reaching changes; all they want is more of the good things of life. But if one defines revolution more broadly as 'violent civil disturbances that cause the displacement of one ruling group by another that has a broader popular basis for support',[28] then repressed workers may be potentially revolutionary. Their economic grievances may lead to explosive manifestations of protest ('wild-cat' strikes, general strikes, riots, etc.) which could lead to the displacement of the current ruling group, though more likely by a military than a radical workers' government.

One of the paradoxes of an underdeveloped country such as Kenya is that the urban proletarians, though enjoying a higher income than the bulk of the population, could constitute a disruptive social force. But violent group action is much more a matter of relative than absolute deprivation. As Karl Marx pointed out long ago, a class upheaval does not necessarily require a progressive degradation of the proletariat, but could also occur when workers' economic conditions were improving, though not as quickly as those of the bourgeoisie.[29] If the small political class in Kenya continues to enrich itself while adopting a policy of wage restraint and union restriction, workers will feel increasingly deprived relative to this elite. Any violent industrial and political action in the future might thus pit a small section of 'haves', supported perhaps by urban unemployed, against a much smaller group of 'have-mores'.

Appendix 1

Research Methods

The field research for this study was carried out in Kenya in 1968–70 and the summer of 1972. I selected for investigation eleven of the twenty-eight predominantly African unions which were affiliated in 1968 to COTU, the sole registered federation of trade unions since 1966. Since two of these unions had been formed through amalgamations (the Plantation and Agricultural Workers' Union in August 1963 and the Union of Commercial, Food and Allied Workers in November 1965), their main predecessors were also included in the sample, which thereby totalled fifteen. The object, in selecting unions for study, was to obtain a sample sufficiently large and diverse to permit one to make general statements that would be true of the Kenyan union movement as a whole. Unions were selected on the basis of a number of criteria. First, unions were chosen in each sector of the economy – agricultural, public services, and industry and commerce. This seemed a reasonable criterion since Kenyan unions are organized on an industrial rather than a craft basis. Within each sector of the economy, I selected unions to ensure a wide variety of organizational types: small unions (the Common Services' Union, the Petroleum Oil Workers' Union and the Quarry and Mineworkers' Union) as well as large ones (the Plantation and Agricultural Workers' Union, the Local Government Workers' Union, the Union of Commercial, Food and Allied Workers and the Railway African Union – see Appendix 2); and unions in which there has been a relative ease of informal communication among members (the Dockworkers' Union and the Railway African Union) as well as the majority in which communication was more difficult owing to dispersed memberships.

To overcome the notorious deficiencies of sources of information on African trade unions, I employed several complementary research methods. These included observation of non-agricultural union meetings when this was permitted, interviews and discussions with trade unionists and others, and documentary investigation. I began with the last approach. Especially helpful in developing a chronology of events relating to the selected unions and national union federations were local Kenyan newspapers and journals (the *Daily Nation, East African Standard, Kenya Weekly News, Mombasa Times* and *Reporter*) and selected files and records of defunct and extant national union federations, employers' associations, individual trade unions, and several enterprises. I had access to all the files and records of the Kenya Federation of Registered Trade Unions (1952–5) and the Kenya Federation of Labour (1955–66); these were located in Solidarity Building, Nairobi. In addition, I was allowed to see selected files, reports and memoranda of the Kenya Federation of Progressive Trade Unions (1964–6) and the Central Organization of Trade Unions (Kenya), both of which had been based in Nairobi. The Federation of Kenya Employers gave me copies of its annual reports from 1967 to 1971 inclusive and access to selected files going back to 1956; these mainly contained records of the proceedings of conferences and the minutes of meetings. In addition, the Kenya Bankers' (Employers') Association, the Kenya Coffee Growers' Association, the Kenya Tea Growers' Association and the Sisal Employers' Association (Kenya) provided me with selected documents from their head offices, most of which related to annual reports or industrial relations matters. Information on several other specialized employers' associations was provided by the Federation of Kenya Employers, who handled their affairs. A most useful source of information was the selected files and other documents of the fifteen defunct and extant unions included in my sample. Most of the general secretaries or presidents of these unions were very helpful in supplying me with annual reports, policy statements, collective bargaining agreements, copies of submissions to the Industrial Court, circular letters to the branches, records of conferences and minutes of joint industrial councils (where these existed) and union committee meetings. In some cases a union's files were not very extensive, as the loser in a factional conflict had walked off with many of the records and files. Valuable also were the data on employees, annual reports and records of dealings with the appropriate trade union provided by the East African Cargo Handling Sevices in Mombasa and the East African Railways and Harbour Corporation, formerly based in Nairobi.

But these sources seldom provided a complete picture of a union's activities and internal dynamics. Access to the current and past files of the Ministry of Labour in the Nairobi headquarters and of the dead files in this Ministry's Mombasa office helped fill out the picture, as this governmental agency, long responsible for guiding trade union growth, has maintained detailed records of internal union affairs and activities. Inasmuch as the officials of this department have naturally interpreted events from the point of view of the government's interests (whether colonial or post-colonial), their reports, memoranda and correspondence provide yet another perspective on trade unionism.

The researcher, in these circumstances, must try as best he can to balance off varying viewpoints, fortified by the belief that labour is an important topic that should not be ignored simply because reliable data is difficult to obtain. Hence, after perusing the above documentary sources for ten months, I began pursuing trade unionists and other knowledgeable individuals. In all, I conducted seventy-three lengthy and detailed interviews with past and present national and branch union officials, politicians, management representatives and civil servants, usually after spending considerable time in establishing my trustworthiness with potential respondents. In addition, I engaged in many informal discussions with union officials and union members. While I did not employ a rigorous sampling procedure in selecting trade unionists for interviewing, I was careful to choose respondents within the fifteen unions in my sample who held office at various levels and in various geographical locations. As well, I took advantage of any other opportunities for discussions that arose; one could not afford to miss any chance to speak to such a mobile and busy group of individuals. I did not employ a standard interview schedule but questioned each interviewee on matters about which I expected him to be informed, as well as on his career and attitudes. Previous detailed study of the documentary sources allowed the interviewer to appraise critically the information supplied by respondents and to follow up interesting, though unexpected, ideas or revelations. Owing to the political sensitivity of the research topic, I was regrettably not authorized to undertake a sample survey of workers' attitudes towards their unions, management and political leaders.

Some readers will be disappointed by the absence of references to specific sources for many statements. Since some of the subjects discussed in interviews and discussions involved contentious political and trade union issues, a condition of nearly all such exchanges was that the respondent would remain anonymous. Moreover, I was granted privileged access to some private and governmental files and documents which I cannot specifically identify.

Appendix 2
Trade Union 'voting'* membership, 1952–70

Date of registration	Union	1952	1955	1958	1961	1964	1967	1970
22. v. 52	EAFBCWU	7,530	616	1,960	8,342	1,523	6,154	9,547
3. vi. 52	KD&CWU–KUCFAW	1,300	140	5,806	5,892	10,786	14,919	19,746
4. ix. 53	KLGWU	—	1,909	600	7,560	8,155	21,287	16,919
2. x. 53	RAU(K)	—	1,500	3,900	3,900	16,909	13,549	13,309
20. x. 54	DWU	—	2,044	1,595	3,000	6,137	6,542	7,284
5. viii. 58	KPOWU	—	—	250	1,600	1,936	1,492	1,227
11. viii. 58	KCWU	—	—	668	2,015	1,901	2,832	3,932
7. ix. 59	TPWU	—	—	—	262	Defunct	Defunct	Defunct
29. xi. 60	KUSPW	—	—	—	132	987	2,883	4,843
13. ii. 61	GAWU	—	—	—	27,870	Defunct	Defunct	Defunct
7. ix. 61	KQ&MWU	—	—	—	200	15	1,373	1,486
5. ix. 62	CSACSU(K)	—	—	—	—	548	864	1,683
22. viii. 63	KPAWU	—	—	—	—	43,395	63,160	40,575

SOURCE: Kenya, *Annual Report of the Registrar-General*, various years.

* A 'voting' member is one who is less than thirteen weeks in arrears with his monthly union dues. Note, however, that, prior to the introduction of the 'check-off' system and more rigorous supervision by the Registrar of Trade Unions in the early 1960s, many of the union returns actually report as members all those whose names appear on the union's books, regardless of whether these persons were paid up or not. Thus, before 1964, most figures are inflated.

NOTE: Two of the unions in the sample do not appear in the above list because they were registered and then de-registered within one of the three-year intervals. One of these was the Coffee Plantation Workers' Union, which was registered on 20 November 1959, and de-registered on 12 December 1961. In December 1960 it had a membership of 1,586. The other union was the Sisal and Coffee Plantation Workers' Union, which was registered on 24 August 1962, and amalgamated with two other unions on 12 August 1963. At the end of December 1962 the SCPWU had a reported membership of 25,798.

Appendix 3

The determination of tribal affiliation

The object was to arrive at a rough estimate of the ethnic composition of the branch and national officers of fifteen trade unions at several points in time. Ideally, a researcher would obtain this information by questioning at least one member of each branch and head office executive about the tribal affiliations of his colleagues and himself. In practice, this method is unfeasible. Union branches are located in every part of the country and, indeed, many have no office as all officials are part-time. Moreover, ethnicity is a sensitive subject; a researcher would be likely to raise suspicions by questioning a large number of officials on this topic. Hence, one is thrown back to more indirect and less accurate means of estimating tribal composition. The technique adopted was the attribution of tribe on the basis of name, a method employed in at least two other sociological investigations in Kenya.[1]

The files of the Registrar of Trade Unions in Nairobi provided the names of all present and past national officials of registered trade unions, and of all branch officials since October 1964. The names of members of opposition factions at the head-office level were obtained from various sources, including the files and records of the Registrar of Trade Unions, the Ministry of Labour and individual trade unions. A total of 2,536 names resulted. Of these, 815 names were eliminated from the final list, either because the researcher gained personal knowledge of the ethnic affiliation of union leaders, or because the attribution of tribe was obvious from a superficial knowledge of the naming systems of the main tribes involved. As a check on the validity of name analysis, the names of 75 people were included in the final list of 1,721 names, even though the researcher had personal knowledge of their tribal affiliation.

Lists of the 1,721 names were then distributed to three Kenyan university students – a Luo, a Kikuyu and a Mluhya – each of whom worked independently of the others. They were instructed to categorize each name in terms of one of the following categories: Coastal tribes, Akamba, Kikuyu–Meru–Embu, Kalenjin, Masai, Baluhya-Iteso, Gusii, Luo, 'Others' (i.e., non-Kenyan tribes), and 'Don't Know'. The results showed that the final two categories were confusing because, if a student did not know the ethnic affiliation of a particular name, he could choose to place it in either category. Thus, these two categories were reduced to one.

To provide a check on the reliability of the responses by the three students, a Kikuyu and a Luo friend independently categorized a sample of the 1,721 names appearing on the list. The results are shown in the following table.

[1] See S. K. Karimi, 'The Nairobi African Community as Seen Through the General Elections', paper presented to the East African Institute for Social Research Conference, Kampala, June 1961; and Michael Chaput (ed.), *Patterns of Elite Formation in Kenya, Senegal, Tanzania and Zambia* (Syracuse, Program of East African Studies, Syracuse University, 1968).

Responses of the three students

Names on which the three students agree	850	(49%)
Names on which two students agree	624	(37%)
Names on which there is no agreement, or 'Don't know'	247	(14%)
Total no. of names	1,721	(100%)
Names not on list either because already known or ethnic affiliation obvious from knowledge of naming systems		815
Total no. of names		2,536

Check on reliability

Karanja, the Kikuyu checker, took a sample of every third name, which meant he considered the ethnic affiliation of a total of 554 names.

Ochieng, the Luo checker, took a sample of every fifth name, which meant he considered the ethnic affiliation of a total of 339 names.

To test the reliability of the answers given by the three students, the researcher considered only those names on which at least two of the three students were in agreement on ethnic affiliation. Of Karanja's sample of 554 names, 450 fell into this category; of Ochieng's 339 names, 279 were in this category.

	Agreed with students	Disagreed with students	'Don't know' or 'others'	Total
Karanja				
No. of responses	250	99	101	450
% of total responses	56	22	22	100
Ochieng				
No. of responses	196	36	47	279
% of total	70	13	17	100

Discussion

The results seem to warrant using name analysis as the basis of a rough estimate of tribal composition. It is true that the three students were unanimous on only 49 per cent of the 1,721 names. However, this percentage rises to 66 per cent of the total of 2,536 names when the 815 names excluded from the list on the grounds of personal knowledge or obviousness are added to the 850 listed names on which the students were unanimous. Unanimity, of course, does not necessarily imply correctness of categorization, but it does provide a reasonable assurance of validity, given that the three students and two checkers were drawn from three different tribes. It should be noted that on only 14 per cent of the responses did the three students either not know the ethnic affiliation, or totally disagree. Moreover, the checkers only disagreed with a majority of the three students on 22 per cent and 13 per cent of the names, respectively. Most of these disagreements, as one might expect, were over categorization of a name as either Luo, Gusii or Abaluhya–Iteso, and Kamba or Kikuyu. The fact that at least four of the five people involved in the project agreed on 51 of the 86 names they all considered is significant given that a high proportion of the times on which they disagreed was due to one or two of the analysts being unsure of tribal affiliation, and thus writing 'Don't Know'.

Three further points are worth making in connection with this technique. First, the researcher placed on the list the names of 75 people whose ethnic affiliation he had already established. As one would expect, such names as 'Omido' and 'Ottenyo' were categorized as Luo, though, in fact, their owners were Luhya. Again, 'Mwani-ki' was categorized as both Kamba and Kikuyu, though the person was Kikuyu. But the point is that one becomes aware very quickly which names can belong to more than one tribe, and one can attempt to randomize the categorization of such names. Secondly, the author had a very important advantage over the five other people involved in this project; he knew the geographical location of each branch from which the names of the officials were drawn. If, for example, there is disagreement over whether a name is Luo or Luhya, and the branch is located in Kakamega, then the chances are that the official is a Mluhya. In the same way, an official in a Nyeri, or even a Thika branch is more likely to be Kikuyu than Kamba. Knowledge of the dominant ethnic group in different areas, and knowledge of the important sources of migration to certain industries and areas (e.g., Mombasa) provides the author with a higher degree of accuracy than is suggested by the figures arrived at above. Finally, it should be borne in mind that all that is required for this study is a gross figure, so that one can say, for instance, that one-half or one-third of the branch officials are drawn from a particular tribe or group of related tribes. At this level of approximation, name analysis seems to be a justifiable technique.

Notes

Chapter 1

1 Frantz Fanon, *The Wretched of the Earth* (Harmondsworth: Penguin, 1967), 86, 96–8.
2 For other techniques, see E. J. Berg, 'The Development of a Labor Force in Sub-Saharan Africa', *Economic Development and Cultural Change,* XIII (1965), 394–412.
3 Ann Seidman, *Comparative Development Strategies in East Africa* (Nairobi: East African Publishing House, 1972), 15.
4 International Bank for Reconstruction and Development, *The Economic Development of Kenya* (Baltimore: Johns Hopkins Press, 1963), 18.
5 C. C. Wrigley, 'Kenya: The Patterns of Economic Life, 1902–1945', in Vincent Harlow, E. M. Chilver and A. Smith (eds.), *History of East Africa,* Vol. II (Oxford University Press, 1966), 260.
6 Republic of Kenya, *Development Plan, 1966–1970,* 17.
7 Seidman, *Comparative Development Strategies,* 23, 24.
8 See esp., International Labour Organization, *Employment, Incomes and Equality: A Strategy for Increasing Productive Employment in Kenya* (Geneva, 1972), Chap. 6; and Seidman, *Comparative Development Strategies,* Chap. 3.
9 P. Marris, 'Economics is Not Enough', *East Africa Journal,* III (February 1967), 14–15.
10 For a discussion of many aspects of foreign investment in Kenyan industry, see Technical Paper 16, in ILO, *Employment, Incomes and Equality,* 437–57.
11 For some estimates of foreign control see *ibid.,* 441.
12 National Christian Council of Churches, *Who Controls Industry in Kenya?* (Nairobi: East African Publishing House, 1968), Chaps. 2, 3 and 5. See also Seidman, *Comparative Development Strategies,* 33–6.
13 Seidman, *Comparative Development Strategies,* 37. See also NCCC, *Who Controls Industry,* Chaps. 4, 9, 10, 11, and ILO, *Employment, Incomes and Equality,* 441–2.
14 NCCC, *Who Controls Industry,* 257.
15 ILO, *Employment, Incomes and Equality,* 442, 446.
16 For all these figures, see *ibid.,* Table 126, p. 571.
17 R. Gavin, 'Correcting Racial Imbalances in Employment in Kenya', *International Labour Review,* XCV (Jan.–Feb. 1967), 67.
18 See R. Lacey, 'Foreign Resources and Development', in Goran Hyden, Robert Jackson and John Okumu (eds.), *Development Administration* (Nairobi: Oxford University Press, 1970), 80–1.
19 ILO, *Employment, Incomes and Equality,* 572.
20 For the comparative statistics, see J. R. Nellis, 'Expatriates in the Government of Kenya', paper delivered at the Canadian Association of African Studies Conference, Ottawa, Feb. 16–18, 1973, pp. 10–11.
21 *Ibid.,* 15, 31.

22 For a discussion of the monopolistic nature of the petty-bourgeoisie emerging in Kenya, see C. T. Leys, 'The Limits of African Capitalism: The Formation of the Monopolistic Petty-Bourgeoisie in Kenya', in *Developmental Trends in Kenya*, proceedings of a seminar held in the Centre for African Studies, University of Edinburgh, 28–9 April 1972.

23 For a general assessment of the regime's success, see Peter Marris and Anthony Somerset, *African Businessmen: A Study of Enterpreneurship and Development in Kenya* (London: Routledge & Kegan Paul, 1971).

24 See esp. Chap. 13 of M. P. K. Sorrenson, *Land Reform in the Kikuyu Country* (Nairobi: Oxford University Press, 1967).

25 ILO, *Employment, Incomes and Equality*, Table 25, p. 74.

26 *Ibid.*, 100.

27 For a discussion of the nature and conditions under which tribal identity assumes salience in East Africa, see P. H. Gulliver, 'Introduction', in Gulliver (ed.), *Tradition and Transition in East Africa* (Los Angeles: University of California Press, 1969).

28 See, for example, J. J. Okumu, 'Charisma and Politics in Kenya', *East Africa Journal*, v, 2 (Feb. 1968), 11–12.

29 C. T. Leys, 'Politics in Kenya: The Development of Peasant Society', *British Journal of Political Science*, i (July 1971), 325–32.

30 For fascinating studies of social differentiation, class formation and political conflict in various areas of rural Kenya, see G. B. Lamb, 'Politics and Administration in Murang'a District, Kenya', D. Phil. dissertation, University of Sussex, 1970; A. Sandberg, 'Generational Conflict and Entrepreneurship in Meru', Discussion Paper No. 52, Institute for Development Studies, Nairobi, Dec. 1969; and David Parkin, 'The Monopoly of Ritual: Political Redefinition in a Kenya Rural Trading Centre', unpublished paper presented at the University of Toronto, Jan. 1971. See also ILO, *Employment, Incomes and Equality*, 80.

31 Sorrenson, *Land Reform*, 227.

32 G. Wasserman, 'Continuity and Counter-Insurgency: The Role of Land Reform in Decolonizing Kenya, 1962–70', *Canadian Journal of African Studies*, vii, 1 (1973), 148.

33 These figures on the urban poor are taken from ILO, *Employment, Incomes and Inequality*, 56, 63–4.

34 See T. Shanin, 'The Peasantry as a Political Factor', *Sociological Review*, xiv (1966), 5–27.

35 See R. Cohen and D. Michael, 'The Revolutionary Potential of the African Lumpenproletariat: A Skeptical View', *Bulletin of the Institute of Development Studies*, University of Sussex (Oct. 1973); and Joan Nelson, *Migrants, Urban Poverty and Instability in Developing Nations*, Harvard University, Center for International Affairs, Occasional Paper No. 22, Sept. 1969.

36 For a discussion of the inadequacies of Marxist class analysis in the modern world, see Stanislaw Ossowski, *Class Structure in the Social Consciousness* (London: Routledge & Kegan Paul, 1961), esp. p. 184.

37 R. Cohen, 'Class in Africa: Analytical Problems and Perspectives', *The Socialist Register, 1972* (London: Merlin Press, 1972), 248. On the same point, see Oginga Odinga, *Not Yet Uhuru* (London: Heinemann, 1967), 303.

38 See J. R. Nellis, 'Is the Kenyan Bureaucracy Developmental? Political Considerations in Development Administration', *African Studies Review*, xiv, 3 (Dec. 1971), 391.

39 ILO, *Employment, Incomes and Equality*, 101. See also, Seidman, *Comparative Development Strategies*, 97–8.

40 Ann Seidman, 'Old Motives, New Methods: Foreign Enterprise in Africa To-day', in C. Allen and R. W. Johnson (eds.), *African Perspective* (London: Cambridge University Press, 1970), 262–3, 268–9; and G. Arrighi, 'International Corporations, Labour Aristocracies, and Economic Development in Tropical Africa', in R. I. Rhodes (ed.), *Imperialism and Underdevelopment* (New York: Monthly Review Press, 1970), 256–7.

41 For the employers' view, see the article by an Executive Officer of the Federation of Kenya Employers, David Richmond, 'Employer Attitudes to Wage Policies in Developing Countries', in Anthony D. Smith (ed.), *Wage Policy Issues in Economic Development* (London: Macmillan, 1969). For the Government's view, see Chap. 7 below.

42 Leys, 'Politics in Kenya', 311–12.

43 Quoted in P. Krauss, 'From Devil to Father Figure: The Transformation of Jomo Kenyatta by Kenya Whites', *Journal of Modern African Studies*, IX, 1 (1971), 131–7.

44 Leys, 'The Limits of African Capitalism'.

45 Figures on wage employment, unless otherwise indicated, are drawn from *Economic Survey, 1970*, Tables 9.1 and 9.2, pp. 128–9. For the sake of comparison, Zambia had about the same proportion in wage employment as Kenya while only about 10 per cent of the labour force in Tanzania and Uganda were wage-earners. See K. C. Doctor and H. Gallis, 'Size and Characteristics of Wage Employment in Africa: Statistical Estimates', *International Labour Review*, XCIII, 2 (Feb. 1966), 159.

46 Twenty-eight of these unions, which included those with the largest memberships and with predominantly African memberships, were affiliated to COTU, the sole registered trade union federation.

47 *Statistical Abstract, 1971*, Table 203, p. 189.

48 For a summary of the results of the 1961 Industrial Census, see S. H. Ominde, *Land and Population Movements in Kenya* (London: Heinemann, 1968).

49 Walter Elkan, *Migrants and Proletarians: Urban Labour in the Economic Development of Uganda* (New York: Oxford University Press, 1960), 131–2.

50 Kenya, Colony and Protectorate, *Report of the Committee on African Wages* (Nairobi, 1954). (This is usually referred to as the 'Carpenter Report'.)

51 Alice Amsden, *The Development of Industrial Relations in Kenya*, Ph.D. dissertation (University of London, 1968), 139. See also, J. B. K. Hunter, 'The Development of the Labour Market in Kenya', in I. G. Stewart (ed.), *Economic Development and Structural Change* (Edinburgh: Edinburgh University Press, 1969), 120–1, 133–4.

52 K. Bissman, 'Industrial Worker in East Africa', *International Journal of Comparative Sociology*, X (March-June, 1969), 27.

53 H. Rempel, 'The Rural-to-Urban Migrant in Kenya', *African Urban Notes*, IV, 1 (Spring, 1971), 70.

54 See Amsden, *The Development of Industrial Relations in Kenya*, 138–53.

55 Kenya, *The Pattern of Income, Expenditure and Consumption of African Middle Income Workers in Nairobi, July 1963* (Nairobi: Government Printer, 1964).

56 Rempel, 'Rural-to-Urban Migrant in Kenya', Table 6, p. 62. A somewhat conflicting finding is that of Bissman's that 77 per cent of Kenyan industrial workers interviewed held land that was presently being worked. Bissman, 'Industrial Worker in East Africa', 28.

57 Marc Ross, *Politics and Urbanization: Two Communities in Nairobi*, Ph.D. dissertation (Northwestern University, 1968), 68.

58 H. Wolpe, 'Port Harcourt: Ibo Politics in Microcosm', *Journal of Modern African Studies*, VII, 3 (1969), 489–90; and R. Melson, 'Ideology and Inconsistency: The "Cross-Pressured" Nigerian Worker', *APSR*, LXV (March 1971), 161–71.

59 See G. Bennett, 'Tribalism and Politics in East Africa', in P. H. Gulliver (ed.), *Tradition and Transition in East Africa* (Los Angeles: University of California Press, 1969), 71–9.

60 Arrighi, 'International Corporations, Labour Aristocracies and Economic Development,' 234–9, 256.

61 For a comparative analysis of working-class radicalization, see R. Sandbrook, 'The Working Class in the Future of the Third World', *World Politics*, XXV (April 1973), 448–78.

62 See R. Sandbrook, 'Patrons, Clients and Factions: New Dimensions of Conflict Analysis in Africa', *Canadian Journal of Political Science*, V (March 1972), 104–19; and B. J. Berman, 'Clientelism and Neo-Colonialism: Center-Periphery Relations and Political Development in African States', paper prepared for delivery at the IXth World Congress of the International Political Science Association, Montreal, 19–25 August 1973, esp. pp. 8–17.

63 Fanon, *Wretched of the Earth*, Chap. 3.

64 Both of these features have characterized the first decade of Kenya's independence. I do not have space here to outline the increasing authoritarianism of the ruling elite – its elimination of opposition parties, meaningful popular participation and constitutional limitations on the exercise of power. These aspects are discussed at length in Cherry Gertzel, *The Politics of Independent Kenya* (London: Heinemann, 1970), esp. Chaps. 2–6 and the Appendix; and in Y. P. Ghai and J. P. W. B. McAuslan, *Public Law and Political Change in Kenya* (Nairobi: Oxford University Press, 1970), Chaps. 5–8, 11 and 13.

65 J. D. Powell, 'Peasant Society and Clientelist Politics', *American Political Science Review*, LXIV (June 1970), 411–12.

66 See Gertzel, *Politics of Independent Kenya*, Chap. 3; D. Koff, 'Kenya's Little General Election', *Africa Report*, XI, 7 (Oct. 1966), 57–60; and J. J. Okumu, 'The By-election in Gem: An Assessment', *East Africa Journal*, VI (June 1969), 9–17.

67 N. K. Nicholson, 'The Factional Model and the Study of Politics', *Comparative Political Studies*, V, 3 (1972), 299.

68 See Okumu, 'Charisma and Politics', 12; and S. Rohio, 'Ideology and Rural Development', *East Africa Journal*, IX, 5 (May 1972), 29–31.

69 Cf. A. Weingrod, 'Patrons, Patronage and Political Parties', *Comparative Studies in Society and History*, X (July 1968); and E. Wolf, 'Kinship, Friendship and Patron–Client Relationships in Complex Societies', in Michael Banton (ed.), *Social Anthropology of Complex Societies* (London: Tavistock Publications, 1966).

70 This point is made by H. Alavi, 'Peasants and Revolution', *The Socialist Register, 1965* (London: Merlin Press, 1965), 274; and C. Landé, 'Networks and Groups in South-east Asia', paper presented to the South-east Asia Development Advisory Group, New York, March 1970, p. 36.

71 The most comprehensive source on recent Kenyan politics is Gertzel, *Politics of Independent Kenya*.

72 *Ibid.*, 61. See also, J. E. Hakes, 'Intra-Elite Bargaining and Co-optation in the Kenya Parliament', paper presented at the African Studies Association Meeting, Philadelphia, 8–11 November 1972.

73 See R. Stren, 'Factional Politics and Central Control in Mombasa, 1960–69',
   Canadian Journal of African Studies, IV (Winter 1970); W. O. Oyugi, 'The
   Ndhiwa By-Elections', *East Africa Journal*; and Lamb, 'Politics and Administration in Murang'a District', Chap. 3.
74 J. Okumu, 'The Socio-Political Setting', in Goran Hyden, R. Jackson and J.
   Okumu (eds.), *Development Administration: The Kenya Experience* (Nairobi:
   Oxford University Press, 1970), 32; and G. Hyden, 'Government and Co-operatives', in Hyden *et al.*, *Development Administration*, 306–7.
75 Since the author could not carry out a systematic attitudinal survey, this reference to the workers' own testimony is based on a considerable number of
   informal discussions with workers and their representatives in various parts of
   Kenya, especially Nairobi and Mombasa.
76 W. H. Friedland and D. Nelkin, 'African Labor in the Post-Independence
   Period', paper presented at the 1967 meeting of the African Studies Association,
   p. 4.
77 William H. Friedland, *Vuta Kamba: The Development of Trade Unions in
   Tanganyika* (Stanford: Hoover Institution Press, 1969), 152–3.
78 Robert H. Bates, *Unions, Parties, and Political Development: A Study of the
   Mineworkers in Zambia* (New Haven: Yale University Press, 1971), 56, 63.
79 Bates, *Unions, Parties, and Political Development*, 98–104.
80 See A. M. Ross, *Trade Union Wage Policy* (Berkeley: University of California
   Press, 1948), 27; and Joel Seidman, 'The Labor Union as an Organization', in
   Arthur Kornhauser *et al.* (eds.), *Industrial Conflict* (London: McGraw-Hill,
   1954), 109–20.
81 See especially, Clark Kerr, J. T. Dunlop, F. H. Harbison and C. A. Myers,
   Industrialism and Industrial Man, 2nd ed. (New York: Oxford University
   Press, 1964), 60–1.
82 Jean Meynaud and Anisse Salah-Bey, *Trade Unionism in Africa* (London:
   Methuen, 1967), 160.
83 Bates, *Unions, Parties, and Political Development*, 27.
84 Ioan Davies, *African Trade Unions* (Harmondsworth: Penguin, 1966), 222.
85 Readers interested in the methodology employed in this study, including the
   sample of unions selected for investigation, are referred to Appendix 1.

Chapter 2

1 See Roger Scott, *The Development of Trade Unions in Uganda* (Nairobi: East
   African Publishing House, 1966), 158; and William Tordoff, 'Trade Unionism in
   Tanzania', *Journal of Development Studies*, II (July 1966), 423.
2 See Robert H. Bates, *Unions, Parties, and Political Development: A Study of
   the Mineworkers in Zambia* (New Haven: Yale University Press, 1971), 126; and
   L. N. Trachtman, 'The Labour Movement of Ghana: A Study in Political
   Unionism', *Economic Development and Cultural Change*, X (Jan. 1962), 183–4.
3 See William H. Friedland, 'Cooperation, Conflict and Conscription: TANU–
   TFL Relations, 1955–1964', in Jeffrey Butler and A. A. Castagno (eds.),
   Boston University Papers on Africa: Transition in African Politics (New York:
   Praeger, 1967), 96; and Donald Chesworth, 'The Evolution of Trade Unions in
   Tanganyika', paper delivered at the Institute of Commonwealth Studies,
   University of London, November 1966, p. 7.
4 This distinction is derived from G. H. Williams, 'The Concept of "Egemonia" in
   the Thought of Antonio Gramsci', *Journal of the History of Ideas*, XXI (Oct.–Dec.
   1960), 586–97.

5 Y. P. Ghai and J. P. W. B. McAuslan, *Public Law and Political Change in Kenya* (Nairobi: Oxford University Press, 1970), 506.

6 See W. H. Friedland, 'Paradoxes of African Trade Unionism: Organizational Chaos and Political Potential', *Africa Report* (June 1965), 6–13.

7 R. Murray, 'Militarism in Africa', *New Left Review*, No. 38 (July–August 1966), 46.

8 See esp. A. Clayton and D. C. Savage, *Government and Labour in Kenya, 1895–1963* (London: Frank Cass, 1974). See also Makhan Singh, *History of Kenya's Trade Union Movement to 1952* (Nairobi: East African Publishing House, 1969); R. Sandbrook, 'The State and the Development of Trade Unionism', in Goran Hyden, R. Jackson and J. Okumu (eds.), *Development Administration: The Kenyan Experience* (Nairobi: Oxford University Press, 1970), 252–94; and S. Stichter, 'The Development of a Working Class in Kenya', in R. Sandbrook and R. Cohen (eds.), *The Development of an African Working Class* (forthcoming, 1975).

9 The Attorney-General, H. C. Willan, described the object of the bill in these terms in his speech moving the bill. See Kenya Colony, *Legislative Council Debates*, II (1937), col. 48.

10 See Trade Unions (Amendment) Ordinance, 1939 and Trade Unions and Trade Disputes Ordinance, 1943. The latter bill replaced all preceding trade union legislation. In 1940, the Colonial Secretary's position vis-à-vis intransigent colonial governments was greatly enhanced by the Colonial Development and Welfare Act. One section provided that, where money was spent under the Act, the law of the colony concerned should furnish 'reasonable facilities' for the establishment of trade unions.

11 See Singh, *History of Kenya's Union Movement*, 141–57.

12 *Ibid.*, 202–69.

13 Political organizations were allowed to form on a district basis in June 1955.

14 A KFL file entitled 'British TUC, 1953–60' contains references to several instances in which the TUC General Secretary responded to a request by Mboya by making representations to the Colonial Secretary.

15 The Congress was held in late May 1955. See Tom Mboya, *The Kenya Question: An African Answer* (London: Fabian Colonial Bureau, 1956).

16 See *Kenya Weekly News* (20 January 1956), 2–3.

17 See George Bennett, *Kenya: A Political History* (Oxford: Oxford University Press, 1963), 139.

18 *E.A. Standard* (13 March 1956).

19 Mboya, 'Annual Report by the General Secretary to the KFL Annual Conference' (13 September 1958).

20 An unspecificable number of African employees did stay home on 15 April, but rail and road transport and other public services were unaffected. Predictably, the highest absentee rate on Good Friday was among Kikuyu coffee estate workers in Kiambu, probably the most politically-conscious segment of the work force.

21 Federation of Kenya Employers, 'Notes of the Chairman for Meeting of the Management Board, 22 April 1960'.

22 It was rumoured that the two politicians had made a secret pact with the Colonial Secretary to keep Kenyatta in detention. See G. Bennett and C. G. Rosberg, *The Kenyatta Election* (Oxford: Oxford University Press, 1961), 131–3.

23 Orde Browne, *Report on Labour Conditions in East Africa* (London: HMSO, 1946), Col. 193. This Report stated that 'the need for their appointment is to

ensure that the growth of a Trade Union movement...should be on sound and wellproved lines, and that it should not fall into the hands of unscrupulous persons anxious to exploit it for their own ends.'

24 Mboya, *Freedom and After* (London: André Deutsch, 1963), 31.
25 See Elliot Berg and Jeremy Butler, 'Trade Unions', in James Coleman and C. G. Rosberg (eds.), *Political Parties and National Integration in Tropical Africa* (Berkeley: University of California Press, 1964), 371.
26 KFL, 'Resolutions Adopted at the General Council Meeting Held on Saturday–Sunday, December 1st and 2nd, 1962'.
27 *E.A. Standard* (Coast edition) (11 February 1963).
28 For C. K. Lubembe's policy, see COTU(K), 'A Statement of Policy', Nairobi, 8 November 1966. For J. D. Akumu's policy, see *E.A. Standard* (25 February 1969).
29 Their proposals were published by the Government Printer in Nairobi as 'The Policy on Trade Union Organization in Kenya', on 1 September 1965; it was referred to as the 'Presidential Declaration'.
30 In practice, President Kenyatta has always respected the democratic principle by appointing those with the largest number of votes to these posts. He has never revoked the appointment of any COTU official. Finally, the Labour Minister has initiated two committees of inquiry into COTU's affairs; one in 1967, and the other in 1968.
31 Kenya Colony, *Report of the Committee on African Wages* (Nairobi, 1954).
32 Kenya Colony, *The Pattern of Income and Consumption of African Labourers in Nairobi, October–November, 1950* (Nairobi, 1951).
33 See Kenya Colony, *Report of the Commission of Inquiry Appointed to Examine the Labour Conditions in Mombasa* (Nairobi, 1939); Kenya Colony, *Brief Comments on Certain Sections of the Phillips Report on Labour Unrest in Mombasa* (Nairobi, 1946); and Kenya Colony, *Report on the Economic and Social Background of the Mombasa Labour Disputes* (Nairobi, 1947).
34 Reginald Green, 'Wage Levels, Employment, Productivity and Consumption', in James R. Sheffield (ed.), *Education Employment and Rural Development* (Nairobi: East African Publishing House, 1967), 218.
35 'Meeting of Ministers Responsible for Labour in Kenya, Uganda and Tanganyika, held at Kampala, August 1962' (extracts contained in ILO seminar on Industrial Relations, Abidjan, 15–26 October 1963).
36 Refer to *Venture*, xvi, 1 (1964), 11–13.
37 A good summary is contained in F. R. Livingstone, 'The Government, the Worker and the Law in Kenya', *East Africa Law Journal*, iii (1967), 282–315. See also Alice Amsden, *International Firms and Labour in Kenya* (London: Frank Cass, 1971).
38 Kenya, National Assembly, *Official Report*, iv (1965), cols. 7602, 7603.
39 *Daily Nation* (28 August 1969).
40 Kenya, National Assembly, *Official Report*, xxiii (16 June 1971).
41 Some of the boards on which union leaders serve are the Labour Advisory Board, the General Wages Advisory Board, Wages Councils, the National Social Security Fund Council, the Apprenticeship Board and the Factories Committee. Top COTU leaders also have been appointed to the boards of publicly owned or controlled corporations.
42 A 'check-off' system is one in which the employer is obliged to deduct and remit to union headquarters the monthly union dues of all employees who have signed forms acknowledging membership in the relevant trade union. In a 'union shop'

situation, all the employees in an enterprise or industry must pay union dues when a specified proportion of these employees – usually 50 per cent – voluntarily join the union.

43 Kenya, National Assembly, *Official Report*, XXIII (24 June 1971), col. 1473.

Chapter 3

1 Walter Galenson, 'Introduction', in Galenson (ed.), *Labor and Economic Development* (New York: John Wiley, 1959), 13, 14.

2 Several employers and management officials confirmed that this was not an uncommon tactic.

3 Considering that Permanent Secretaries in the Kenyan civil service (except the one in the Office of the President) were paid approximately K£240 per month (until July 1970), trade union leaders making up to K£200 per month are certainly in the top income bracket in Kenya.

4 Such control is an important feature of oligarchical dominance of many American trade unions. See Joel Seidman, 'Some Requirements for Union Democracy', in R. A. Lester, ed., *Labor: Readings on Major Issues* (New York: Random House, 1965), 164.

5 See Edna E. Raphael, 'Power Structure and Membership Dispersion in Unions', *American Journal of Sociology*, LXXI (Nov. 1965), 274–84, esp. p. 283.

6 As of December 1968. All union and branch membership figures are taken from the unions' annual returns submitted to the Registrar of Trade Unions.

7 See S. M. Lipset, 'The Political Process in Trade Unions', in Morroe Berger, Charles Page and Theodore Abel (eds.), *Freedom and Control in Modern Society* (New York: Van Nostrand, 1954), 101.

8 The first estimate was provided by J. D. Akumu, General Secretary of the union until 1965; the second by Juma Boy, who has been General Secretary since May 1966.

9 Interview, Johnstone Mwandawiro, General Secretary (until August 1969), RAU(K), 14 July 1969.

10 These figures are compiled from the annual returns which FKE members submitted to that body in 1967.

11 Chakufwa Chihana, the Malawian editor, was a trusted lieutenant of Clement Lubembe while the latter was the President of KUCFAW and Secretary-General of the KFL and COTU(K). Chihana also edited the KFL's 'Department of Information Bulletin'. He was expelled from the country after Lubembe fell from power.

12 Interview, Sammy Muhanji, General Secretary of KUCFAW, 12 August 1969.

13 GAWU, 'Mid-Year Report, 1961, Delivered by H. A. Oduor, General Secretary, on June 30, 1961' (mimeo.).

14 Interview, James Karebe, General Secretary of the KLGWU, 6 September 1969.

15 The evidence is necessarily fragmentary because few unions consistently provide detailed audited annual accounts. Moreover, the various unions employ differing categories of expenditures.

16 The concepts 'moral' and 'contractual' ties are taken from F. G. Bailey, *Stratagems and Spoils: A Social Anthropology of Politics* (Oxford: Basil Blackwell, 1969).

17 These are federations of independent unions from various countries that represent workers in particular occupations or industries. They are closely associated with the International Confederation of Free Trade Unions.

18 Most unions simply provide such gross figures as 'Working Expenses: Head Office' and 'Working Expenses: Branches'.

19 See J. P. Windmuller, 'External Influences on Labor Organizations in Under-developed Countries', *Industrial and Labor Relations Review*, XVI, 4 (July, 1963), 559–73. I know of cases in which the following governments allocated scholar-ships to Kenyan trade unionists: the USA, USSR, UK, Canada, Yugoslavia, West Germany, Austria, Cuba, Israel, UAR and Sweden.

20 'Minutes of the Executive Committee of the KFL Held in Solidarity Building on 30 November 1962'.

21 Lubembe, 'Report in the Form of a Speech from Sen. C. K. Lubembe, Deputy General Secretary', Address to the KFL Biennial Conference of 17–18 August 1963.

22 M. of L. files, Nairobi.

23 Wages councils are statutory wage-determination bodies established for trades or industries in which there are a multiplicity of small employers. A perusal of the *Kenya Gazette* between 1952 and mid-1969 revealed the existence of thirteen such bodies.

24 Smock reports that leaders of the Nigerian Coal Miners' Union used their influence on promotions within the Coal Corporation to reward supporters and punish opponents. See David Smock, *Conflict and Control in an African Trade Union* (Stanford: Hoover Institution Press, 1969), 12.

25 Seidman, 'Some Requirements of Union Democracy', 165.

26 Interview, Mr S. O. Tala, the Assistant Registrar of Trade Unions, July 1969.

27 The former figures were obtained from the reports of the supervising M. of L. officials; the latter ones were found in the unions' Annual Returns to the Registrar.

28 Of course, the Ministry was acting as a judge in its own cause in these cases. The one case in which an investigator found some grounds for complaint was a flagrant attempt by a labour officer to manipulate a branch election in favour of his former comrades within his old union. Since so many of the labour officers and industrial relations assistants who supervise union elections are former trade unionists themselves, it is not surprising that some of them allow old loyalties to outweigh their official obligation to remain impartial.

29 The police are responsible for ensuring that election meetings are orderly, and that 'non-members' are kept from the meeting place.

30 Intervention by national officials in branch elections is often admitted by union leaders, but it is justified in terms of the necessity to ensure that the best people are elected. One General Secretary remarked that the head office sometimes 'imposed a branch candidate in order to ensure that the right people are elected to branch office. We can't have illiterates as branch leaders'.

31 The head office, for example, may permit (or advise) the branch secretary to set the time for the branch general meeting during working hours. It may then request only selected employers to allow union members time off to attend the meeting. Since one tribe may be more numerous in one firm than another, this stratagem may aid the incumbent branch leaders.

32 The 1965 Presidential Declaration stipulated that all unions would hold elections every three years. However, a few unions continue to hold annual conferences at which the national officers present their reports on the previous year.

33 The constitution of the Dockworkers' Union could not be easily evaded because all annual conferences were supervised by Labour Department officials since the union's creation. The history of several other unions is also largely free of manipulation by union leaders. Most flagrant violations occurred during the

periods 1960–2, 1964–5 and 1971–2, when strife was at its height owing to struggles between national union federations, backed by 'Cold War' supporters.

34 Officials of the Dockworkers' Union are elected by the members at large, so there may be as many as 6,000 people voting in an election.

35 Letter to the Labour Minister, Nov., 1968. M. of L. files, Nairobi.

36 See *E.A. Standard* (18 and 21 January 1971).

Chapter 4

1 Cf. B. C. Roberts, *Trade Union Government and Administration in Great Britain* (London: Bell and Sons, 1956), 243.

2 Unanimous unopposed elections were common in other unions.

3 These comments are based on a perusal of the two unions' minutes of meetings and conferences and other union files, reports on the 1965 and 1968 elections by M. of L. officials, and interviews with various union officials.

4 The President, in his own words, felt he was treated 'just like a picture on the wall which doesn't know where, why, when, how things happen that way'. Both these charges were contained in correspondence passing between Ogutu and Nyerenda in 1960–1, and in the minutes of the Second Annual Conference, held from 8 to 10 September, 1961 at Solidarity Building, Nairobi. Correspondence and minutes are in the KCWU's files, Nairobi.

5 This policy is clearly formulated in the union's policy statement entitled *Union Tasks Ahead* (n.d., circa 1966).

6 Philip Taft, *The Structure and Government of Labor Unions* (Cambridge, Mass.: Harvard University Press, 1956), 65.

7 This statement is a translation from the Swahili minutes taken at the meeting. All the national officials, auditors and branch delegates present at the central committee meeting were returned unopposed at the following election.

8 Seymour M. Lipset, Martin Trow and James Coleman, *Union Democracy: The Internal Politics of the International Typographical Union* (Garden City, New York: Anchor Books, 1956), 270–92.

9 *Ibid.*, xi.

10 The concept 'majority-bent faction' is adapted from Maurice Durverger's use of the term 'majority-bent party' in *Political Parties: Their Organization and Activity in the Modern State* (London: Methuen, 1954), 283–5.

11 See F. G. Bailey, *Stratagems and Spoils* (Oxford: Basil Blackwell, 1969).

12 These restrictions were particularly stringent in their application to members of the Kikuyu, Embu and Meru tribes. It was these tribes, moreover, from whom the bulk of union leaders and members were drawn prior to 1953.

13 The files of the M. of L. reveal that these tactics were often quite successful.

14 In terms of internal squabbles, peculation of union funds and administrative chaos, the CPWU was beyond redemption when its registration was cancelled in December 1961.

15 A copy of this letter is in the M. of L. files, Nairobi.

16 In April 1963, the Registrar of Trade Unions refused to register the Co-operative Creameries Workers Union (Kenya), even though he discovered that the Distributive and Commercial Union had only 43 members in the Kenya Co-operative Creameries Ltd. out of a total of approximately 607 employees. Moreover, 38 of these 43 had not paid any subscription for four months, and five had only joined in January 1963. Correspondence was in the M. of L. files, Nairobi.

17 Emphasis is mine. The advice was furnished to the Assistant Registrar in a letter of March 1964, in the context of an application for registration by a union named

the 'Kenya Union of Railway Workers'. Later, the Registrar refused registration. Correspondence is in the M. of L. files, Nairobi.

18 This is how Tom Mboya, then Minister for Justice and Constitutional Affairs, described the purpose of the Act in the Kenyan National Assembly. See *Official Report*, III, Part 2 (7 August 1964), col. 1473.

19 Saeed Cockar, the President of the Industrial Court, is also the Chairman of the Tribunal. He usually sits with two members. The procedure of the Tribunal is similar to that of the Industrial Court. Each party is supposed to submit a memorandum and then to elaborate orally on this before the Tribunal. Witnesses can be called and cross-examination is permitted.

Chapter 5

1 David Smock, *Conflict and Control in an African Trade Union* (Stanford: Hoover Institution Press, 1969), 43–4, 13, 84.

2 *Ibid.*, 13.

3 R. D. Grillo, 'The Tribal Factor in an East African Trade Union', in P. H. Gulliver (ed.), *Tradition and Transition in East Africa* (Los Angeles: University of California Press, 1969), 306, 307, 328.

4 Roger Scott, 'Trade Unions and Ethnicity in Uganda', *Mawazo*, I (June 1968), 44–5, 51.

5 Arnold Epstein, *Politics in an Urban African Community* (Manchester: Manchester University Press, 1958), 233.

6 M. of L., *Annual Report, 1967*, p. 12.

7 Owing to the absence of records, it is impossible to know the precise proportion of manual workers among the total memberships of the various unions. However, leaders of thirteen of the fifteen unions studied (the Common Services and Petroleum Oil Workers' Unions being the exceptions) stated definitely that such workers comprised the bulk of the members of their unions.

8 Personal interviews with the union's officials.

9 This impression was gained through the author's contact with branch officials of various unions in different parts of Kenya.

10 Kenya, M. of L., *Annual Report, 1967*, p. 12.

11 United Kingdom, *African Labour Efficiency Survey* (The 'Northcott Report') (London: HMSO, 1949), 23.

12 Information supplied by the EAR Corporation, Nairobi.

13 Grillo, 'The Tribal Factor...', 301.

14 Until the end of the Second World War only the skilled or clerical grades were fairly stable, with a fairly high turnover of unskilled employees. The turnover rate then declined. See *African Labour Efficiency Survey*, 74.

15 The composition of the factions changed in the course of two years, though several key leaders remained throughout. Among the opposition's nineteen foremost activists were twelve Luo, six Luhya and one Kikuyu, whereas the incumbent's eleven-man team was composed of five Luo, one Luhya, two Kikuyu, two Kamba and one Coastal. The predominance of Luo and Luhya is understandable, given the fact that the two tribes together constituted 47.7 per cent of the African labour force of the EARH in Kenya in 1962. Source: EARH, Nairobi.

16 By early 1969, the basic minimum wage of railwaymen in Nairobi was KSh200, an increase of 121 per cent over nine years. In October 1960, Ohanga sponsored a resolution at a Mombasa general meeting of 4,000 railwaymen to the effect that the minimum wage must be raised to KSh250. See *E.A. Standard* (12 October 1960).

17 RAU files, Nairobi.

18 'Reasons which Necessitated Convening of Meeting of the Executive Council so Urgently, by Acting President, P. J. Muinde, to Delegates to Extraordinary Conference, November 3rd, 1960'. RAU(K) files, Nairobi.
19 Mango was a stationmaster who soon became an executive assistant in charge of the Commercial Section of the Traffic Department. He was ousted in April 1972.
20 Ottenyo, a Luhya, was selected for the RAU post by Mango and his executive.
21 On the concept 'occupational community' see Seymour Lipset, Martin Trow and James Coleman, *Union Democracy* (Garden City, New York: Anchor Books, 1956), 77–117.
22 Partial support for the view that these figures are not too inaccurate is provided by a sophisticated 1969 survey of a random sample of 1,092 African migrants in Kenya's eight largest urban areas. The distribution of ethnic groups in the sample was the following:

	%
Kikuyu, Embu and Meru	38
Abaluhya and Kisii	18
Luo	21
Kamba	12
Coast tribes (plus Tanzanians and Ugandans)	10
Others	1
Total	100

Source: Henry Rempel and Michael Todaro, 'Rural–Urban Labour Migration in Kenya', paper delivered at the seminar on Population Growth and Economic Development, Nairobi, Dec. 1969.
23 The author's survey.
24 This conclusion is based on interviews and discussions with a wide array of trade unionists who have attended annual or triennial conferences.
25 This is also a common practice in American trade unions. See Jack Barbash, *American Unions: Structure, Government and Politics* (New York: Random House, 1967), 134–5.
26 Both the Plantation and Agricultural Union and the Commercial, Food and Allied Workers have had high rates of revocation after triennial elections in which all tribes did not have an equal chance to elect union leaders. Of course, no record has been kept of the tribal affiliation of either members or those who have revoked membership, but the statements of shop stewards suggest a relationship.
27 This observation is based on discussions and interviews with trade unionists in all parts of Kenya and on a perusal of the minutes of national conferences held by unions in the sample. The sensitive nature of the topic did not permit a more systematic survey.
28 This table is based on a detailed analysis of the internal politics of the thirteen unions in my sample on which sufficient information could be gathered.
29 The term 'potential membership' rather than 'membership' is used for two reasons. First, although it is possible to arrive at a rough estimate of the tribal composition of the labour force in a particular industry or enterprise, it is more difficult to assess the ethnic composition of a union's actual membership. One cannot assume that membership reflects the composition of the labour force as a whole because union recruiters may favour one tribe, or workers from particular tribes may tend not to join the union. Moreover, unions keep no statistics on the tribal affiliation of their members. Second, the distinction between members and non-members is not crucial because of the ease with which any worker can join

the union. He has merely to sign a 'check-off' form to become automatically a member.

30 Cf. St Clair Drake, 'Some Observations on Interethnic Conflict as One Type of Intergroup Conflict', *Journal of Conflict Resolution*, I (1957), 162.

31 Boy attacked Akumu for his continued affiliation to the so-called 'imperialist-dominated' ICFTU through his affiliation to the KFL. But Boy also was willing to accept assistance from such KADU leaders as Ronald Ngala and S. T. Omari, who wished to eliminate Akumu's trade union base. Akumu was a staunch KANU supporter at this time.

32 The Giriama and Digo are two of the most numerous of the nine 'sub-tribes' of the Mijikenda. The Taita are a separate tribe whose home area is near the Coast.

33 Boy has been associated with the Msanifou Kombo KANU faction in Mombasa, which has struggled to wrest control of Mombasa away from the Ngala faction.

34 Again, this conclusion is necessarily impressionistic, based on many discussions with union members and officials on the fate of certain union leaders who were clearly successful or unsuccessful in fulfilling their formal function.

Chapter 6

1 E. M. Kassalow, 'Unions in the New and Developing Countries', in Kassalow (ed.), *National Labor Movements in the Postwar World* (Chicago: Northwestern University Press, 1963), 231; Stephen Low, 'The Role of Trade Unions in the Newly Independent Countries of Africa', in Kassalow (ed.), *National Labor Movements*, 219–20; Bruce H. Millen, *The Political Role of Labor in Developing Countries* (Washington: Brookings Institute, 1963), 91.

2 Information on COTU's pressure group activities was gathered from interviews and from the correspondence, memoranda, resolutions, press statements and minutes of COTU's governing bodies contained in selected COTU files to which the author had access at Solidarity Building, Nairobi.

3 J. Jupp, 'Trade Unions and Politics in Australia', University of London, Institute of Commonwealth Studies, *Collected Seminar Papers on Labour Unions and Political Organizations* (Jan.-May, 1967), 71.

4 Rolf Gerritsen, 'The Evolution of the Ghana Trades Union Congress Under the Convention Peoples Party: Toward a Reinterpretation', *Transactions* (Journal of the Ghana Historical Society), December 1972.

5 *Ibid.*

6 See the discussion of clientelism in Chap. 1.

7 The most notable exception was Tom Mboya, who always played a prominent national role even though his Nairobi power base was anything but secure after 1963. But Mboya retained the backing of the Kenya Federation of Labour and its successor, the Central Organization of Trade Unions, which compensated for weak regional support.

8 See, for example, the debate on a motion introduced into the National Assembly in 1967 to dismiss Tom Mboya from the cabinet because of his alleged association with the Central Intelligence Agency. National Assembly, *Official Report*, XII (July 14, 1967). See also, G. E. Lynd, *The Politics of African Trade Unionism* (New York: Praeger, 1968), Chap. 4.

9 This became clear when I sought to understand why Ochola Mak'Anyengo, a prominent KPU leader in 1968–9, retained the respect and loyalty of his mainly anti-KPU membership. He was, up to his second detention in 1969, one of the most capable union leaders in Kenya.

10 Those readers who would like to pursue this matter further are referred to my

'Patrons, Clients, and Unions: The Labour Movement and Political Conflict in Kenya', *Journal of Commonwealth Political Studies*, x (March 1972), 3–27.

11 This was also the situation, for example, in Northern Rhodesia before 1963–4. See Elizabeth Colson, 'Competence and Incompetence in the Context of Independence', *Current Anthropology*, VIII (February–April 1967), 94. In exchange for the services offered by the European or Asian, the African could only offer deference, and acquiescence to a demeaning, paternalistic system.

12 Legum, 'What Kind of Radicalism for Africa?' *Foreign Affairs*, XLIII (January 1965), 245–6.

13 While Odinga has not been reticent about the financial assistance he has received from communist sources, Mboya always denied publicly that he received money from United States sources. But both pro and anti-Mboya men in Kenya universally accepted that Mboya did receive such funds. How else, some implied, could Mboya have afforded to service such a far-flung clientage network? At the very least, the Kenya Federation of Labour, which Mboya formally headed until August 1963, received thousands of Kenyan pounds from the International Confederation of Free Trade Unions and Western sources, as evidenced by the KFL's audited annual returns in the Registrar of Societies office, Nairobi. On Odinga's foreign source of funds, see his *Not Yet Uhuru* (London: Heinemann, 1967), 200, and J. K. Cooley, *East Wind Over Africa* (New York: Walker and Co., 1965), 63–4.

14 Jay Hakes, *The Parliamentary Party of the Kenya African National Union: Cleavage and Cohesion*, Ph.D. dissertation (Duke University, 1970), 262–3.

15 Jay Hakes, 'Patronage and Politics in Kenya: A Study of Backbencher Membership on Statutory Boards', unpublished paper (Nairobi, 1970), 4.

16 John Okumu, 'The Socio-Political Setting', in Goran Hyden, R. Jackson and J. Okumu (eds.), *Development Administration: The Kenya Experience* (Nairobi: Oxford University Press, 1970), 33.

17 My interpretation is based mainly on confidential interviews and discussions conducted with a wide array of Kenyan politicians and trade unionists between July 1968 and January 1970.

18 See John Spencer, 'Kenyatta's Kenya', *Africa Report*, XI (May 1966), 11.

19 These are the terms used by Cherry Gertzel in *The Politics of Independent Kenya* (London: Heinemann, 1970), 54.

20 *Ibid.*, 57.

21 *Ibid.*, 61.

22 See, e.g., *E.A. Standard* (20 August 1962) and (24 August 1962).

23 See, e.g., the statement by O. O. Mak'Anyengo in *E.A. Standard* (24 August 1962).

24 *Reporter* (Nairobi), II, 36 (1 September 1962), 9–10.

25 'Resolutions of the Trade Union Leaders' Conference on 25–26 August 1962, held at Solidarity Building', in KFL files, Nairobi. These resolutions were later endorsed by the Federation's Executive Committee.

26 See speeches and statements by the two men in the following issues of the *E.A. Standard*: 2 January 1964; 17 May 1965; 17 February 1966.

27 Letter to Kenyatta of 5 April 1964, in M. of L. files, Nairobi.

28 H. A. Oduor, 'Reorganization Plan for KFL', dated 9 May 1964, in KFL files, Nairobi.

29 See, e.g., the speeches on the Trade Unions (Amendment) Act, in House of Representatives, *Official Report*, III, Part 2 (7 Aug 1964), and on the refusal to register the Federation of Progressive Trade Unions, in *ibid.* (15 September 1964).

30 Kenya, Ministry of Labour, *Report of a Board of Inquiry into (i) The Claim of the Dockworkers Union to Represent Certain Categories of Workers in Mombasa and (ii) Industrial Unrest in Mombasa in the Year 1964*, report dated May 1965 (mimeo).
31 *E.A. Standard* (12 September 1970).
32 *E.A. Standard* (12 July 1972).
33 For a thorough study of factional politics in Mombasa, see Richard Stren, 'Factional Politics and Central Control in Mombasa, 1960–69', *Canadian Journal of African Studies*, IV (Winter 1970).
34 G. B. Lamb, *Politics and Administration in Murang'a District, Kenya*, D.Phil. dissertation (University of Sussex, 1970).
35 *Ibid.*
36 See *E.A. Standard* of 10 and 12 March 1969 for reports of this dispute.
37 Initially, Gachago barely won the KANU preliminary election, with a vote of 5,865 to a combined vote of almost 10,000 for his two opponents. But the propriety of this election was successfully challenged in the courts. A second election was held in June 1970, in which Gachago was defeated. Since only one national party existed after October 1969, the winner of the preliminary election automatically became the M.P. for the constituency.
38 Correspondence in the M. of L. files, Nairobi, and confidential interviews.
39 Letter from Njoka to E. N. Mwendwa, Labour Minister, of 30 August 1968, copied to Gachago. '*Bega kwa bega*' is a Swahili phrase meaning 'shoulder to shoulder'.
40 When Akumu became Secretary-General of COTU in February 1969, he tried to secure Njoka's reinstatement as Estate Manager. This was one aspect of Akumu's attempt to limit the rules of the game in union politics so that a defeated union leader would not be hounded out of his job as well. While Njoka never secured reinstatement, he found other channels for his considerable energy. By the time of my return to Kenya in 1972, he was a successful Nairobi businessman, having got his start as a middleman in the wholesale–retail trade.

Chapter 7

1 Sidney and Beatrice Webb, *The History of Trade Unionism*, 2nd ed. (London: Longmans, Green, 1920), 1.
2 For the distinction between 'consumptionist' and 'productionist' unions see Isaac Deutscher, 'Russia', in W. Galenson (ed.), *Comparative Labor Movements* (New York: Prentice-Hall, 1953), 505. See also William H. Friedland, 'Basic Social Trends', in Friedland and Carl Rosberg (eds.), *African Socialism* (Stanford: Stanford University Press, 1965), 19–21.
3 'Excerpts from a Speech Given by the Hon. Mwai Kibaki at the Opening of the COTU(K) Joint Seminar on the Role of the Trade Union Movement in Economic Planning and Development..., and Workers' Participation in Management, at the Management Training and Advisory Centre, Nairobi, on 15th November, 1971', mimeo., p. 3.
4 *E.A. Standard* (26 January 1971).
5 For an analysis of a similar situation in Tanganyika see W. H. Friedland, *Vuta Kamba: The Development of Trade Unions in Tanganyika* (Stanford: Hoover Institution Press, 1969), 110–11.
6 The typology of union–management relations to be presented is similar to that developed by F. H. Harbison in the context of Egypt. See Harbison, 'Egypt', in W. Galenson (ed.), *Labor and Economic Development* (New York: John Wiley,

1959), 168–76. See also F. H. Harbison and J. R. Coleman, *Goals and Strategy in Collective Bargaining* (New York: Harper and Brothers, 1951), and Robert Dubin, 'A Theory of Conflict and Power in Union–Management Relations', *Industrial and Labor Relation Review*, XIII (July, 1960), 501–18.

7 All of these actions became more dangerous after independence because those involved in them could be accused of subversive activities. Sabotage was most frequently carried out on Nyanza sugar plantations, where cane fields were set on fire.

8 Kenya Coffee Growers' Association, 'Annual Report, 1964', by the chairman.

9 This association was renamed the Federation of Kenya Employers in 1959. For a favourable interpretation of the employers' associations' contribution to the development of trade unionism in Kenya, see Alice Amsden, *International Firms and Labour in Kenya* (London: Frank Cass, 1971).

10 Overseas Employers Federation, *Newsletter* (18 January 1956), 5.

11 Association of Commercial and Industrial Employers, 'Joint Consultation Reports', drafted by a select committee of the association in August 1957, and later approved by a General Meeting. These documents were retained by the FKE.

12 R. Scott, *The Development of Trade Unions in Uganda* (Nairobi: East African Publishing House, 1966), 103.

13 Once employers granted 'check-off', they usually discovered that there were fewer industrial disturbances. Union officials no longer had to precipitate crises in order to persuade 'members' to pay their dues.

14 Information for this case study was obtained from the M. of L. files, Mombasa, selected files of the Landing and Shipping Company of East Africa (now with the East African Cargo Handling Services Company), newspaper reports and confidential interviews with major participants in the events of 1958–9, both from management and the union.

15 In addition to this company, there were four small stevedoring companies on the docks. Together, they comprised the Port Employers' Association.

16 As Williams remarked in a letter to the president of the Harbour Asian Union of East Africa in May 1958: 'Since I have been in a position to do so, I have treated the development of responsible trade unionism as a vocation.' L. and S. Co. files, Mombasa.

17 'Circular to Directors by the General Manager', dated 14 January 1958. L. and S. Co. files, Mombasa.

18 'Minutes of the 59th Meeting of the Joint Industrial Council for the Dock Industry, Mombasa, held in the Board Room of the Landing and Shipping Co. on April 24th, 1958'. Emphasis is mine.

19 This was reported by a management informant. See 'Notes Taken of a Meeting held in Tononoka Hall by the DWU on Sunday, May 11th, 1958'. L. and S. Co., files, Mombasa.

20 M. of L. Files, Nairobi.

21 'Minutes of the Special Meeting of the J.I.C. for the Dock Industry, Mombasa, held in the Board Room of the Landing and Shipping Co. on October 2nd, 1958.'

22 Letter from the Chairman, PEA, to Denis Akumu of 4 October 1958. L. and S. Co. files.

23 'Report of the Dockworkers' Union election', by the Senior Labour Officer, Coast, dated 27 February 1959. M. of L. files, Mombasa.

24 Kenya Colony, *Report of the Board of Inquiry Appointed to Inquire Into Employment in the Port of Mombasa* (Nairobi, 1959).

25 Letter dated 24 March 1961. KFL files, Nairobi.

26 Interview with Herman Oduor, Kitale, June 1972.
27 *Ibid.*
28 Kenya National Archives, DC Nakuru File 2/10, District Monthly Report, Sept./Oct. 1961.
29 FKE files, Nairobi.
30 Kenya Coffee Growers' Association, 'Annual Report, 1964', by the Chairman, Major V. E. Kirkland.
31 This charge was made at the Special Conference called to discuss Oduor's dismissal. See KPAWU, 'Minutes of the Special Conference held in Nakuru on 20th September 1964'. In confidential interviews, seven present and former officials of this union said that this theme had been used against Oduor.
32 *E.A. Standard* (31 July 1964).
33 KCGA, 'Annual Report, 1964', by the Chairman.
34 One highly-placed official of the KPAWU told the author that he even feared accepting an employer's invitation to tea when he was visiting a farm or estate.
35 These generalizations are based on my perusal of the M. of L.'s strike reports for 1960–72. These reports, which local Labour Officers were supposed to submit to headquarters as soon as possible after work stoppages, provide information on the causes, circumstances, duration and terms of settlement of strikes. Also helpful were official boards of inquiry into particular disputes and interviews with the trade unionists involved in decisions to employ the strike weapon.
36 Speech by Martin Shikuku on measures to curb unemployment, in National Assembly, *Official Report*, xix (27 February 1970), col. 792.
37 H. Wamalwa, COTU's Director of Industrial Relations, claimed in June 1972 that 'almost 99 per cent' of 'wild-cat' strikes had the full backing of the relevant union. At the same time, he asked rhetorically 'Do you think that where "human dignity" and "African personality" are concerned such theoretical and academic arguments of illegal strikes could apply to us...?' See his letter to the editor in *Sunday Nation* (Nairobi), 11 June 1972. Note that there are no statistics that separate official from unofficial work stoppages.
38 The first article was by Alan Rake, the last by Dharam Ghai. Both were in *African Development* (January 1971).
39 Peter Gutkind, 'The Energy of Despair: Social Organization of the Unemployed in two African Cities', *Civilisations*, xvii (1967), 191n.
40 Ghai, 'Unemployment: The National Obsession', 13.
41 H. Rempel and M. P. Todaro, 'Rural–Urban Labour Migration in Kenya: Some Preliminary Findings of a Large-Scale Survey', paper delivered to the seminar on Population Growth and Economic Development, Nairobi, December 1969.
42 J. R. Harris and M. P. Todaro, 'Migration, Unemployment and Development: A Two-Sector Analysis', *American Economic Review*, lx (March 1970), 126–42. See also Dharam Ghai, 'Employment Performance, Prospects and Policies', *East Africa Journal*, vii, 11 (1970), 9.
43 Kenya, *Report of the Salaries Review Commission* (Nairobi, 1967), 23.
44 See Samir Amin, 'Levels of Remuneration, Factor Proportions and Income Differentials with Special Reference to Developing Countries', in Anthony D. Smith (ed.), *Wage Policy Issues in Economic Development* (London: Macmillan, 1969), 284–5; and J. B. K. Hunter, 'The Development of the Labour Market in Kenya', in I. G. Stewart (ed.), *Economic Development and Structural Change* (Edinburgh: Edinburgh University Press, 1969), 133.
45 W. E. Whitelaw, 'Nairobi Household Survey: Some Preliminary Results', Institute for Development Studies, University of Nairobi, Staff Paper No. 117, 1971, p. 6.

46 See Margaret Peil, *The Ghanaian Factory Worker: Industrial Man in Africa* (Cambridge: Cambridge University Press, 1972), 207–12, and G. Pfeffermann, *Industrial Labor in the Republic of Senegal* (New York: Praeger, 1968), 166.
47 R. G. Hendrickse, 'Some Observations on the Social Background to Malnutrition in Tropical Africa', *African Affair*, LXV (Oct. 1966), 346, 347.
48 See F. I. Ojow, 'Labour Organizations in Economic Development: A Survey of Some Views', *Eastern Africa Economic Review*, II (June 1970), 28, and E. Kassalow, 'Labor in Development: A Critique of Some Current Concepts', *Industrial Relations Research Association Annual Proceedings*, 1969.
49 V. L. Allen, *Power in Trade Unions* (London: Longmans, Green, 1954), 24.
50 'Recommendations of the Participants: COTU(K) Seminar on "Wages and Incomes Policy in Kenya"', May 1971, mimeo. The Secretary General, Denis Akumu, made somewhat the same conditions in his speech opening the seminar.
51 For a comparison of wage increases in Kenya, Uganda and Nigeria, see J. F. Weeks, 'Wage Policy and the Colonial Legacy: A Comparative Study', *Journal of Modern African Studies*, IX (Oct. 1971), 361–87.
52 Dharam Ghai, 'Incomes Policy in Kenya: Need, Criteria and Machinery', Discussion Paper No. 66 of the Institute for Development Studies, Nairobi, June 1968, 2.
53 Compiled from information supplied by the East African Cargo Handling Services, Mombasa.
54 G. E. Johnson, 'The Determination of Individual Hourly Earnings in Urban Kenya', Institute for Development Studies Discussion Paper No. 115, Nairobi, Sept. 1971, 31.
55 National Assembly, *Official Report*, XIX (27 February 1970), cols. 769–75.
56 See the text of the 'Agreement on Measures for the Immediate Relief of Unemployment' in Ministry of Labour, *Annual Report, 1964*, 37–9.
57 *E.A. Standard* (9 October 1970).

Chapter 8

1 V. L. Allen, 'East African Workers in Transition', *Africa Today*, IX, 5 (1962), 6.
2 W. A. Warmington, *A West African Trade Union* (London: Oxford University Press, 1960), 120.
3 Calculated from data supplied by H. Wamalwa, Director of Industrial Relations, COTU(K), in August 1972.
4 For evidence of racial inequalities in Kenya – in terms of occupation, wealth, ownership of the means of production, and education – aided by colonial discriminatory practices, see Donald Rothchild, 'Ethnic Inequalities in Kenya', *Journal of Modern African Studies*, VII, 4 (1969), 693–6. For some African attitudes towards these inequalities, derived from a questionnaire answered by 653 respondents, see pp. 701–4 of the same article.
5 Kenya Colony, *Report of the Board of Inquiry Appointed to Inquire into Labour Unrest at the Macalder–Nyanza Mines and into the Machinery for Negotiations with the Kenya Quarry and Mine Workers Union* (Nairobi, June 1963).
6 Kenya, Ministry of Labour and Social Services, *First Report of a Board of Inquiry Appointed to Inquire into a Trade Dispute in the Sugar Industry* (November 1962), mimeo.
7 Kenya, Ministry of Labour and Social Services, *Report of a Board of Inquiry into the Arrangements within the City Council of Nairobi for Regulating Labour Relations and Negotiating Terms and Conditions of Service* (February 1963), mimeo.

8 A perusal of the strike files of the M. of L., Nairobi revealed that the largest number of 'wild-cat' strikes on this apparent pretext occurred just prior to independence, in the 1961 to 1963 period.

9 RAU(K), *Press Release of November 23rd, 1959*, issued by the General Secretary, J. B. A. Ohanga. Eight days after the strike began the union added wage demands onto its original grievance.

10 See, e.g., *E.A. Standard* (24 February 1962). Railwaymen have most recently gone on strike over the issue of workers' dignity in February 1971, when 200 employees walked off the job after one of their number was 'abused' by a senior foreman.

11 KUCFAW, *Board of Inquiry: Memoranda of a Trade Dispute between KUCFAW and the Kenya Meat Commission*, KUCFAW files Nairobi, dated 1969, p. 74.

12 *E.A. Standard* (24 October 1970).

13 Kenya, Ministry of Labour, *Report of a Board of Inquiry Appointed...to Inquire into a Trade Dispute between the KDCWU and the Distributive and Allied Trade Association* (December 1963), typewritten.

14 Report to the Minister for Labour, M. of L. files, Nairobi.

15 KLGWU, 'Report by the General Secretary', in *Proceedings of the 14th Annual Conference, 23rd and 24th September, 1967*, mimeo.

16 KLGWU, *Review of the Past Work of the Union: Report on Activities by the National General Secretary*, August 1967, 6, mimeo. Emphasis is mine.

17 Mak'Anyengo was politically unpopular, the reader will recall, because of his connections with Oginga Odinga and the opposition KPU. He was detained both in August 1966 and November 1969.

18 For a report of this Industrial Court case, see *E.A. Standard* (13 September 1969).

19 See, e.g., KANU's May Day policy statement on trade unionism issued by R. Matano, KANU's Acting Secretary General, in *E.A. Standard* (1 May 1970).

20 Interview with Okoe Clottey, Director of Projects, Ghana TUC, Accra, July 1972.

21 KFL, Education Centre, 'First Year's Report' (29 July 1965), p. 4.

22 *Ibid.*, 6.

23 Mboya, *Freedom and After* (London: André Deutsch, 1963), 200–3.

24 *E.A. Standard* (26 February 1969).

25 Interview with Okoe Clottey, Director of Projects, Ghana TUC, Accra, July 1972. But note that this TUC has an important advantage over COTU: it can rely on a large monthly income owing to a union shop system.

26 'Excerpts from a Speech Given by the Hon. Mwai Kibaki at the Opening of the COTU(K) Joint Seminar on the Role of the Trade Union Movement in Economic Planning and Development..., and Workers' Participation in Management..., on 15th November 1971', mimeo.

27 For a brief discussion of the operation of a 'Workers' Development Corporation' in Tanzania, see William Tordoff, 'Trade Unionism in Tanzania', *Journal of Development Studies*, ii (July 1966), 425–6.

28 Lubembe, 'Secretariat Report to the Governing Council of COTU(K) of 19 September 1968', mimeo., COTU files, Nairobi, p. 2.

Chapter 9

1 E. J. Berg and J. Butler, 'Trade Unions', in James S. Coleman and C. G. Rosberg (eds.), *Political Parties and National Integration in Tropical Africa* (Los Angeles: University of California Press, 1964), 366.

2 *Ibid.*, 370.
3 On the same point, see C. Allen, 'African Trade Unionism in Microcosm: The Gambian Labour Movement', *Africa Today*, xviii (Jan. 1971), 393–5.
4 Berg and Butler themselves try to dispel the notion that the Kenyan union movement is a monolithic entity. See their 'Trade Unions', 360–1.
5 See C. Peter Magrath, 'Democracy in Overalls: The Futile Quest for Union Democracy', *Industrial and Labor Relations Review*, xii (July 1959), 503–25.
6 V. L. Allen, *Power in Trade Unions* (London: Longmans, Green, 1954), 63–4.
7 Robert H. Bates, *Unions, Parties, and Political Development* (New Haven: Yale University Press, 1971), 1.
8 *Ibid.*, 74–94.
9 See Douglas Rimmer, 'The New Industrial Relations in Ghana', *Industrial and Labor Relations Review*, xiv (Jan. 1961), 202–26; L. N. Trachtman, 'The Labor Movement in Ghana: A Study in Political Unionism', *Economic Development and Cultural Change*, x (1961–2), 185; and St Clair Drake and L. A. Lacy, 'Government Against the Unions: The Sekondi–Takoradi Strike, 1961', in Gwendolen Carter (ed,), *Politics in Africa* (New York: Harcourt and Brace, 1966), 86–7. See also, R. Gerritsen, 'The Evolution of the Ghana Trades Union Congress under the Convention People's Party: Toward a Reinterpretation', *Transactions* (of the Ghana Historical Society) (Dec. 1972).
10 Drake and Lacy, 'Government Against the Unions', 115.
11 Dennis Austin, *Politics in Ghana, 1946–1960* (London: Oxford University Press, 1964), 401.
12 Drake and Lacy, 'Government Against the Unions', 97.
13 Ghana, *Report of the Commission on the Structure and Remuneration of the Public Services in Ghana* (Accra, 1967), p. 41.
14 *Ghanaian Times* (10 September 1971).
15 *Daily Graphic* (13 September 1971).
16 See the *Spokesman* (Accra) (18 January 1972).
17 This was the finding of the Morgan Commission, which was established in October 1963 to study wages and salaries in the public services. See Emile R. Braundi and Antonio Lettieri, 'The General Strike in Nigeria', *International Socialist Journal*, i, #5–6 (Sept.–Dec. 1964), 603.
18 See R. Melson, 'Nigerian Politics and the General Strike of 1964', in Robert Rotberg and A. Mazrui (eds.), *Protest and Power in Black Africa* (New York: Oxford University Press, 1970), 777–82.
19 Walter Schwarz, *Nigeria* (London: Pall Mall Press, 1968), 155.
20 Quoted in Braundi and Lettieri, 'General Strike in Nigeria', 608.
21 *Daily Nation* (7 May 1971).
22 Kenya, *Report of the Commission of Inquiry (Public Service Structure and Remuneration Commission, 1970–71)* (Nairobi, 1971), para. 104.
23 *Ibid.*, para. 101.
24 *Ibid.*, see tables and figures on pp. 322, 332, 333.
25 Kenya, National Assembly, *Official Report*, xix (18 February 1970), col. 359.
26 National Assembly, *Official Report*, xix (27 February 1970), col. 794.
27 Samuel P. Huntington, *Political Order in Changing Societies* (New Haven: Yale University Press, 1968), 264.
28 James C. Davies, 'Toward a Theory of Revolution', *American Sociological Review*, xxvii (1962), 6n.
29 Karl Marx and Fredrick Engels, 'Wage Labour and Capital', *Selected Works*, Vol. i (Moscow: Foreign Languages Publishing House, 1955), 94.

Index